KT-568-713

101 822 431 9

SAP Enterprise Portal

SAP PRESS and SAP Technical Support Guides are issued by
Bernhard Hochlehnert, SAP AG

SAP PRESS is a joint initiative of SAP and Galileo Press. The know-how offered by SAP specialists combined with the expertise of the publishing house Galileo Press offers the reader expert books in the field. SAP PRESS features first-hand information and expert advice, and provides useful skills for professional decision-making.

SAP PRESS offers a variety of books on technical and business related topics for the SAP user. For further information, please visit our website: *www.sap-press.com*.

Jens Stumpe, Joachim Orb
SAP Exchange Infrastructure
Learn everything about Routings, Mappings, Proxies, and Business Process Monitoring
2005, approx. 270 pp., ISBN 1–59229–037-X

Chris Whealy
Inside Web Dynpro for Java
A guide to the principles of programming in SAP's Web Dynpro
2005, 356 pp., ISBN 1–59229–038–8

Andreas Schneider-Neureither (Ed.)
The ABAP Developer´s Guide to Java
Leverage your ABAP skills to climb up the Java learning curve
2005, 495 pp., ISBN 1–59229–027–2

Frédéric Heinemann, Christian Rau
Web Programming with the SAP Web Application Server
The complete guide for ABAP and Web developers
2003, 528 pp., ISBN 1–59229–013–2

Sigrid Hagemann, Liane Will
SAP R/3 System Administration
2004, 520 pp., ISBN 1–59229–014–0

Arnd Goebel, Dirk Ritthaler

SAP Enterprise Portal

SAP PRESS

SAP PRESS is an imprint of Galileo Press,
Boston (MA), USA
Bonn, Germany

Translation Lamoine International, Inc.,
Salt Lake City, UT
Copy Editor Nancy Etscovitz, UCG, Inc.,
Boston, MA
Cover Design department, Cologne, Germany
Printed in Germany

ISBN 1-59229-018-3
ISBN13 978-1-59229-018-5
1st edition 2005, 3rd reprint 2007

Contents

9 Java iView Development 161

10 Connectivity 215

11 Portals and Security 223

Preface

Portal *[from Medieval Latin porta (city gate)]: the often imposing entrance to a church or cathedral. A portal provides access to the holy of holies.*

At first glance, the use of the term *portal* in information technology appears inappropriate. In the main sense of (IT) portals—the combination of Web content and applications—one could just as well speak of a center, much as one does of a call center. But portals are much more. They involve not only bundling information and applications, but also the targeted processing of decision-making documents so that employees, customers, and partners can make optimal decisions. Because such decisions require information from the *most holy* of IT systems, the term portal does not seem so inappropriate.

First, portals do more than use Web technologies to provide information and applications. They unify the information and applications so that users can work from an integrated interface. Portals also tailor information and applications so users don't have to expend considerable energy creating the configuration themselves. In addition, portals integrate structured and unstructured data from the Internet, a company's intranet, and other applications into the environment that is most conducive to supporting the users' productivity. Portals therefore help users to find, organize, and access information efficiently and effectively.

Secondly, portals build an integration platform for users; the actual technical components can hide behind the platform. A portal can partially fulfill user-oriented success factors for an application, such as *usability* and *look and feel*, and increase the acceptance of those applications that are critical to a company's success. This approach makes it much easier to exchange applications. Laborious product training and complicated installation procedures to heap the frontends of applications onto employees' personal computers are no longer needed. Even non-Web-enabled legacy applications can be integrated with a portal framework. And applications can be made available to customers, vendors, and partners instantly. Portals therefore can also lighten the load on administrators by reducing IT overhead.

Lastly, portals create consistent and context-sensitive access to Web services—the programming technology of the near future. In terms of technology, Web services consist of a structured, uniform, and content rich question–answer protocol that, by its very nature, does not include a user interface. A Java server page (JSP) or an active server page can be written quickly; however, if a Web service were to run alone in a Web browser, the page would have to handle all the context information and menu prompts itself. A portal also handles those tasks; it is the generic graphical user interface (GUI) of the future.

But the plug-and-play installation of portals is still at least several years away. The problem arises not because of the portals, but due to today's often extremely heterogeneous IT infrastructure. In the world of Web services, a portal installation consists primarily of configuration procedures. Today, however, various information and application sources must be adjusted to fit the portal, which can involve considerable effort. The critical precondition for a portal is that the company that wants to implement it can clearly identify *to whom* specific content should be displayed and *who* should make what decisions regarding IT support. That's why most portal projects are assembled with the discovery or rediscovery of company processes and structures. Technical, operative, and even social hurdles must be overcome.

This book takes a unique approach to these considerations. The authors demonstrate the various phases of a portal project and, based on their practical experience, show how to lead a portal project to a successful conclusion. Security is certainly an integral part of success: without appropriate security measures, a portal project poses an extremely high risk for the company—the risk of offering on a platter data worthy of protection to any Internet user interested in it. The authors address this concern thoroughly and offer several options to ensure the security of a portal.

Initially, portals were looked at with skeptical amusement. The benefits of portals were often questioned, especially after the hype related to e-business. But the changing basic IT architecture and Web services will make portals indispensable in the near future. This book contributes to the successful implementation of this important component of tomorrow's IT architecture.

Dr. Sachar Paulus
December 2004

1 Introduction

I would not lead you willingly astray,
But as regards this science, you will find
So hard it is to shun the erring way,
And so much hidden poison lies therein,
Which scarce can you discern from medicine.
Here too it is the best, to listen but to one,
And by the master's words to swear alone.
To sum up all--To words hold fast!
Then the safe gate securely pass'd,
You'll reach the lane of certainty at last.
Johann W. von Goethe, Faust—Part I

A great deal of time has passed since SAP crossed the narrow boundaries of enterprise resource planning (ERP) and introduced mySAP.com in 1999, and increasingly addressed communications and business processes among companies. Since then, the SAP portfolio of products—marketed today as *mySAP Business Suite*—has changed and expanded in a manner that could hardly be fathomed by those who can recall the good old days of SAP R/3. While the mapping and optimization of processes *within* a company—with the use of *one* comprehensive software package—characterized the 1990s, since then, the focus has effectively changed. The ability to map processes *between* companies, facilitate communication among employees working from widely separated locations, combine information from various sources into one uniform interface, and realize seamless collaboration between several applications characterize today's market.

Three levels of integration

The levels of integration that SAP now calls *the* challenge for the development of business software can be summarized as follows:

- Integration of customers, employees, and business partners
- Integration of existing information
- Integration of business processes

SAP NetWeaver

With its new integration and application platform, *SAP NetWeaver*, SAP has realized these three levels. *SAP Enterprise Portal (SAP EP)* plays a vital role here: it functions as a central component for the first two integration levels. It's well-suited to integrate and personalize the contents of a PC interface in ways that have long been impossible, and it closely aligns a company's business partners with its employees.

But the functions of SAP EP go even further. Based on various technologies developed over the years, such as Drag&Relate or collaboration functions, SAP EP enables the display and smooth linking of information from the most varied of sources, and it fosters collaboration among widely separated employees of one or more companies.

Portal as a standard interface

SAP Enterprise Portal has an important place in the overall strategy of SAP. It has been the standard interface for mySAP CRM since Release 3.1, and we can assume that it will increasingly replace the dynpro interfaces of additional solutions in mySAP Business Suite. In the long term, an SAP system landscape without SAP Enterprise Portal is simply inconceivable.

This book provides a detailed look at the technical abilities of SAP EP and its numerous options for integrating applications and information. It offers a solid foundation on several topics, including system requirements, installation, linking content, and security issues. In light of current development work, we intentionally wrote the book so that it would be valid for both SAP EP 5.0 and SAP EP 6.0; the text highlights the difference between the two releases where appropriate.

Structure of the book

Chapter 2 addresses the system landscape, including the requirements for installing SAP EP. It examines operating systems individually and deals with the peculiarities of individual components of the portal during installation.

With the use of a sample installation, **Chapter 3** illustrates how to set up SAP EP 5.0 in a Windows NT/2000 environment. Then, it shows you how to install SAP EP 6.0 in a UNIX environment. This chapter also explains how to create users and roles.

Chapter 4 describes a business application from the portfolio of mySAP products and an essential component of SAP NetWeaver—the SAP Business Information Warehouse (SAP BW). The functionality of these products is explained so far, that readers could understand, in terms of how to integrate content from SAP BW in the portal.

Chapter 5 builds on the topics covered in Chapter 4 and illustrates sample integration for the reporting, administration, and extraction levels. The chapter ends with an introduction to Drag&Relate functionality.

Chapter 6 provides a general overview of customer relationship management (CRM) and the characteristics of CRM that are specific to SAP.

A project scenario describes the interaction of mySAP CRM, SAP BW, and SAP EP.

Chapter 7 defines the unification server, the unifier for SAP R/3, SAP BW, and the database unifier. It describes the installation and configuration and guides readers through the creation of a unification project with the use of a sample.

Chapter 8 gives readers a detailed overview of iViews. Whether they were created with technologies such as Java or Microsoft .NET or, if they currently exist as ready-made components in business packages, iViews are a central component of SAP EP. They fill the portal with content, permit interaction and collaboration between applications, and display information from various data sources. Self-created iViews allow users to tailor their portal components to reflect their needs. SAP offers an easy-to-use, integrated development environment (IDE) to help users in this process.

Chapter 9 introduces Java-based iView programming. It provides an overview of the Java programming language and then examines specific Java technologies, such as Java servlets, Java Server Pages (JSPs), and Enterprise Java Beans (EJBs). Java portal components build on these technologies.

Information exchange and integration are integral to SAP EP—not only with SAP systems, but also with almost every application and the Internet. **Chapter 10** explains how you can use numerous connectors to realize process integration between systems of various manufacturers.

Chapter 11 looks at portal security. Secure connections, authentication, authorization, single sign-on (SSO), digital signatures, and network infrastructure allow companies to protect their sensitive data from unauthorized access.

Chapter 12, the final chapter, looks ahead at new key technologies that will be used in the portal environment. SAP EP and SAP Exchange Infrastructure (SAP XI) are discussed in the context of the SAP Web Application Server (SAP Web AS). Lastly, SAP NetWeaver Developer Studio (NWDS) is introduced as an innovative SAP development platform for applications based on Web Dynpro technology.

The **appendices** include a glossary of important terms that are associated with enterprise portals, a table of the presentation objects in SAP EP 5.0 and SAP EP 6.0, and a list of sources and suggestions for additional reading. An index lists every keyword in the book so that you can quickly and easily find any term in question.

Note Our goal is that this book will give you a technological compendium with which you can use SAP Enterprise Portal. Because the portal environment includes very heterogeneous topics, we couldn't avoid using certain terms in some parts of the book and explaining them in more detail in later sections. To avoid excessive redundancies, these instances always include a reference to the corresponding section.

Acknowledgements We want to thank our colleagues for their expert support, proofreading, and helpful comments and suggestions: Stefanie Garcia Laule, Dr. Sachar Paulus, and Gerlinde Zibulski from security project management; Klaus Kiefer, Rainer Kreft, and Christoph Roller for support in the area of digital signatures; Martina Armbruster and Kai Ullrich in the area of security portals; and our consulting colleague, Yann Floch, for his support with the description of installation and configuration.

We would also like to thank the following colleagues for their review of the content of the book: Simone Bruckert, Markus Fuchs, Tobias Kaufmann, Timo Kirchner, Stefan Kraus, Markus Kupke, Sven Leukert, Joachim Mette, Barbara Neumann, Michelle Peiser, Serge Saelens, Eric Schemer, Marko Schroeter, and Thomas Volmering.

Finally, we thank the publisher, and especially our editor, Florian Zimniak, for their fine work and enjoyable collaboration.

2 System Landscape and Requirements

This chapter deals with the components that are indispensable for a working portal and provides an overview of the platforms on which a portal can be installed.

2.1 Overview of Components

This section introduces you to the most important portal components (see Figure 2.1):

- Portal infrastructure
- Unifier
- SAP Knowledge Management (SAP KM)
- Search and classification engine
- LDAP server

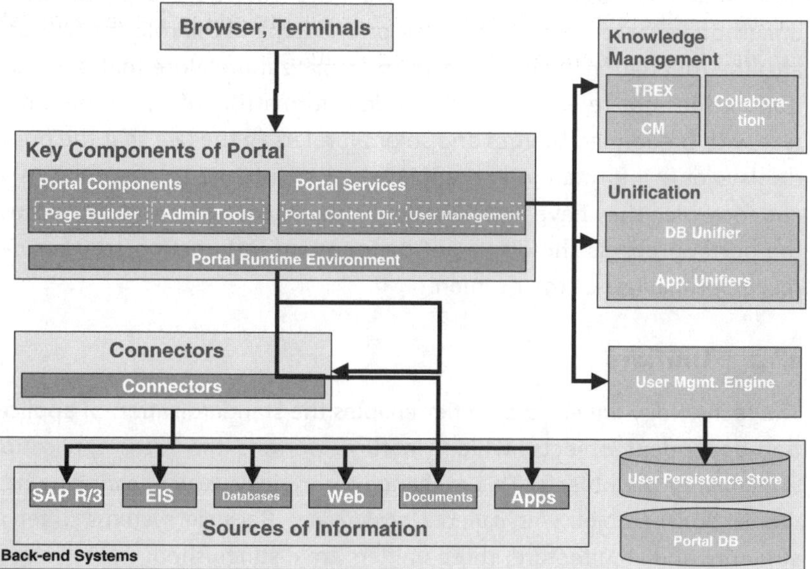

Figure 2.1 Components of SAP Enterprise Portal

Later chapters examine individual components in more detail. The goal here is to provide you with an initial overview before we create a test system in the next chapter. This section does not describe well known standard software components, which are necessary for this scenario, that you can presuppose to exist, and whose functions are familiar (such as Web browsers and servers).

2.1.1 Portal Infrastructure

Because later chapters will deal with the portal in great detail, in this section, we have provided only an abstract introduction to the terms associated with an enterprise portal.

Integration of information

A *portal* is a modular application that enables end users to enjoy uniform access to numerous applications, information, and services within a company. The portal server acts as the technological foundation for the portal solution from SAP. The portal can link both structured and unstructured information and present it to end users as iViews.

Portal server

The portal server interacts with the remaining components connected to the portal: see below for information on these components. To ensure that the data and information in the portal can be tailored to meet and reflect the needs of individual users, the portal uses the techniques of roles and personalization. These techniques exclude the possibility of unauthorized access to sensitive company data, and the role concept creates the foundation for user-specific personalization. Note that personalization does not refer to user-dependent formatting of the portal interface with predefined themes and so on. It refers to the fact that the portal displays only information and applications of interest to particular users and for which they have authorization. This concept is important because the portal prevents the display of unimportant information so users can make optimal use of their screen.

2.1.2 Unifiers

Drag&Relate

The technology linked to a unifier enables the standardization of application-dependent objects, which, in turn, permits the cross-application exchange of the objects. This exchange technology, which leads to a harmonization of objects, is called *Drag&Relate*. Because systems differ in structure and architecture, three unifiers are distinguished:

- **SAP R/3 unifier (application unifier)**
  This unifier can make traditional SAP R/3 systems capable of Drag&Relate.
- **SAP BW unifier (application unifier)**
  For business intelligence scenarios

- **Database unifier**
  Also used for legacy systems and third-party applications

Use of the unifiers enables problem-free execution of complex Drag&Relate operations between individual SAP business processes. However, the use of this technology is more complex than merely connecting data.

The first step involves setting parameters on the SAP servers in use, installing plug-ins, and assigning roles to specific user IDs. The corresponding unification server is built on a portal server, although you can install the unifier on separate hardware for better performance. Installation of a plug-in you can download also enables the underlying SAP R/3 systems for *single sign-on (SSO)*: see Chapter 11. See Chapter 7 for additional details, including the required DCOM connector.

iPanel

SAP EP 5.0 enables access to Drag&Relate functionality with the *iPanel*, a type of informational bulletin board with a hierarchical structure that provides users with data in an organized form. The iPanel permits the exchange of objects between heterogeneous applications; that is, SAP EP uses the unifier to enable seamless switching among various applications.

Navigation panel in SAP EP 6.0

The current release, SAP EP 6.0, uses a navigation panel (instead of the iPanel) that includes an area for Drag&Relate target objects. Administrators can adjust the navigation panel to reflect individual needs and enhance it with additional functionality, such as iViews.

2.1.3 SAP Knowledge Management (SAP KM)

SAP Knowledge Management (SAP KM) is an integrated environment for dealing with documents and includes software for formatting data. You use SAP KM to publish, version, and edit documents. Portal-side access to such a system occurs over a *Web-based distributed authoring and versioning* (WebDAV) interface. SAP KM also determines access authorizations with an *access control list (ACL)*.

Search and classification engine (TREX)

"Search all"

The search and classification engine is a fundamental component of SAP KM and is installed along with it. It supports searching unstructured data, which is often the norm with SAP KM, and searching structured data, which is the norm with SAP BW, unification servers, and so on. It enables functionality to "search all," including any connected company applications.

Content Management (CM)

Dealing in information

In general, *content* refers to information present in a structured, soft-structured, and unstructured form that others use as an object of exchange or, that can be given to others. *Content management* refers to a framework for the systematic generation and presentation of this information. Therefore, the term CM pertains to services for SAP KM to deal with and present unstructured or prestructured content.

Collaboration

Virtual networks

Collaboration refers to integrated tools in the portal environment that enable collaboration in real time. Possible uses of these tools include chat forums, Web-based application sharing, and virtual work areas called *collaboration rooms*. Such rooms involve locally administered portal pages that users can create themselves with predefined templates.

The *launch pad*, a simple, dynamic application, enables access to collaboration services and contacts. It displays the online status of the members of a team. It also offers ad hoc workflows and a central list of tasks. These functions support users in monitoring and coordinating the processing of tasks that are subdivided into several substeps and on which various employees work at any given time.

2.1.4 LDAP Server and UME

Dealing with user management

Lightweight Directory Access Protocol (LDAP) is a directory access protocol borrowed from TCP/IP. It refers to an open protocol to and by directory services to deal with user management. Business applications use LDAP to enable transparent access to information from various directory services, which enables these applications to have *Novell directory services (NDS)*, active directory, and others without requiring any special modification.

SAP EP 6.0 includes *SAP User Management Engine (SAP UME)*, which offers expanded functionality for user management. SAP UME has more memory options and therefore allows flexible management of user accounts and information. Relational databases and SAP WEB AS function as storage locations for user data. You can also select various memory locations and parallel use of memory locations for user accounts by employing various memory adapters (a separate software level and interface built into SAP UME).

2.1.5 Connectors

To integrate the multifaceted systems illustrated in Figure 2.1, you need various connectors bundled in integration architecture. Use of connectors makes originally disparate systems interoperable and available for linkage to the portal. SAP delivers some connectors itself; SAP partners offer others and make them available on the basis of open interfaces. This integrative approach allows for central, role-specific access to information, regardless of the predominate system boundaries.

2.2 Platforms and PAM

This section deals with the hardware requirements necessary to ensure that the portal can be used in production and guarantee good performance. It examines the hardware requirements of a portal in light of specific releases and platforms. This section also clarifies the configurations (OS, DB, browser, and so on) that can support use of the portal, and therefore looks at the *platform* or *Product Availability Matrix (PAM)* of SAP.

The portal consists of the components listed in Figure 2.1. They offer several options for which applications reside on which physical system components. Before we look at the hardware requirements, we must first discuss the various alternatives.

2.2.1 Scenarios for Distributing Portal Components on Various Instances

Of course, you can simply install all the components on one server platform. However, the approach taken for the installation of the remaining components from the mySAP Business Suite family of solutions, which distributes them across two hardware components, has proven itself valuable. Because multiple end users use a portal concurrently, we recommend that you avoid using a compact installation on a single component.

Because content management must access a database for cross-system storage of documents and forms, including searching for and classifying them, it's preferable to use the same database for the portal itself, so that both subcomponents use only one database.

A fundamental problem develops when aiming for the most compact installation possible on anything other than a Sun Solaris operating system. Because you generally cannot do without use of the search and classification engine as a subcomponent (this server enables "search all" functionality), you must access a separate hardware component here. The limitation arises because currently, the search and classification server can run on only a Sun Solaris platform.

The combined use of content management and the portal presents another important restriction because both applications must be installed on identical hardware. If you use a cluster of portals, a requirement exists to have all hardware components on which J2EE applications run for the portal use the same operating system.

Unless the unification server is set up by the standard installer for SAP EP, it must be installed on separate hardware.

2.2.2 Hardware Requirements

The following hardware recommendations refer to a standard installation. Of course, the benchmark data given here is to be considered as only a rough guideline. Practical experience has shown that simple demo portals, used (simultaneously) by a small number of users, can even be installed on commonly available PCs and laptops.

A key factor for the hardware requirements is the available memory. On average, you shouldn't have less than 2GB of available memory.

The requirements for a hard disk no longer present any real restrictions. The simple installation of a portal application requires about 1GB; installation of the required databases requires an additional 6 to 10GB. In addition to the data volume needed, the transfer rate that the hard disk can achieve is more important. A simple rule of thumb applies—the faster the better.

At the beginning, we noted that portals are set up so that many end users can access them simultaneously. The natural consequence is that many parallel processes run on the database and application server. It's best to use a multiprocessor machine. As a minimal requirement, the portal requires a machine with two processors, each running at 700 MHz.

2.2.3 Software Requirements

As noted, the software requirements refer to the PAM, which you can access from SAP Service Marketplace (*http://service.sap.com/pam60*). The PAM distinguishes availability by phase and components (operating system, database, and so on).

Requirements for SAP EP 5.0

Table 2.1 lists the software components required to install SAP EP 5.0 and which products can be considered.

Software Component	Product
Operating system (OS)/DB	Windows 2000 Server 32-bit/MS SQL Server 8.0 Windows 2000 Server 32-bit/Oracle 8.1.7
J2EE application server	JRun In-Q-My
Web server	IIS
Windows client (browser)	IE 5.01 and above Netscape 4.7
Proxy	Microsoft ISA Server 2000 iPlanet Web Proxy Server 3.6 Netscape Proxy Server 3.5 Novell Border Manager 3.6
Portal LDAP	iPlanet Novell Microsoft
Connectors	File system Web server WebDAV-compatible server Lotus R5 Exchange 2000 SAP Content Server

Table 2.1 Software Components for an Installation of SAP EP 5.0

Requirements for SAP EP 6.0

The availability of SAP EP 6.0 has undergone three phases, as indicated by the following:

1. Ramp-up phase 1
2. Ramp-up phase 2
3. Unrestricted shipment or global availability

Among the three phases, differences exist in product support for individual software components, as shown in the following table.

Software Component	Phase/Product
UNIX	
Operating system (OS)/DB	Phase 1: Sun Solaris 8.0/Oracle 9.2, 64-bit UTF8 HP-UX 11 and 11i/Oracle 9.2, 64-bit UTF8
	Phase 2: AIX 5.2/Oracle 9.2, 64-bit UTF8
	Phase 3: AIX 5.2/IBM DB2/UDB
J2EE application server	As of Phase 1: SAP J2EE engine 6.20
Web server	As of Phase 1: Apache Web server 1.3x
Linux client (browser)	As of Phase 2: Netscape 6.2
Corporate LDAP	Phase 1: Novell eDirectory 8.6.1 and above Sun ONE Directory Server 5.0 and above
	Phase 2: Siemens DirX V6
Windows	
Operating system (OS)/DB	Phase 2: Windows 2000 Server 32-bit/MS SQL Server 2000, US English version Windows 2000 Server 32-bit/Oracle 9.2, 64-bit UTF
	Phase 3: Windows Server 2003 32-bit/MS SQL Server 2000, US English version Windows Server 2003 32-bit/Oracle 9.2, 32-bit
J2EE application server	As of Phase 2: SAP J2EE engine 6.20
Web server (optional)	As of Phase 2: IIS 5.0
	Phase 3: IIS 6.0

Table 2.2 Software Components for an Installation of SAP EP 6.0 on UNIX and Windows

Software Component	Phase/Product
Windows client (browser)	As of Phase 1: IE 5.5 SP 2 and above, IE 6.0, and Netscape 6.2
	As of Phase 2: Netscape 7.0
Corporate LDAP	Phase 1: Novell Directory 8.61 and above Sun ONE Directory Server 5.0 and above Microsoft ADS 2000
	Phase 2: Siemens DirX V6
	Phase 3: Microsoft ADS in Windows Server 2003

Table 2.2 Software Components for an Installation of SAP EP 6.0 on UNIX and Windows (cont.)

The PAM undergoes frequent revisions, so we recommend that you download the current versions from *http://service.sap.com/pam*.

Note: This Web site requires Client Authentication, however, you can request this certificate identification from this page.

3 Portal Installation, Configuration, and Customizing

This chapter describes the procedure for installing SAP Enterprise Portal as a test installation on a local test system. It also examines various combinations of LDAP directories.

The installation of SAP Enterprise Portal that is described in this chapter assumes that we are working with the same system landscape that was used in Chapter 2. The installation of a test system, which is performed here as an example, requires far fewer resources than a productive system, where hundreds or even thousands of users will later work. Before installing a portal that will be used as a productive system, we encourage you to get some experience working with a portal installation on a smaller computer so that the entire procedure will run more efficiently and you can avoid stumbling blocks.

Note

The next section describes a test installation of SAP EP 5.0 SP 5; Section 3.3 looks at the details of installing SAP EP 6.0. Please note that changes might have occurred between the writing of this book and its publication. The screenshots are intended as support only during installation; however, they might vary slightly due to recently released versions of the product at the level of service packs.

3.1 Sample Installation of a Test System: SAP EP 5.0

Installation options

SAP Enterprise Portal offers three server variations during installation: standalone, lock , or cluster server. Each option is intended for a different use. Typically, either a standalone server, as is the case for this test installation, or a combination of lock and cluster servers is installed.

Required components

The test installation requires prior installation of a number of components to ensure a smooth operation of the portal. The components include the following:

- Database server
- Directory server
- Java Development Kit (JDK)
- SAP Java Application Server (J2EE Engine)

- Internet Information Server (IIS)
- Database client
- Microsoft Data Access Components (MDAC)
- A file from the Novell Developer Kit (NDK)

The following installs each component and describes the procedure step by step. The test installation installs the database and directory server on the same computer, but you can also install them on separate computers.

LDAP The test installation will set up SAP EP 5.0 on a Microsoft SQL database (MS SQL). You should already have some experience with an LDAP directory server, although you don't need to make any extensive settings other than inserting three branches. The variants of LDAP servers that can be used are discussed later. An introduction to LDAP servers or the LDAP protocol exceeds the subject matter of this book and therefore, is not addressed here. See the related literature on these subjects in the appendices.

PDK If you prefer that a given installation not use a database or LDAP server, see Section 9.2.1 for a discussion of installing the *Portal Development Kit (PDK)* for SAP EP 5.0 and SAP EP 6.0. The PDK for SAP EP 5.0 requires no other software components than a J2EE engine (Apache Tomcat) and works solely at the database level. But don't be afraid. Installation of a portal is an exciting and interesting task. The greater your prior experience with installing portals, the more your knowledge of the related components will increase. The LDAP protocol and LDAP server were new even to us when SAP Enterprise Portal came on the market two or three years ago.

3.1.1 Database Server

Installation of Microsoft SQL Database (MS SQL) is rather simple. After you insert the CD, the setup menu appears automatically and asks the user which components are to be installed. Select **SQL Server 2000 Components** here and **Install Database Server** on the next screen. Then, select the computer on which you want to install the database (**Local Computer**, see Figure 3.1) and then **Create a new instance of SQL Server** (see Figure 3.2).

After you enter the license data and agree to the conditions, select **Server and Client Tools** (see Figure 3.3).

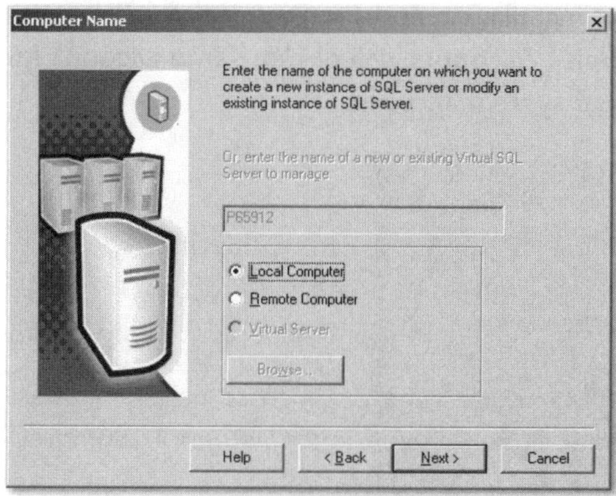

Figure 3.1 Selecting the Computer on which to Install the Database

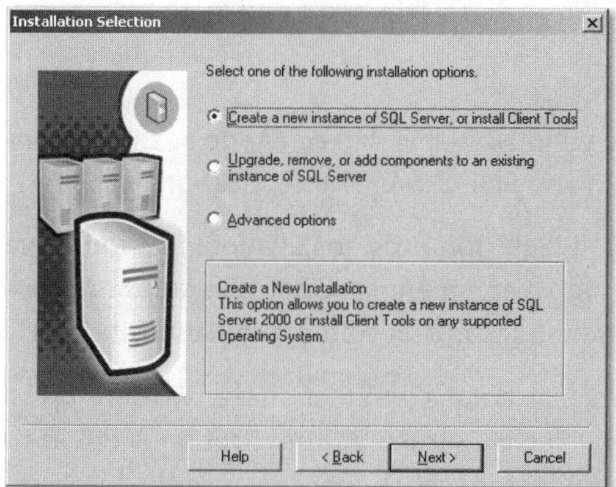

Figure 3.2 Creating a New SQL Server Instance

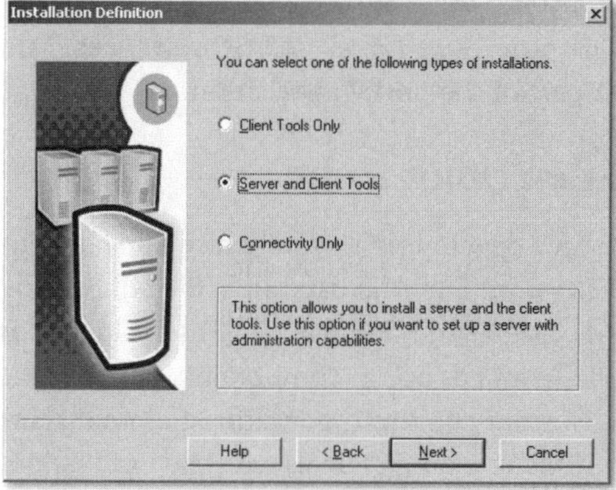

Figure 3.3 Selecting the Type of Installation

Setup Type Select the option for **Default** installation and then **Typical** for the setup type (see Figure 3.4). For Service Accounts, select **Use same account for each service** and **Use the local system account**.

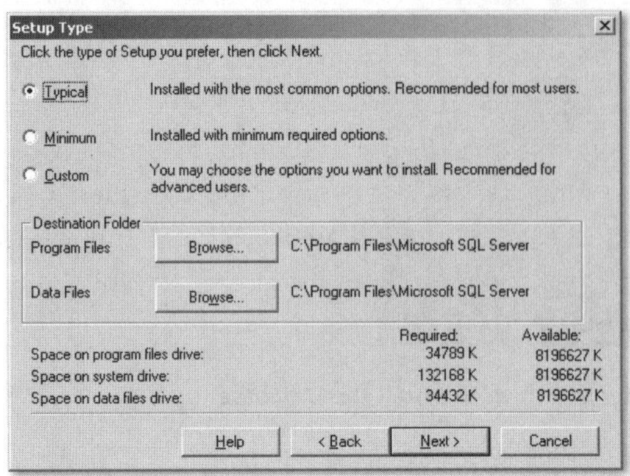

Figure 3.4 Selecting the Setup Type

Authentication In the **Authentication Mode** window, select **Mixed Mode** as the authentication method for Windows and SQL Server Authentication.

Password You can set the password to "blank" for a test installation. In productive operations, however, that's not recommended. The next steps are self-explanatory: select the license model and close the installation.

If you already installed an MS SQL database server, make two settings so that it can operate as a portal server: set the Authentication Method to **MS SQL and Windows** and set all services so that they use the local system account. Follow the menu path **Start · Settings · Control Panel Services**. Select the **MS SQL** service and right-click to display the context menu, where you select **Properties**. Under the **Log On** tab, select **Local System Account**. Perform this procedure for all MS SQL services. You have now completed the first part of the portal installation.

3.1.2 Java Development Kit (JDK)

If you're already familiar with Java development, you're also familiar with the Java Development Kit (JDK) from Sun Microsystems. If not, it's time to become acquainted with it, particularly because we'll use it in a later chapter when we develop Java iViews as portal components. In that section, we'll also provide a brief introduction to the Java programming language and work with the JDK. This section first deals with the installation.

Download

Licensing considerations prohibit delivery of the Java Development Kit with SAP Enterprise Portal, so you'll have to download it from Sun's Web site. For SAP EP 5.0, you actually need a version that is no longer current, SDK 1.3. You can download it from *http://java.sun.com/j2se/1.3/download.html*.

After you download the file, start the setup and install the JDK in the root directory of the portal computer, in directory *c:\jdk1.3* for example. After a successful installation, you must set three environment variables. Follow the menu path **Start • Settings • Control Panel • System** and select the **Advanced** tab. Select **Environment Variables** and insert the following settings under **System Variables:**

- Assign "CLASSPATH" the value "<JAVA-Root>\src.jar"
- Assign "JAVA_HOME" the value "JAVA-Root"
- Add "<JAVA-Root>\bin" to the PATH variable

In all three settings, replace the placeholder (<JAVA-Root>) with the path to your JDK directory, such as *c:\jdk1.3.1*. To test whether the JDK is being found, follow the menu path **Start • Run,** enter `cmd` to start a DOS console, and then enter the command `java -version`, which displays the version of the JDK you just installed. You've now completed the second step.

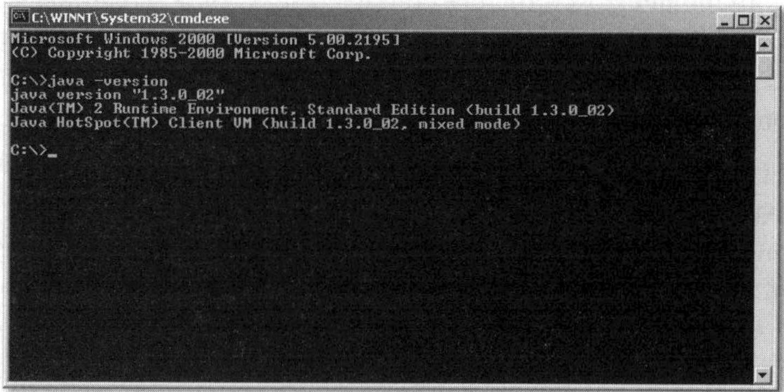

Figure 3.5 Display of the JDK Version in the DOS Console

3.1.3 Java Application Server (J2EE Engine)

Of the Java application servers available, SAP Enterprise Portal currently offers support for only the J2EE application server (J2EE Engine), which is delivered with SAP EP. When you insert the CD, you'll find the following two files in the directory: *sapj2ee620s_8—10001969.sar* and *sapcar.exe*;

you might encounter slight variation in the **.sar* file names. Select the correct file name in the following steps.

Follow the menu path **Start • Run** and enter `cmd` to open another DOS console, and change to a temporary directory. In the console, enter `<CD drive>\sapcar -xvf sapj2ee620s_8-10001969.sar`. *SAR* files are unpacked SAP directory containers. Your temporary directory will now contain a file named *visual.bat*. Start the program to begin installation of the J2EE Engine. After a welcome screen, licensing matters, and entry of your user information, select the path in which to install the J2EE Engine. Select the *<Root>* directory. After selection of the program directory and of all groups, you must then select the Java Virtual Machine (JVM). Select JRE from your *<Java root>* directory, which was installed together with the JDK. The installation procedure begins after you confirm a display that summarizes the settings.

Configuration

The next step configures the J2EE Engine for collaboration with SAP Enterprise Portal. To do so, you must modify some parameters with the J2EE configuration tool, register the engine as a Windows service, start the service, and ensure that the installation and configuration were finished successfully. The following describes each step in sequence.

Start the configuration tool with **Start • Programs • SAP J2EE Engine • Tools • Config Tool** or start the *configtool.bat* file under *<J2EE engine>\configtool*. In the directory structure on the left side of the screen, select **Alone** by double-clicking, which opens the parameter settings in the right side of the screen. Select the **NT Service** tab and then **Enabled**. Select **Apply** from the menu.

Port numbers

It's important to note that the port numbers of the J2EE Engine (for HTTP and HTTPS) differ from those of the IIS. In the tree structure on the left, once again select **Alone • Services • http**. If the IIS HTTP port is set to 80, change the HTTP port of the engine to 8100 or another value of your choice. It's important that no other application use this value. The same holds true for the HTTPS port. If that port is set to 443 in the IIS, select 8443 or another value of your choice. To change the values, click on the parameter, change it in the lower area of the screen, and then select **Add**.

Note

These values are generated automatically during installation of the portal. If you want to change them after installation, modify the file *<ROOT>\Enterprise Portal\Data File\multiplexer.dat* as needed.

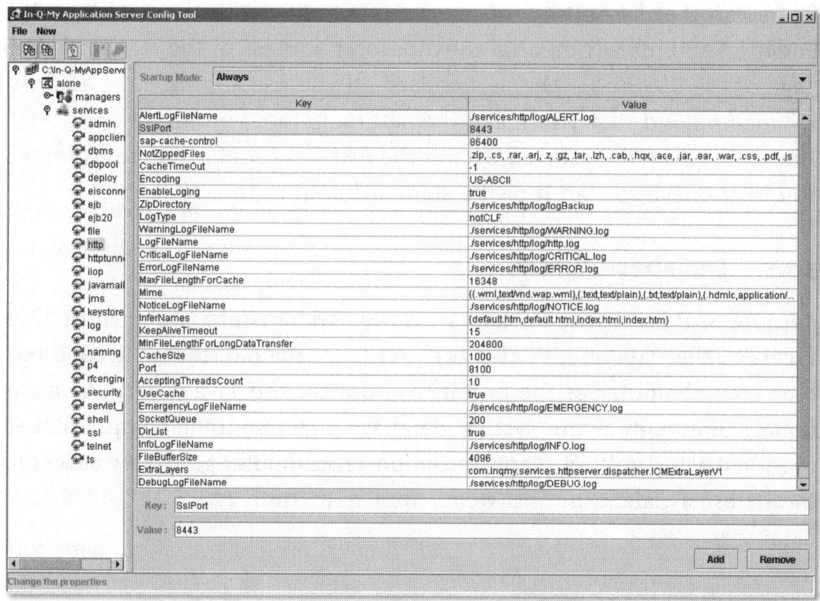

Figure 3.6 Configuration Tool of the J2EE Engine

The value for **EnableZippedResponse** must also be modified. Set it to **false**. To save the parameters, select **Apply** from the menu again and then close the configuration tool.

Windows service

Now you must set up the J2EE Engine as a Windows service. To do so, open a DOS window by following the menu path **Start • Run** and entering `cmd`. When the DOS window opens, change to the *<SAPJ2EE-Engine\configtool>* directory and enter `service -install`. This action records another entry in the service directory of Windows. To start the service, select **SAP J2EE Engine Alone** from the Windows Service Manager and then select the start button or use the context menu.

Testing the installation

To test the successful installation of the J2EE Engine, open a browser window and enter *http://<localhost>:8100* or the port number that you assigned. If the opening documentation page of the J2EE Engine appears, the installation was successful. If problems develop, check the settings again, especially the port number. Ensure that all services have started successfully.

3.1.4 Internet Information Server (IIS)

The Internet Information Server (IIS) is the only Web server currently supported for SAP EP 5.0. It must be installed on every portal server and configured so that its port addresses do not conflict with those of the J2EE Engine. SAP Enterprise Portal uses the port address of the standard Web page of the IIS (80 or 1080 is standard). If you use another port address, we recommend that you make the setting before you install the portal. The IIS is generally installed during the installation of a Windows server. You might have to start it or the standard Web page.

3.1.5 Database Client

Because SAP Enterprise Portal has its own system database, it must have access to this database. If, as is the case here, the database is installed on the same computer as the portal, you don't need to perform any additional steps. But, if the system database is on another computer, you must install a database client on the portal computer to enable access to the external database. This point applies to both MS SQL and Oracle databases.

3.1.6 Microsoft Data Access Component (MDAC)

SAP EP requires yet another component, the Microsoft Data Access Component (MDAC) 2.6x. You can download it from *http:// www.microsoft.com/downloads/details.aspx?FamilyID=6a7d785f-c2e0–471d-a33b-82ad1d514737.*

If the components are not yet installed on your computer, you must install them now. Simply execute file *MDAC_TYP.EXE* and follow the instructions on the screen.

3.1.7 Novell Developer Kit (NDK)

Before you can start the portal installation, SAP Enterprise Portal requires the presence of a particular Novell DLL file in a specific file folder on the portal server. The file is part of the Novell Developer Kit (NDK). Installation of this file is required regardless of the LDAP server you use.

Download

To install the NDK, you must first download it from *http://developer.novell.com/ndk/cldap.htm* (without documentation and examples). You can download the NDK free of charge, but you must register to get a user profile.

Installation

After you download the program, start it from its current location. The *cldap.exe* file is copied and opened. When the security warning appears and you're asked if you want to execute the setup program, select **Yes**. Follow the instructions given in the NDK Wizard and install the NDK files in a temporary directory on the portal server. Select **Finish** and note the directory in which the DLL files are stored. Copy the *ldapssl.dll* file from your temporary directory (or from *<ROOT>\Novell\NDK\cldapsdk\win32\bin*) into your *<Windows>\system32* directory. You have now completed this part of the installation.

3.1.8 Directory Server—LDAP

Except for the LDAP directory server, you have now installed all the components required for installation of the portal.

You have some freedom in selecting the LDAP directory server. To provide a better understanding of the issues involved, the following sections describe the LDAP servers required for installation. As noted, if you don't want to install an LDAP directory server and database, you should install the portal development kit (PDK 5.0 for SAP EP 5.0). Section 9.2.2 explains the installation of the PDK.

Corporate LDAP

SAP EP requires two LDAP servers, the first of which is the corporate LDAP server that is typically already operating at a company and is responsible for managing user information during operations. It supports the authentication of users and grants them access to the needed systems and data. SAP Enterprise Portal can use an existing corporate LDAP server. Only read access occurs on the corporate LDAP server. Except for anonymous users, every portal user must be registered with this directory server.

SAP Enterprise Portal currently supports the following LDAP servers:

- iPlanet from Netscape
- Microsoft Active Directory
- Novell eDirectory

Portal LDAP

An additional LDAP, the portal LDAP, is required for user mapping, role management, and storing additional attributes: it handles management of user information. You don't have to install this LDAP server on a separate instance, it can run on the same computer as the existing corporate LDAP server. However, only Netscape iPlanet and Novell eDirectory currently support this option.

The portal LDAP server stores information on portal users or mapping information entered by the portal administrator, or users themselves.

To use a company's existing corporate LDAP server as a portal LDAP server, you must ensure that Novell eDirectory or Netscape iPlanet is being used. You must also insert portal-specific branches that enable the portal to store user information.

Whether you use an existing LDAP for the portal or create a new instance, you must create three new branches on the portal LDAP server (see Table 3.1).

Branches	Explanation	Authorization
ou = UserMapping	User mapping: of portal user **Peter Miller** to SAP user **MillerP,** for example.	Read and write authorization
ou = Roles	Roll and user assignment: Peter Miller to the Sales-Representative role, for example.	Read and write authorization
ou = CustomAttributes	Attributes that you can maintain	Editing of schemes and enhancing authorizations (only at the beginning, you can reduce them later).

Table 3.1 Creating Branches in the LDAP Directory

After all the components have been installed, you must still check additional installation requirements.

3.1.9 Checking the Installation Requirements

During installation of the portal, you must have your user ID and the associated passwords at hand.

User data and authorizations

First, the user who starts the Setup Wizard must have local administration rights on the computer. The user must also have administrator rights for the database (which is assumed here). During installation, a user is queried for a user ID and password for authentication purposes. Both user management of the portal and the IIS require a Windows user with authorizations sufficient to access all network resources of the portal components and portal server, including write authorization for the Windows registry. You can use an existing Windows user (with sufficient authorizations) or create a new user.

The administrator ID and password for the J2EE Engine were assigned during installation. By default, the ID is set to "Administrator" and the password is blank. If the password has been changed, enter the correct password.

An administrator ID is also required for the database. The standard user is "sa" and the password is either blank or the result of an entry you made during installation. In either case, the password is required.

An ID for Yahoo! services is optional. You can request these services from your SAP consultant. You can also enter them later.

3.1.10 SAP Enterprise Portal

Setup Wizard

After you have completed all the previous steps to install and configure all the required components, you can begin the actual installation of the portal. The Setup Wizard guides you through the installation step by step. It checks the individual components that we have installed and issues a notification if problems occur during installation. In most cases, however, the windows in which the messages appear are too small for detailed information. Therefore, references to log files are displayed, which are most easily viewed in a text editor. This approach has an advantage: the messages remain even after the installation has aborted. Therefore, you can remedy any problems more easily if need be.

To begin installation of the portal, ensure that all components have been installed correctly and that you have the required user authorizations, user IDs, and passwords. Check again to ensure that the database and the Java application server (J2EE Engine) have been started.

Now, insert the SAP Enterprise Portal CD (main installer) into the CD drive of the portal server. Setup should start automatically. If it doesn't, start file *Start.hta* in the main directory of the CD. Select **EP 5.0 SP5** from the Portal Installation column, as shown in Figure 3.7.

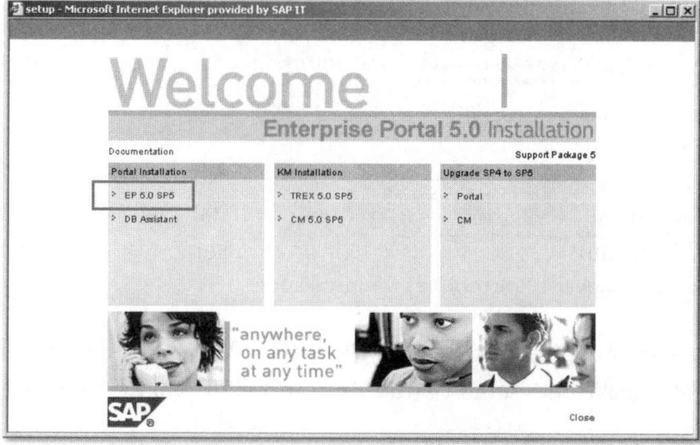

Figure 3.7 Welcome Screen of Portal Installation

Starting additional components

If, at a later point, you want to start SAP KM (CM and TREX), the SAP R/3 unifier, or an upgrade, you can do so from this menu. However, you must first install SAP Enterprise Portal as the first component. When the file download menu appears, select **Run this program from its current location** (see Figure 3.8).

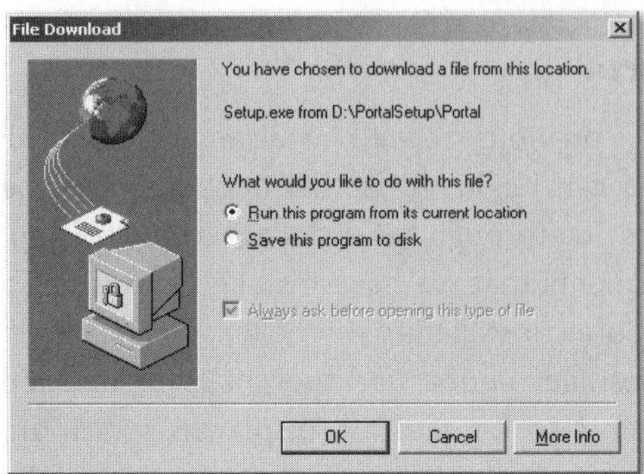

Figure 3.8 Run File—Do Not Save

You can close the security notice by selecting **Yes**. Then, click on **Next** (see Figure 3.9). Since we are performing only a test installation, select **Standalone Installation** from the list of installation types (see Figure 3.10).

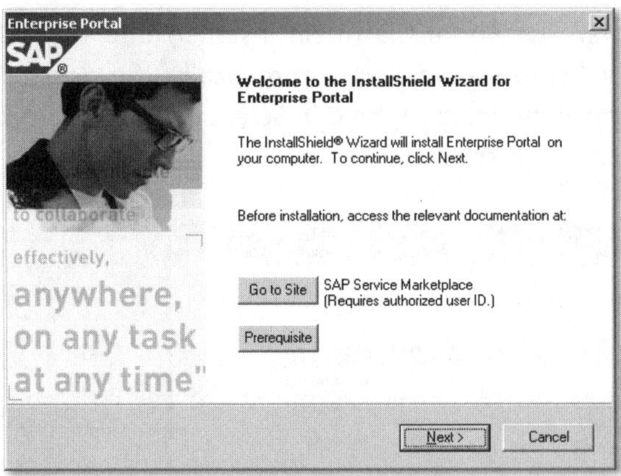

Figure 3.9 Option to Check the Prerequisites for Installation

You are now prompted to specify the directory in which you want to install the portal. Leave the default entry as is and click **Next** (see Figure 3.11).

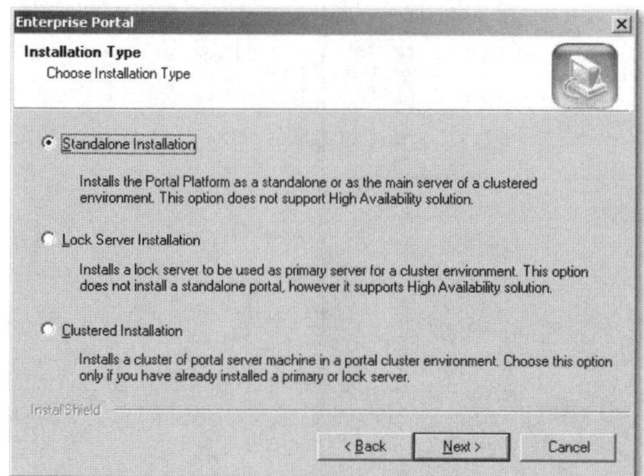

Figure 3.10 Selecting the Type of Installation

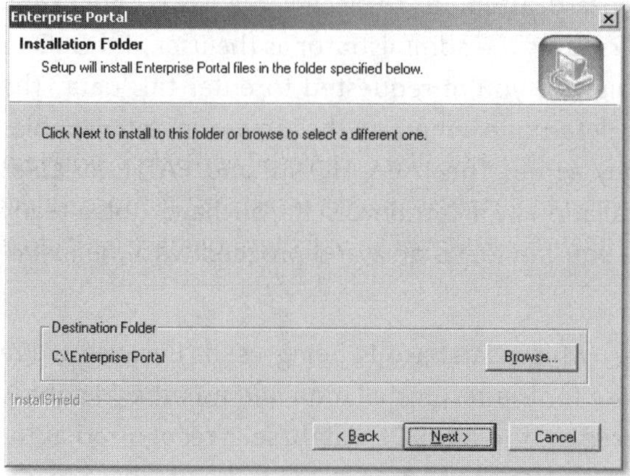

Figure 3.11 Selecting the Installation Directory

When you're asked for the program directory, leave the default entry as is. You can select the portal from this directory later on.

Authentication

Now, you're prompted for user information and therefore, you must authenticate yourself. Enter the Windows user information noted above and an encryption code for your passwords (see Figure 3.12). The Windows user is required to enable the first logon for the portal administrator. Enter the Windows user in the following format: "<domain>\<user_ID>". The user ID is sufficient for a local installation. You can choose any character string for the encryption code, which is used to encrypt sensitive data. You should use the same code for the portal and the unification server so that both products can exchange information with each other.

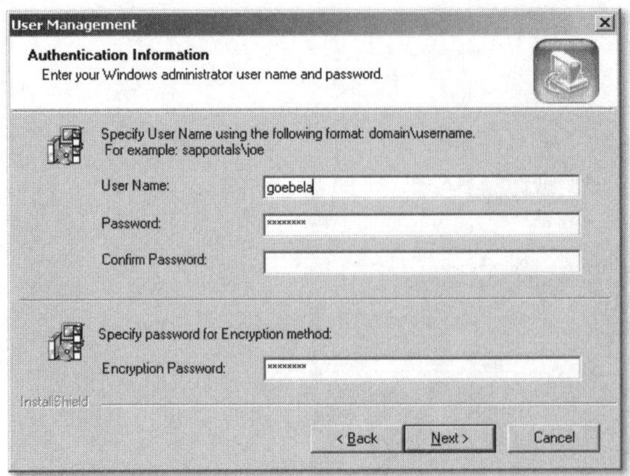

Figure 3.12 Entering the Password and User ID

J2EE Engine In the next step, the Wizard attempts to access the Java Application Server (J2EE Engine). It first uses the administrator as the user. If this ID or a password has been assigned, you're requested to enter this data. The Wizard then checks to determine whether the environment variables have been set and if they agree. The JAVA_HOME and PATH variables must be set or the installation will terminate. If you have not already maintained these values, you can do so now and proceed with the installation.

Database The next step determines which database is being used. Because we're using the MS SQL database for the test installation and no other database is running on the portal server, the MS SQL database is recognized automatically. You must now have the connection data for the database ready. Enter the name of the host on which the SQL server was installed. Simply enter the name without any other information. The standard TCP/IP number for the SQL server is already assigned. At this point, you still need the user ID and the password of the system administrator (sysadmin) or the security administrator (securityadmin). We have already assigned "sa" as the user ID without a password. If you assigned a password, enter it now (see Figure 3.13).

You're now requested to enter the user ID and password of the owner of the database, so that the portal can use this information to access the database (see Figure 3.14). A user with sysadmin authorization is created on the database server as are the required databases. The path to the database is found automatically because it resides on the portal server. Figure 3.15 reviews the entries made for the installation.

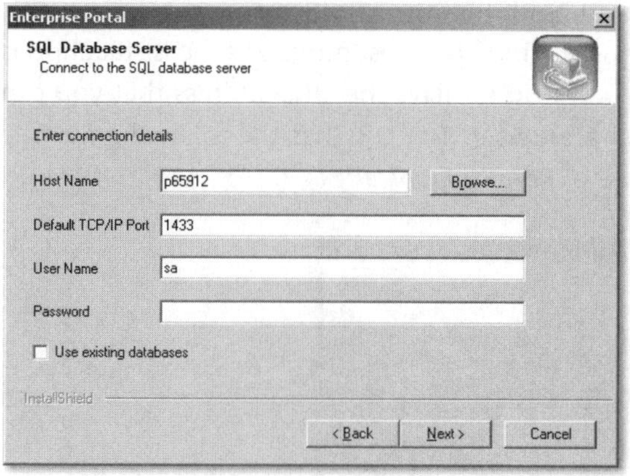

Figure 3.13 Connection Data for the Database

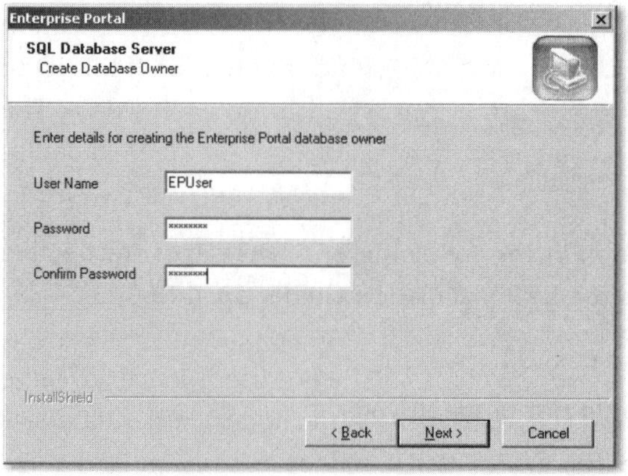

Figure 3.14 Creating the Database Owner

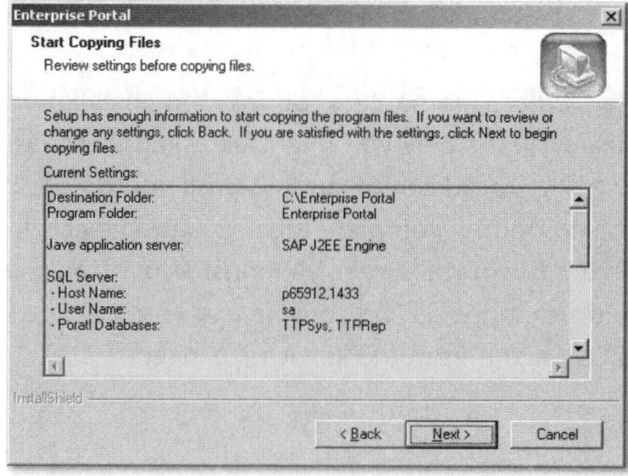

Figure 3.15 Display of Entries for the Installation

URL address of the portal

If the installation occurred without any problems and you haven't received any error messages, a window that summarizes the installation is displayed (see Figure 3.16). It also displays the URL address that you can use to call the portal from a browser. The URL has the following format: *http://<complete_hostname>:<Port>/sapportal*.

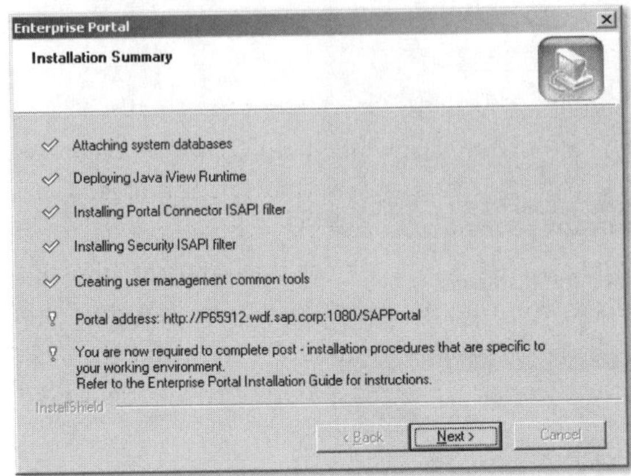

Figure 3.16 Summary of the Installation

Error messages

The summary can also contain the following error messages (respective solutions can be found in the SAP Installation Guide, pp. 119-123):

- Databases could not be created
- Java iView Runtime could not be deployed
- Installing Portal Connector ISAPI Filter
- Installing Security ISAPI Filter

It's important that you restart the IIS and the Java application server: the Installation Wizard prompts you to do so.

It might be impossible to replace some files during the installation because they were being used. That's why you might be asked to restart the computer. In that event, the portal cannot be run until you do so. If you don't have to restart the computer, complete the installation by clicking **Finish**. If you have restarted the portal server, you must also restart the IIS and the J2EE Engine. To do so, open a DOS console and enter `iisreset`. You can restart the J2EE Engine from the services manager.

Installation Log

Installation creates a log file (*TTInstall.log*) in the *\Enterprise Portal\Installation\Logs* directory. Check the *sql_run.log* file in the *\Enterprise Portal\Installation\Logs* directory for any errors that occurred.

The installation is now complete. Check the following items:

- Verify the connection to the J2EE engine
- Set IRJ and media library parameters

Connection to the J2EE Engine

Start the IIS enterprise manager from the following menu path: **Start · Settings · Control Panel · Administrative Tools · Computer Management · Services and Applications · Internet Information Services**. Right-click on **Internet Information Services** to display the context menu: select **Settings**. In the window that opens, select the **Internet Information Services** tab and **Edit** in the **Master Properties** area. Another window opens, where you select the **ISAPI Filters** tab. Verify that the **J2EE connector** is installed correctly, that a green, upward arrow is displayed, and that the priority is set to **High**, as shown in Figure 3.17.

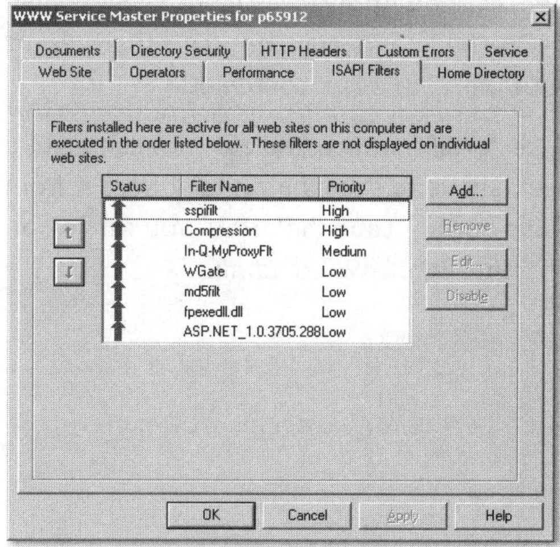

Figure 3.17 ISAPI Filters

If the J2EE connector appears multiple times, delete all but one entry and then restart the IIS. The display should show only one instance.

IRJ and media library parameters

Check the correct mapping of the URLs for the J2EE Engine in the *SAPJ2EE.ini* file in directory *\Inetpub\Scripts*. Ensure that the following values have been set in the **URL.Mapping** area:

http:/irj/servlet->http://<complete_portal_server_name>:<port>
https:/irj/servlet->https://< complete_portal_server_name >:<port>

Ensure that the complete name (not "local host") of the portal server is given in both cases and that the syntax is correct.

Virtual directories Virtual directories were created in the IIS on the portal server during installation of the portal. These directories contain pointers to libraries in portal installation files in the file system. To achieve the optimal performance of the portal, you must adjust the values for the HTTP header settings that enable recognition of an expiration date for Web content. Change the settings for three virtual directories in the IIS manager:

- Common tools
- SAPPortal
- Irj

To change the settings, proceed as follows. In the IIS manager, select **Default Website · Common Tools** and then display the context menu by right-clicking the mouse. Select **Properties**. In the **HTTP Headers** tab, select **Enable Content Expiration** and **Expire After**. You can enter a rough value, such as "9999" days. Then, click on **Apply** (see Figure 3.18). Follow the same procedure for the *SAPPortal* and *irj* branches, and then restart the IIS in a console window with the `iisreset` command.

The installation of SAP Enterprise Portal is now complete. You can open a browser and enter the URL given above to start the portal, or call it from the start menu (**Start · Enterprise Portal · Launch Portal**). You can log on to the portal with user name admin and password admin.

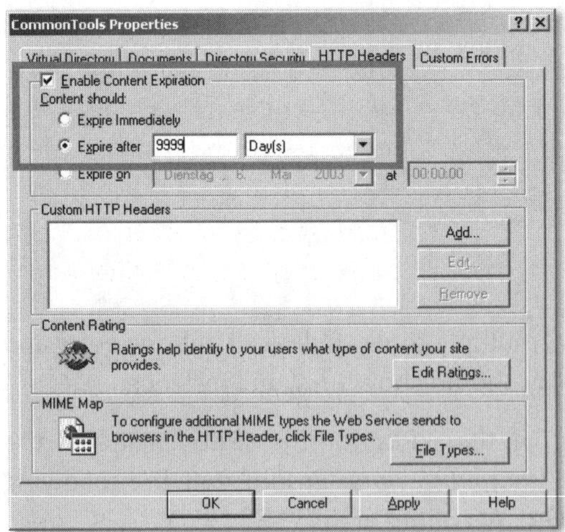

Figure 3.18 HTTP Header in IIS Manager

License key

A notification will inform you that you do not yet have a license key. To create the key, select **System Configuration • License** and then **Install Temporary License Key** from the top-level navigation. You must then restart the SAP J2EE Engine and the IIS, as described above.

Configuration of user management

You logged on to the portal with admin as the user name and admin as the password. To prevent unauthorized access to the portal, you should change these values as quickly as possible. We also want to create additional users we can use to log on to the portal.

As you know, SAP Enterprise Portal works along with an LDAP server that manages a directory of portal users. In most cases, companies already operate an LDAP server. For our test installation, you must now create five directory branches on the LDAP server: one for user groups, one for users, and three more for the portal itself (*UserMapping*, *CustomAttributes*, and *Roles*). You can later assign groups or users to portal roles. Groups allow abstraction and simplification of role assignment. Create a test user under the **User** branch in your LDAP server. We don't need groups right now. Note the LDAP administrator name and the password, the port for the LDAP server (389 is typical), and where you created the directory branch. Unfortunately, we can't use individual LDAP servers here. Our test uses Netscape iPlanet LDAP. It's easier to install than Novell eDirectory, but its functionality is more limited. **LDAP**

In the portal, select **System Configuration • User Management Configuration**. Create a new configuration by entering a name (without special characters) in the field behind **Create New.** Select **Create**: you have now generated a new confirmation with the new name. Reenter the administrator ID and password. The ID can remain `admin`, but you should change the password. Under **NT User Impersonation**, enter the local Windows administrator, as you did during installation, and click **Apply**. Now select the **Directory Server** tab. Here you specify the data for the LDAP server. Select your **LDAP server** (Netscape, Microsoft ADS, Novell, or Other) and enter the server name, port (generally `389`), and the administrator name (as `cn = directory manager, ou = services, and o = sap`) and password. If the data is correct, use the **Browse** button behind **Groups Root** to display the directory nodes of the LDAP. Select the correct node and do the same for **People Root**. **Portal**

Authentication method

Then select the method used to maintain hierarchies in your LDAP (flat or deep). Click on **Apply**. An **Authentication Server** is displayed. Here you define how users are authenticated: either by an external system, such as Netegritys Siteminder, Windows NTLM, an SAP system, or an LDAP server. First, select **LDAP**. In a later section we'll discuss how to authenticate with Windows NTLM. You can copy the data from the fields of the previous tab by using the **Copy** function. You can also use the copy function to copy data to the **Portal Roles** and **Portal Mapping** tabs. You must simply select the correct directories from the LDAP with the **Browse** function. In each case, click on **Apply**. No entry is needed in the **Certificates** tab. Now restart the J2EE Engine and the IIS.

You now have a portal that can operate and log on to the portal from the LDAP server directory with a user. This user has no administrator rights in the portal, only usage rights. The following section discusses how to assign roles and authorizations.

3.2 Setting Up the Portal for Users and Roles

Users

SAP Enterprise Portal is designed for various users and groups within a company, including users in the financial, controlling, sales, production, human resources, consulting, marketing, and other departments. Not all portal users need the same systems, applications, and authorizations. That's why you can form groups of employees who belong to a given department. Administrators save a great deal of time by assigning authorizations to only one group, rather than to individual employees. Employees are then simply assigned to a group with the Membership function of the LDAP and have exactly the authorizations they need to perform their functions. As a precondition, a given user and the group must exist in the LDAP.

Roles

For its part, the portal contains roles. Not every individual application needs to be assigned to a user, only channels, entire directories, or work sets. You can use roles to assign these items to a user or a group with one action. If you're already familiar with SAP products, imagine that SAP Enterprise Portal has a role called *sales employee*. Specific transactions are assigned to the sales employee in SAP R/3. For example, you would assign these transactions to a role in SAP Enterprise Portal and then assign the role to the *sales* user group from the corporate Lightweight Directory Access Protocol (LDAP) in the portal. With one action, you have given the group the required authorizations. The difference between a role in SAP R/3 and a role in SAP Enterprise Portal is that in addition to recording authorizations to SAP R/3 transactions, portal roles can also record authorizations for access to any other system, such as a Baan, Siebel, or PeopleSoft system, or to Web services on the Internet.

Some roles are already preconfigured in the portal, such as the portal administrator role or the standard portal user role. The *admin* administrator that you used for your first logon to the portal has, by default, the *Portal_Admin* and *Portal_User* roles.

Assigning roles

To illustrate how to assign roles, we'll assign only administrator rights to a test user in the user directory of the LDAP (people). To do so, log on as the *admin* user and select **Portal-Admin • Role Assignment** from the top-level navigation (TLN). Select **Search <user>** in **Users** and click **Go**. Select your user and then select **Edit**. The left half of the screen will now display the user's data: the authorizations assigned to the user appear in the upper-right section and all available authorizations are displayed in the lower section. Select the *Portal_Admin* role and click **Add**. In the left area, select **Save** (see Figure 3.19)

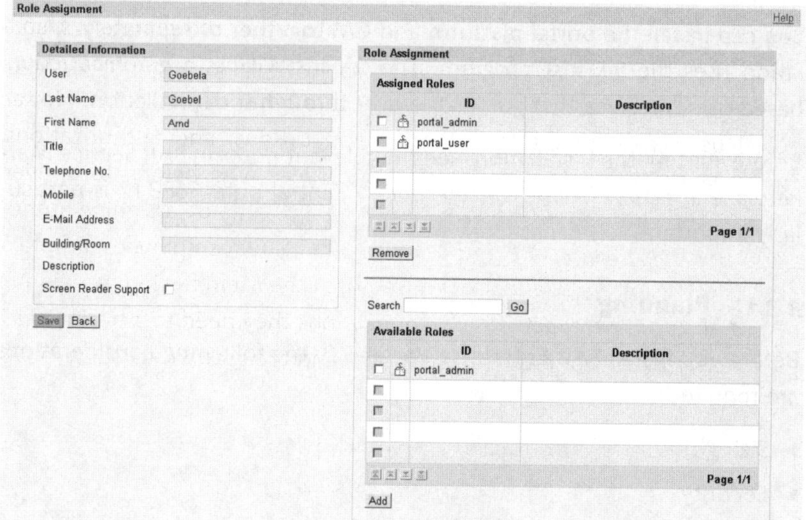

Figure 3.19 Assigning a User to the Portal_Admin Role

Now close your browser and restart SAP Enterprise Portal in a new browser session. Log on with the data of the new user, who now has administrator rights. You can assign roles to a user group just as you assigned roles to a user. Experiment with this task to familiarize yourself with the role concept. For more information on roles, see Section 8.1, "Roles and Navigation in the Portal," in Chapter 8.

3.3 Sample Installation for a Test System with SAP EP 6.0

Chapter 2 has already presented the system landscape and system requirements you require to operate SAP Enterprise Portal 6.0. At the time this book was written (service pack 2), SAP EP 6.0 comprised the following components:

Component

- Portal platform
- Connector to SAP R/3
- Connector for database applications via JDBC
- Content management (CM)
- Text retrieval and classification (TREX)
- Unification server

This section looks at the installation of the standalone portal platform of SAP EP 6.0 with the application connectors under UNIX and without content management.

You can install the portal platform and CM together or separately. Installation uses the SAPinst program. The SAPinst GUI is a graphical, Java-based user interface that guides the user through the installation.

Before starting the installation, see the relevant notes in SAP Service Marketplace at *http://service.sap.com/notes*. Central note 668312 is particularly important.

3.3.1 Planning

Before you install SAP Enterprise Portal 6.0, the following considerations are required:

- Sizing
- Security
- Load balancing
- System requirements (see Chapter 2)

Performance

To ensure good performance of the portal, think about an optimal approach that distributes individual portal components across several computers. The portal and content management platform and the unification and database servers are all components that require sufficient system resources to provide good performance.

If you have many users, you will have to operate several servers in parallel and use network load balancing (NLB). Doing so offers ensures reliability and greatly enhances performance.

Security

Today security is particularly important. When you consider the architecture of a solution such as SAP Enterprise Portal, you must always keep an eye on security. Chapter 11 examines in detail the following subjects associated with security: encryption, authentication, and separation of the Internet, intranets, and a demilitarized zone.

3.3.2 Preparations

Before you begin an installation, you must do some preparatory work, which includes the following:

- Preparation of the database installation
- Configuration of the portal host
- Installation of the Java Development Kit (JDK)
- Preparation of the SAPinst installation
- Oracle JDBC libraries
- Java cryptographic toolkit

Database server

SAP Enterprise Portal requires a database server. As was the case with the installation of SAP EP 5.0, the SAP EP 6.0 installation prompts you for information on the database server. When this book was being written, the portal supported the Oracle database for both UNIX and Windows and the Microsoft SQL database for Windows. In this context, it's important to note that although the portal and the database can run on different servers, they must still run on the same operating system. This test installation uses the Oracle database.

You can install the Oracle database on a separate server before you install the portal. Content Management (CM) can also use this database. For improved performance, however, we recommend that you install the database server on a separate computer for a productive system. To enjoy even better performance, you should also use a separate database for CM. This test installation places the database and the portal on the same computer. You can do the same when running the SAPinst program.

Please consult the current notes on the current patch sets for the Oracle database when installing SAP Enterprise Portal. You can download the current patch sets from SAP Service Marketplace.

As mentioned, the SAPinst program allows you to install the Oracle database separately from the portal or, as part of the standard installation, together with the portal and CM. If you select the standard installation, you must install the updates and patches for the Oracle 9i database after SAPinst ends.

Portal server Now you must configure the computer for the J2EE engine and the SAPinst installation. To do so, you'll need the OS dependencies guidelines that you can find at SAP Service Marketplace: *http://service.sap.com/instguides* (**SAP Components · SAP Web Application Server · <Release> · SAP Software on Unix: Dependencies**). Follow the instructions in subsection 1 and in the area applicable to your database.

Java Development Kit (JDK) For SAP EP 6.0 (as for SAP EP 5.0), you must install the JDK. Please consult the Product Availability Matrix (PAM) at *http://service.sap.com/pam* and in Chapter 2 to see which versions are currently supported. If you already installed the Oracle database on your server, the JDK was installed with it and you can skip this step.

SAPinst installation You need a Java Runtime Environment (JRE) for the SAPinst GUI, which was installed along with the database or, which you installed separately with the JDK. The SAPinst GUI requires the same JRE version as the SAP Web Application Server (SAP Web AS). SAP does not deliver the JRE. You must set some environment variables to install the GUI. $JAVA_HOME must point to the JDK directory (for example, for Solaris: `setenv JAVA_HOME /opt/j2sdk1_3_1_06`, for HP: `setenv JAVA_HOME /opt/java1.3`, and for Windows see JDK installation with SAP EP 5.0). The PATH variable must point to the *bin* directory of the JDK.

The JRE *ext* directory cannot contain any **.jar* files from other applications because they will cause error messages from the SAPinst GUI. For the duration of the installation, rename all **.jar* files so that they no longer end in **.jar* (change *xerces.jar* to *xerces.xxx*, for example). The *ext* directory is located at *<JAVA_HOME>/JRE/lib/ext* under UNIX and at *<JAVA_HOME>\JRE\lib\ext* under Windows.

Note Remember to rename the files with their original names after the installation.

Oracle JDBC To install the portal, you'll need an Oracle JDBC driver. If the database server and the portal server are identical, as is the case in this test installation, you don't need to do anything. If they are not identical, you must copy the file *<$ORACLE_HOME>\jdbc\lib\classes12.jar* from the database server into the *home* directory of the user on the portal server.

Java cryptographic toolkit

To use Java encryption for SAP Web AS, you need the Java cryptographic toolkit. Download the toolkit from SAP Service Marketplace at *http://service.sap.com/download* (note the export control: see note 397175). Extract the toolkit into a temporary directory and copy the **.jar* files into the *home* directory of the user before you begin the installation.

3.3.3 Installation under UNIX

At the time of writing this book, SAP EP 6.0 was available for UNIX and Windows platforms. The description of the installation examines only a local, standalone installation under UNIX.

For the installation of SAP EP 6.0, ensure that your DISPLAY and JAVA_HOME variables (see above) are set. Log on to the installation computer as "Super user (root)." Insert the installation CD locally. Create an installation directory for SAPinst with `mkdir <SAPinst_directory>`. This directory cannot be located directly under the *root* (/) directory: it must be located at least one level lower. Under Sun Solaris, the directory cannot be located in */tmp* or one of its subdirectories because a restart deletes */tmp* and all its subdirectories. Set the authorizations with `chmod 777 <SAPinst_directory>`. Enter `umask 022`. Use `cd <SAPinst_directory>` to change to the *<SAPinst_directory>* directory and start the *install* script from the installation CD with `<Installation_CD>/SAPINST/UNIX/<platform>/INSTALL`.

During installation, SAPinst uses ports 21212 and 21213 to communicate with the SAPinst GUI. If one or both of the ports is already in use, you must call the installation as follows: `<Installation_CD>/SAPINST/UNIX/<platform>/ INSTALL -port <free_port_number>`, where `<free_port_number>` and `<free_port_number> +1` represent the free ports. For example, if you enter 9000 for `<free_port_number>`, ports 9000 and 9001 are selected. SAPinst is now located in the *<SAPinst_directory>* directory and the SAPinst GUI is started automatically.

If the installation program asks you to specify the directory that contains the file *LABEL.ASC*, enter the *<SAPinst CD root directory>* directory.

Installation now begins with a Welcome screen. It then displays the license conditions and directs you to the selection of installation options. Here you can select either the standard installation or individual components. If you have not yet installed the database separately, the standard installation will do so. If you want to install the portal separately, you must install the database before the portal. See the special guidelines, *Installing Oracle 9.2 Database Server for SAP Enterprise Portal 6.0 SP2*, at SAP Service Marketplace at *http://service.sap.com/instguides* (**SAP Components · SAP Enterprise Portal · Enterprise Portal 6.0 · Installation · Installation Guide—EP 6.0 SP2**). Extract the *EP6SP2_Installation_final9.zip* file in a separate directory. The file for installation of Oracle 9i is *EP6SP2_Installing_OracleDB_v2_final.pdf*.

Deploying the portal platform

The next step in the portal installation is the deployment of the portal platform. You install it on a new system and select this option. Because the test installation installs only the portal, select the portal platform option (without CM and collaboration) in the next step. Assign a system name that can be between 4 and 20 letters. The name is used only internally. Don't select "portal" because it can lead to an error. Enter an instance number between 00 and 99. The instance number is used to determine the ports from which the portal can be called. Two portals cannot run on the same instance. If you're already using an instance number, you'll see an error message and must select another one. You are now asked for the maximum heap size for the Java Virtual Machine (JVM). Select **half of the main memory**, but not less than **512 MB** and not more than **1,536 MB**. Don't select a value higher than the maximum Java heap value of your platform (see JDK documentation). The new system is installed under */usr/sap/<SYSTEM_NAME>/j2ee/j2ee_<instance_number>/....*

For portal installation under UNIX, SAPinst uses the system user *j2eeadm* from user group *sapsys*. If the user does not exist, the program displays a notification that prompts you to create the group. You then create user *j2eeadm*.

If the Java cryptographic toolkit wasn't extracted into the *home* directory of the user, the next window asks for the location of the files.

Connection data for the database

Now you must enter the connection data for the database. You need the host name, the system ID (SID), the Oracle listener port, the ID of the portal scheme, and the user ID and password for the portal scheme. By default, the SID is POR, the port is 1527, and the user name is PCD.

If the JDBC libraries weren't extracted into the *home* directory of the user, the next window asks for the location of the files.

Distinguished name

You are then asked for the value of the distinguished name (DN) for the keystore. The DN identifies the portal server as an authorized issuer of certificates for SAP logon tickets. The DN is a combination of the following character strings:

- CN—system ID
- OU—organizational subunit
- OU—organizational unit
- O—organization
- C—Country

Enter your values for CN, OU, and OU. O and C are generally given the standard values of "SAP Trust Community Portals" and "US". For CN, you can select only the following values: A–Z, a–z, blank, and 0–9. The same limitations apply to the OUs. You can use the administrative tool to change these values later.

Now, the installation process begins. After a successful installation, you'll see a confirmation that the process has ended. As occurred with SAP EP 5.0, a URL that you can use to call the portal is displayed. Make a note of the URL and to access it more easily, add it to the Favorites list in your browser.

The portal URL is *http://<complete_portal_server_name>:*<HTTP*_port_of_the_portal_server* >*/irj*. You can calculate the portal number to call the portal as follows: port = 50,000 + (100 * <instance number>). If you use SSL, the URL begins with *https* instead of *http*.

Errors during installation

If errors occur during installation, follow the instructions in Table 3.2.

Problem	Solution
Installation error during the dialog phase	Check the **view logs** to determine whether a system error exists. If it does, contact your system administrator to change the kernel settings. Stop the installation, correct the error, and then restart the installation.
Installation error during the process phase	Check the **view logs** to determine whether a system error exists. If it does, contact your system administrator to change the kernel settings, or try to solve the problem yourself with *SAPinst Troubleshooting Guide* in SAP Service Marketplace (*http://service.sap.com/sapinstfeedback*). Continue the installation after the error has been corrected. If you can't correct the error, stop the installation.

Table 3.2 Notes on Error Correction

Under UNIX, you should monitor the installation process. The files stored in */usr/sap/<SYSTEM_NAME>/j2ee/j2ee_<instance_number>cluster/server/managers/console_logs* provide information on the status of the installation. The most current files are *<YY_MM_DD>_at_<HH_MM_SS>_*

error.log and *<YY_MM_DD>_at_<HH_MM_SS>_output.log*, where *<YY_MM_DD>* stands for the date and *<HH_MM_SS>* stands for the time of creation. You can use the command tail -f <YY_MM_DD>_at_<HH_MM_SS>_error.log to trace the installation process exactly. If the *error.log* file does not contain an entry stating "**Portal installation done,**" the installation was unsuccessful. The *output.log* file must contain an entry stating "**Starting service servlet.jsp.**"

You can use the analyzer for further investigation of errors. You can find it in the */analyzer* directory on the portal CD.

If you can solve the problem, continue with the installation. If you have not yet stopped the installation, select **Retry**. SAPinst will try to continue the installation with the new entries. If you already stopped the installation, you have two options—continue the installation or restart.

To continue the installation, you must first ensure that no Java processes are running with the SAPinst GUI. To do so, you can use `ps -ef | grep java` via a console. You can recognize SAPinst GUI processes when the character string `...java -cp JAR/instgui.jar...` appears in the output. Verify that the environment variables (see above) are set. Start SAPinst from your *<SAPinst_directory>* directory with `./sapinst`. The installation process will continue.

New installation

If you want to restart the installation from scratch, you have two options—restarting from the CD or from the file system. As described above, you can restart from the CD and confirm the notification that all files in the installation directory can be deleted or overwritten. If you restart from the file system, enter `/newinstall` in your *<SAPinst_directory>* directory. The old log files will be stored in the *<SAPinst_directory>/log_<timestamp>* directory. In most cases, you'll have to uninstall any components that have already been installed before you can start a new installation.

3.3.4 Proxy Settings

You now need the name of your proxy server, the proxy HTTP port, the proxy exception list (with local host), the name of the portal server (local host), and the HTTP port of the portal server. With this data, you can start a UNIX console with user *j2eeadm*. Change to the */usr/sap/<SAP J2EE instance name>/j2ee/j2ee_<instance_name>/cluster/server/* directory and open the files *cmdline.properties* and *go* with an editor (vi, for example). Then insert the following lines into each file:

```
-Dhttp.proxyHost=<complete proxy server name>
-Dhttp.proxyPort=<HTTP port of the proxy server>
-Dhttp.nonProxyHosts="<proxy exception list, separated by
pipes (|)>|<complete name of the local host>"
-Dstatusicons.mimes.name=http://<complete portal server
name>:<HTTP port of the portal server>
/irj/services/htmlb/mimes/mimesinfo.xml
-Dhtmlb.useUTF8=x
```

The following lists some sample values:

Proxy Server Name	proxy.mycompany.corp
HTTP port of the proxy	8081
Proxy exception list	*.mycompany.corp, localhost
Portal server (local host)	portal-server.mycompany.corp
HTTP port of the portal server	50000

For this example the above string provided would appear as follows:

```
-Dhttp.proxyHost=proxy.mycompany.corp
-Dhttp.proxyPort=8081
-Dhttp.nonProxyHosts="*.mycompany.corp|portal-
server.mycompany.corp"
-Dstatusicons.mimes.name=http://portal-server.mycom-
pany.corp:50000
/irj/services/htmlb/mimes/mimesinfo.xml
-Dhtmlb.useUTF8=x
```

Note

The string cannot contain any blanks or line breaks.

3.3.5 Logging On

You can now enter the URL to call the portal in your browser and log on. Because the portal is not yet configured for use of an LDAP server or other user management, you must configure it now. Log on to the portal with the user ID of a super user. Use this user for the initial login to create the connection to the LDAP server or user management. Afterward, you can log on to the portal with your own user ID.

Initial login

For the initial login, enter "sap*" as the user ID and "06071992" as the password (the date in European format of the first delivery of SAP R/3 on July 6, 1992). You can now configure user management.

3.3.6 User Management

An important improvement in SAP EP 6.0 is the use of the SAP user management engine (SAP UME), which enables parallel reading and writing user information to and from various sources. See Section 11.7.2 for more details on SAP UME.

You have two options to determine how the sources of user information should be used and how the portal can connect to user information:

- SAP UME provides preconfigured files that contain settings for some standard scenarios, including reading the data of existing users from an LDAP directory server and storing it as new information in a database.
- If the entries in these files are inappropriate, you can modify them. To do so, you'll need exact and detailed data on the data sources. Right now, this type of configuration is supported on a project basis only . Please consult your SAP customer service consultant. The only exception to this approach exists when you want to map the physical attribute names from your LDAP directory to the logical attribute names in the Java API of SAP UME. In this case, you can modify the files.

The following describes how you can use the preconfigured files so that SAP UME can access the user information of the data sources that you want to use for your application.

LDAP as source

If you want to use an LDAP directory server as a source of user information, the structure of the directories in SAP UME must support such use. You must have stored groups as a tree or you must use a flat hierarchy. With the first method, users are located beneath the group entry to which they belong. A deep hierarchy is present. The disadvantage here is that users appear at only one location in the directory tree and therefore can only be members of a group (and the group's superordinate group).

Flat hierarchy

The second method involves the use of a flat hierarchy. Groups and users are stored separately. In this case, groups receive attributes that refer to users or users receive attributes that refer to the groups to which they belong. Of course, users can belong to several groups. If you add users, they are not automatically members of a group. It takes some administrative effort to assign users to groups.

Configuration

To configure user management, proceed as follows:

1. Start user management in the portal with **System Administration • System Configuration • UM Configuration**.

2. Select the combination of sources to which you wish to link user management.
3. Enter the connection data.
4. If you use an LDAP server, select the **LDAP server** tab and enter the URL for the LDAP server, the LDAP port, the directory manager (*cn = directory manager*), the directory manager's password, the distinguished name of the user path (only with a flat hierarchy, such as *Ou = corporate users*, *c = us*, and *o = my company*), and the group path (such as *ou = corporate groups*, *c = us*, and *o = my company*). If you want to use an SSL-protected connection, select **SSL**. In this case, additional configuration is required: see Chapter 11 for more information. Test the connection and then save your entries.
5. If you use an SAP R/3 system, select the **LDAP server** tab. In the SAP system you need a *SAPJSF* user of type *communication user*. The user needs authorizations to read user data and to authenticate remote users. The user also needs RFC authorizations. For this purpose, SAP Web AS 6.20 recognizes the *SAP_BC_JSF_COMMUNICATION_RO* role, which contains the required authorizations.

   Use of an SNC-secured connection requires assignment of the SNC name used by the SAP system to the user. In SAP R/3, start Transaction SU01. Select the **SNC** tab and enter the name of the SAP system. You can find the SNC names in Table USRACL. For the SAP system, you'll need the client, the user *(SAPJSF)*, the user's password, and the system language.

   If you use load balancing and the *sapmsg.ini* file is available on every portal server, you'll also need the name, and possibly the group, of the message server. Use of load balancing without the *sapmsg.ini* file on every portal server requires the name, the group, and the host address of the message server.

   If SAP R/3 does not use load balancing, you'll need the address and system number of the application server. As options, you can also enter the maximum number of open connections in a connection pool and the maximum time that an incoming query should wait for a connection. Save your entries.
6. If you use a database, you don't need to make any other entries because the connection data was already specified during the installation of the J2EE Engine. However, if you want to use a new connection pool, you can specify it in the J2EE Engine. To do so, change the `ume.db.connection_pool_type` setting in the *sapum.properties*

file to `ume.db.connection_pool_type=jdbc/<name_of_connection_pool>`.

7. Restart the J2EE Engine.

3.3.7 Licensing

Unlike SAP EP 5.0, SAP EP 6.0 automatically generates a temporary license during installation. The license is valid for four weeks. During this period, you must request a permanent license. SAP EP 6.0 displays the license key in **System Administration · System Configuration · Portal Licensing**.

3.3.8 Setting Up Roles

Make sure that you are logged on to the portal as the super administrator. In top-level navigation, select **User Administration · Role Assignment**. Search for the user to whom you want to assign a role. Under **Available Roles**, select the role and then click **Add**. The role is assigned to the user. Save all your settings.

4 SAP Business Information Warehouse

SAP Business Information Warehouse (SAP BW) displays and analyzes structured data. It is a significant source of information for SAP Enterprise Portal. This chapter examines SAP BW as a central component of SAP NetWeaver.

4.1 Functional Overview

4.1.1 Advantages of the Implementation

The principal task of SAP BW is to offer a transparent, uniform, and internally coherent view of events in a company in an optimal form and as close to real time as possible. It also lightens the load on operative (source) systems by handling reporting itself. In addition to the improved performance with reports and other advantages that such a system can offer, SAP BW also drastically reduces the duration of a BW implementation project with the targeted use of business content. Consequently, business content is continually enhanced so that as many business areas and industries as possible can profit from it.

The motives for using a portal for targeted integration of business warehouse content—or for accessing a standard business software—are complex and should be clarified from the start.

New realities on the market

Companies often face increased competition, new market realities (virtual networks of customers; the loss of long-term partner, customer, and vendor relationships; various information sources, and so on), and an extremely heterogeneous system landscape. The output parameters of one system often serve as input for another system. In most cases, combining data and information from various sources contributes to a vast improvement in the ability of the information and data to convey important knowledge.

Integration of heterogeneous applications

That's where the portal comes into play: it integrates heterogeneous applications in a uniform interface that focuses on the user. Consequently, in addition to having central access to various applications, users also have access to various sources of information, most of which are designed differently. SAP BW is the instrument to collect structured data and make it available for reporting and analysis. Therefore, it occupies a central position as a supplier of information for the portal.

4.1.2 Three-Layer Architecture

Three-layer architecture of SAP BW

SAP BW is based on a three-layer architecture, as illustrated in Figure 4.1. The three layers are the subject of this chapter and are mirrored in the divergent process flow of SAP BW content integration into the portal (see Chapter 5).

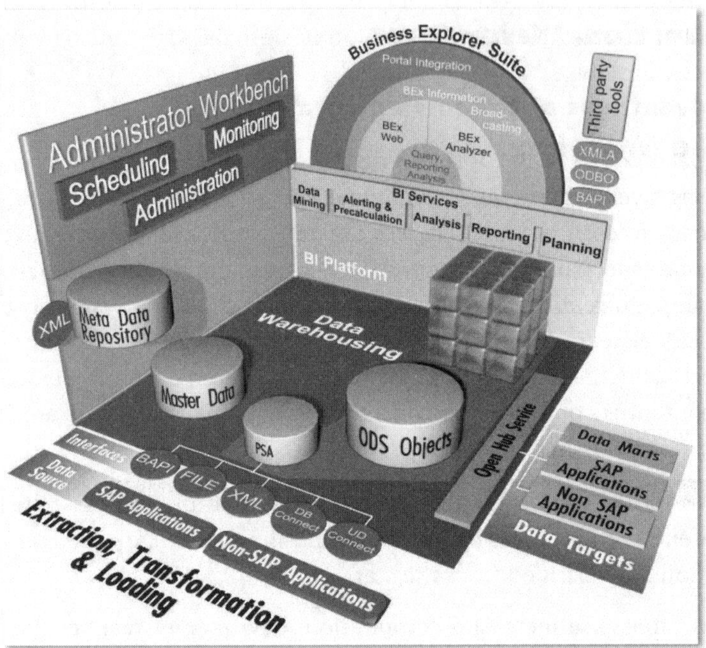

Figure 4.1 Three-Layer Architecture of SAP BW

4.2 The Extraction Layer

The extraction layer of SAP BW refers to functions for the *extraction*, *transformation*, and *loading (ETL)* of data from numerous sources, including non-SAP sources. The relevant data is first defined, transformed, and then transferred to SAP BW. The transfer process, however, assumes the assignment of fields from the source systems to the data objects (InfoObjects) of SAP BW. In SAP BW, InfoObjects represent the lowest level of granularity for metadata objects. *DataSources* (for master and transaction data) combine InfoObjects as "groups of fields" in a closed business unit. A DataSource that can select a data record that has changed since the last extraction is *delta-enabled*.

Although for the most part SAP BW deals uniformly with DataSources that have been extracted into it, the components in the source system that are hidden behind a DataSource can differ a great deal. They can range from simple tables and InfoSets to complex function modules. All components have the same purpose—to transfer the relevant data into SAP BW over a flat structure. To ensure a simpler selection, the DataSources are assigned by industry or business area to a hierarchy of application components.

DataSources

The openness of SAP BW means that you can transfer data records from any external or legacy system, databases, and external DataProviders into the business warehouse.

4.3 The Modeling Layer

Administrator Workbench

The modeling layer, represented technically in SAP BW by the *Administrator Workbench (AWB)*, functions as the central instance for maintaining, controlling, and monitoring the acquisition and availability of data. If necessary, it compresses, duplicates, and transforms the data of a DataSource with a direct business context and stores it in a data container.

The following sections address the elements and functionalities of the AWB (see Figure 4.2) in more detail.

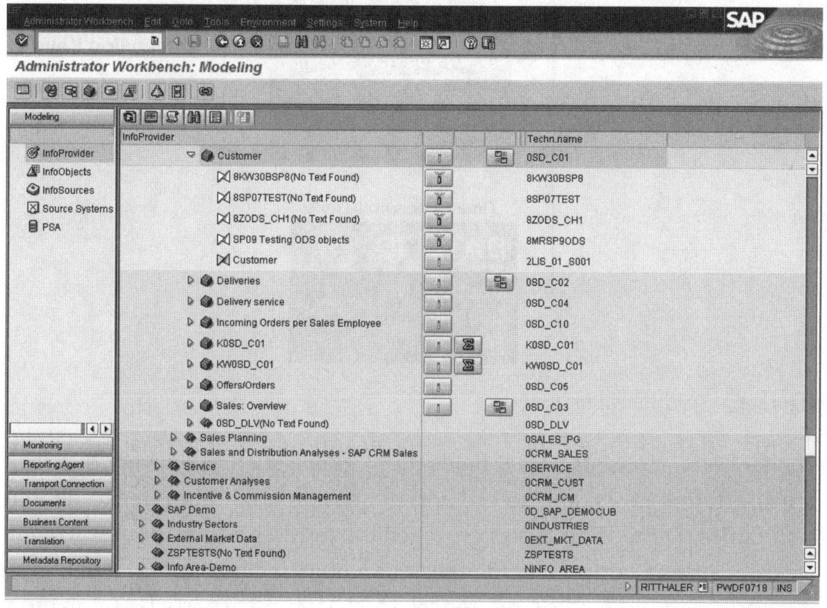

Figure 4.2 Administrator Workbench

4.3.1 Elements of Modeling

Modeling represents the core area of the AWB. The modeling layer is subdivided into InfoProviders, InfoObjects, InfoSources, connections to source systems, and the persistent staging area (PSA).

InfoProviders: InfoCubes and ODS Objects

The (basic) InfoProviders physically store mass data. In addition to the InfoProviders illustrated here, you could also use InfoObjects directly for reporting. Because InfoObjects contain only master data, when using InfoObjects, you'd refer to master data reporting.

InfoCubes InfoCubes store transferred data in a form optimized for reporting, the *star schema* (see Figure 4.3). The star schema consists of a centrally arranged fact table and the dimension tables related to it—up to a maximum of 16. The system populates 3 of the 16 dimension tables with time, request, and units—you can select the remaining tables.

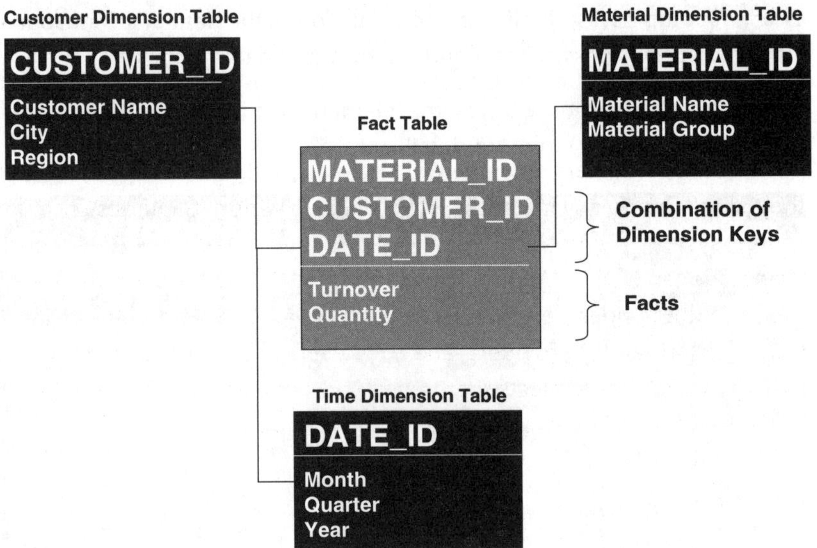

Figure 4.3 Traditional Star Schema

Fact table The fact table consists of fact fields (key figures, such as delivery quantity, transportation costs, and so on) and dimension keys that refer to dimension tables. Dimension tables group characteristics and attributes used in an InfoCube. Examples of dimensions could include a "material;" the dimension would include references to characteristics, such as "material number," "material classification," material group," and so on.

If a dimension contains only one characteristic, it's called a *line item dimension*. In this case, the fact table references master data (SIDs) directly, bypassing the dimension, so that you can enjoy optimal performance with reporting. The programming techniques used to limit the relevant data records in the fact table are relatively simple.

Separate storage of master and transaction data avoids the redundant storage of data. The master data in InfoObjects can be used in as many InfoCubes as you need.

ODS objects

In addition to basic InfoCubes, the *operational data stores* or *ODS objects* are another type of data container. The structure of ODS objects differs significantly from that of the InfoCubes. Instead of using the star schema illustrated in Figure 4.3, they correspond to a database table.

Unlike InfoCubes, ODS objects allow you to change previously stored data records. The clever combination of ODS objects and switching between InfoObjects and ODS objects causes a specific behavior when updating data, which allows for complex loading scenarios. ODS objects are often used for data cleansing, status tracking, InfoSets (joining data), and various other special requirements. All fields in the ODS are separated into key and data fields.

Virtual data containers

Virtual data containers only reference other containers (tables and so on); they don't store any data themselves. In addition to jumps into the source system (RemoteCubes) and being populated by ABAP reports (transactional ODS), MultiProviders or MultiCubes are also frequently used. MultiProviders permit the linking of all SAP BW InfoProviders, including virtual InfoProviders, and they enable very broad reporting. As of SAP BW 3.x, InfoObjects themselves can serve as InfoProviders, which provides the basis for problem-free master data reporting.

InfoObjects

InfoObjects directly correspond to database fields that are made available by extraction from the source system. Each InfoObject corresponds to one field. All InfoProviders use these InfoObjects. In addition to the field type (depending on the InfoObject type), they contain supplemental information, such as reporting parameters, the use of master data, and so on. The term InfoObject is used comprehensively for (time) characteristics, key figures, and units.

Characteristics

Characteristics possess master data, which is divided into texts, attributes, and hierarchies. Texts describe individual characteristic properties in more detail. Attributes, themselves InfoObjects, depend on a basic InfoObject and help display additional information, such as the production location for a material. Navigation attributes are an exception: they can be used as-is for evaluating reports. Hierarchies arrange characteristic properties into a tree that contains roots and nodes to which you cannot post and nodes and branches to which you can post.

Master data history

Separate storage of master data from InfoProviders (and dimension tables) provides more than a current view of master data. Setting a time dependency also allows you to look at particular key data (master data history).

Key figures

A basic setting for key figures is the type of aggregation. Aggregation indicates how the key figures can be selected by characteristics or properties during an analysis. The standard forms of aggregation include "summation," "min," and "max." Other options include exceptional aggregations, such as "last value," "first value," and minimum and maximum depending on a reference characteristic. Reference characteristics usually involve a time characteristic, such as the number of employees on a given date.

For more information related to InfoObjects, such as bracketing, referenced InfoObjects, the consequences of time dependence with master data, and so on, see the relevant literature (see appendix) and the online documentation provided by SAP.

InfoSources

InfoSources represent a business process complete in itself. Figure 4.4 illustrates the place of InfoSources in the overall flow of data. It stores all the business processes related to objects into a mapping structure, the *communications structure*. Figure 4.4 represents the lower two layers of the three-layer model. Replication of DataSources makes the transfer structure (and extract source structure) available in SAP BW; transfer rules transfer it into the communications structure.

Relationship between transfer and communications structures

Speaking pragmatically, an InfoSource combines one or more transfer structures with exactly one communications structure. As Figure 4.4 illustrates, communications structures differ from transfer structures: they operate independently of the source system.

Update rules

Direct updating of data in the data containers occurs in the next step, according to update rules. This structural complexity creates the highest possible flexibility when updating data.

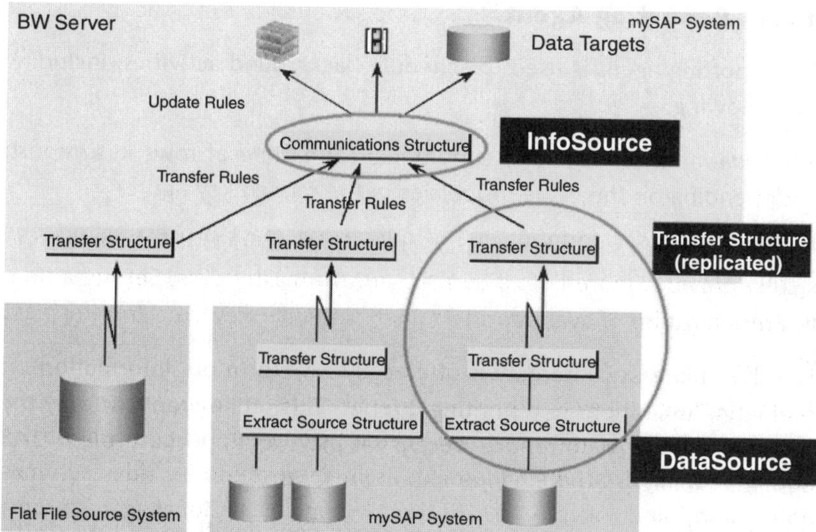

Figure 4.4 DataSources and InfoSources

In principle, you should place routines to modify data as low as possible in the data flow to reduce redundancies. In addition, transfer rules run faster than update rules.

Source Systems

The category of source systems provides an overview of all replicated DataSources for each source system. If a DataSource is reworked or regenerated in the source system, a new replication must occur in SAP BW. The use of plus (+) and minus (-) signs indicates whether the assignment of the DataSource to an InfoSource has already occurred.

Persistent Staging Area (PSA)

Temporary intermediate memory

Every DataSource has a persistent staging area (PSA). Principally, it corresponds to a simple table and helps control the (unmodified) data from the source system. The table features the same field information as the transfer structure.

4.3.2 Monitoring

Status information

Logs are created for the processes that run in SAP BW. Except for application logs, you can view the logs with the monitoring functions of SAP BW. In particular, the monitor displays data during data loads and change runs. For more information, see the online documentation provided by SAP.

4.3.3 Reporting Agent

The reporting agent is used to schedule background activities, including the following:

- *Evaluating exceptions* (for conditional formatting of rows in a report, depending on the value properties of the related key figure)
- *Printing queries* (printing many queries as mass processing on one printer)
- Precalculation of Web reports

See the online documentation offered by SAP for more information on evaluating exceptions and printing queries. This section looks at only the precalculation of Web reports because it plays an important role in *SAP Business Explorer (SAP BEx) information broadcasting*.

Precalculation has two very different goals: considerations of load distribution and the direct consequences of executing reports. In particular, precalculation is always advisable when used with Web applications that demand a lot of patience from their audience due to the applications' complexity and long load times.

Reports without additional navigation

The essential difference between these reports and regular execution of queries is that the OLAP processor (see Section 5.3) is not used here. This approach buys the resulting advantage that additional navigation is no longer possible within the Web application that has been called. In other words, these reports involve purely static reports—a desirable situation in many, but not all cases. However, if you want to retain options for navigation, you can use a control query to execute an entire group of precalculations and therefore simulate a type of navigation when you execute reports later.

With precalculation, it's important to remember that you can access precalculated data only over the Web, and not with the *BEx analyzer* (Excel reports). You can adjust the URL of a Web report (`DATA_MODE` parameter) when executing a report to determine whether the report will access precalculated or new data.

4.3.4 Transport Connection

Please consult the online documentation provided by SAP for information on the use of the regular transport connection.

The import and export functionality for objects via XML files is an important innovation in the transport system of SAP BW 3.x. However, we recommend that you use this functionality with caution because the resulting volume of data can grow vast quickly. However, when you want to exchange objects between systems that have no physical connection with each other, adopting this method is an interesting alternative.

Import and export with XML

4.3.5 Documents

You can create one or more documents in various formats and languages for an individual SAP BW object, and you can do so even on the Web.

Use

Note the following types and classes of documents:

- **Metadata**
  Explanations of SAP BW objects, and so on.
- **Master data**
  Descriptions and technical specifications of materials, order forms (plan, actual, budget, and so on).
- **InfoProvider data**
  Comments on combinations of characteristics.

To be able to use a document created with any desired application external to SAP BW as a document for an SAP BW object, you can import the file into the document management system of SAP BW. Special objects (*items*) exist at the reporting level to allow Web-based access.

4.3.6 Business Content (BC)

Because of its longstanding and comprehensive experience, SAP can provide content for many business areas (logistics, Customer Relationship Management (CRM), controlling, and so on). Business Content (BC) is structured according to industries and applications.

Predefined information model

The idea behind BC is to be able to use a predefined information model, regardless of the particular customer involved. Two types of content exist—content used in the source system as extractors, and content used directly in SAP BW. The latter consists of objects required for the data-modeling process and of data necessary to monitor technical processes in SAP BW.

Content Within the Source System

Before BC can be used within a source system, it must be transferred with the implementation guide (IMG). The transfer itself occurs in two steps. In the first step, the hierarchy of application components is transferred. This step helps to organize the DataSources, which are transferred in the second step, into an application context.

Content Within SAP BW

SAP BW contains predefined objects and properties for all possible types of objects (InfoObjects, InfoProviders, and so on). BC is frequently used as a rough structure or template, which is then tailored to the needs of individual customers. The continual enhancement and improvement of BC not only enriches a possible data-modeling process for a customer, but also significantly reduces the time required for implementation.

Technical Content

Technical content aims to provide an exact log of the numerous processes that occur in SAP BW: loading, rollups, query execution times, and so on.

Associated with the technical content is a predefined workbook that you can use to navigate through several informative statistical reports (the use of queries, performance reports, and so on).

Versioning

All objects that occur in SAP BW can have one of the following statuses:

- D(elivery)
- A(ctive)
- M(odified)

D objects represent an unmodified version from BC. A objects are automatically generated from D objects that have been transferred from BC. If such an object is then modified, it exists as an M object. If you want to use such an object, you must reactivate it.

4.3.7 Translation

Translation enables you to store texts (short or long) for objects in another language in SAP BW.

When you select an object for translation, you also select all its subordinate objects in the work list. This grouping functionality enables you to include objects stored in front of or after the data flow in the translation. Note that you can integrate only active objects in translation.

4.3.8 Metadata Repository

Use

The metadata repository (MDR) in SAP BW makes available technical descriptions and identifiers for active objects and content objects. Generation and activation of objects automatically produces the corresponding metadata in the MDR. The resulting cross-linkages between objects are particularly interesting.

Searching in the MDR

Searching in the MDR is something of a disappointment in the current release. Previous releases included search functionality (in a technical sense as well) as a component of SAP BW itself, however, since SAP BW 3.x , the functionality uses the same technology as knowledge management in the portal—TREX. The technology involves an indexing server that enables searching within object names for a technical name, short text, or long text. A problem arises when SAP BW runs on a UNIX installation because TREX can currently run on only Windows platforms.

4.3.9 Large-Scale Architectures

SAP BW systems that cover large functional areas, manage several source systems, and are used by large numbers of users are called *central data warehouse systems*. Systems with these properties have special requirements regarding architecture, performance, and scalability.

Various configuration scenarios are available to set up SAP BW to meet these requirements, as discussed in the following sections.

SAP BW as a Data Mart

Insular solutions

Because of the great complexity that exists at many large companies, past implementations of a central data warehouse have often ended in failure. That's why the trend is to prefer independent (regionally separate), insular solutions, each with its own supply of data. These satellite solutions are known as *data marts*.

The local orientation of data marts make them an adequate means of lessening the complexity within an enterprise. Of course, weaknesses exist in the central storage of data and in inconsistently defined data.

Data marts in no way represent the ultimate solution to a systemwide data warehouse. However, they do offer a particularly valuable service to the implementation of a companywide data warehouse—especially because they increase the willingness of end users within a company to work with such an application.

Hub-and-Spoke Architecture

Seen abstractly, *hub-and-spoke architecture* is analogous to the data marts approach, especially because insular solutions of data warehouses also come into play here. Unlike a pure data mart approach, this architecture considers the subsystems in use not as autonomous units, but as part of a global data warehouse. In terms of the stored data, that means that a consolidation of the data can ensure the uniformity of the accessed data from the very start.

Properties

Hub-and-spoke architecture involves three actual manifestations, as detailed in the following:

- **Replicating architecture**
  The primary goal of replicating architecture is to prevent bottlenecks during an analysis of data. Data from various data marts is redistributed to provide the required data. Data packages prepared in advance can drastically reduce the effort involved in formatting data for a reporting data mart, which produces the desired improvements in performance.
- **Aggregating architecture**
  In contrast to replicating architecture, the bottleneck here involves data formatting and extraction. The need for aggregated architecture can result from a geographical separation of the source systems, from data volumes that are too large, or from topical heterogeneity. Data is collected from several BW systems and redirected to a central BW system.
- **Virtual hub-and-spoke architecture**
  The idea behind virtual architecture is that data is exchanged between systems only when data analysis of cross-system data starts. The exchange accesses RemoteCubes. Although you can use RemoteCubes just like regular BasicCubes in reporting, they don't contain any data. In other words, you actually use virtual data targets. The advantage of this architecture is that it can simulate both of the aforementioned architectures. To guarantee good performance, ensure that you limit the volume of the data to be transferred.

4.4 The Reporting and Analysis Layer

The reporting and analysis layer represents the third, or highest, layer in the three-layer model of SAP BW. This level handles the definition and processing of queries on the data (containers) stored in SAP BW.

Third-party tools

In addition to the standard front-end solutions delivered with SAP BW, BEx analyzer, and BEx Web (*BEx query designer*, *BEx Web application designer*, *BEx information broadcaster*, and so on), you can also visualize BW data with third-party tools (*inSight/dynaSight*, *Business Objects*, *Cognos*, *Crystal Decisions*, *Hyperion Solutions*, *MIS*, and others). Access to the data occurs with the ODBO interfaces, which is also used with third-party tools. The *object linking and embedding database for online analytical processing* is a standard interface developed by Microsoft that requests the data from BW in a language similar to SQL. The front-end solution of SAP BW, however, was enriched with additional functionalities (exceptions, conditions, cell-based calculations, and so on) that surpass the basic functionalities of the ODBO interface.

OLAP engine

Whether you use SAP or third-party solutions, all query tools use the OLAP (*online analytical processing*) engine, which ensures the optimal processing of data requirements. The OLAP engine is a technology that permits numerous views and presentations of basic data and therefore forms the conceptual basis for solutions to support decision-making in a company. You can achieve multidimensional data storage with a *multidimensional database management system* (MDDBMS). The OLAP engine, however, uses *virtual* multidimensional data storage. The supporting database is a simple relational database.

Regardless of the type of representation, you must first create a query for the target InfoProvider to capture the data for reporting that you want. You create queries with the BEx Query Designer, the most important functions of which are described below.

4.4.1 BEx Query Designer

You can start the BEx Query Designer from the BEx analyzer (see Figure 4.5), via the Web application designer, or directly.

After you open the SAP BEx dialog, you must determine whether you want to create a new query or modify an existing query, and then select the corresponding InfoProvider. The dialog also contains comprehensive extended functionalities (searches that include periods of time, and so on), which we cannot delve into further detail here.

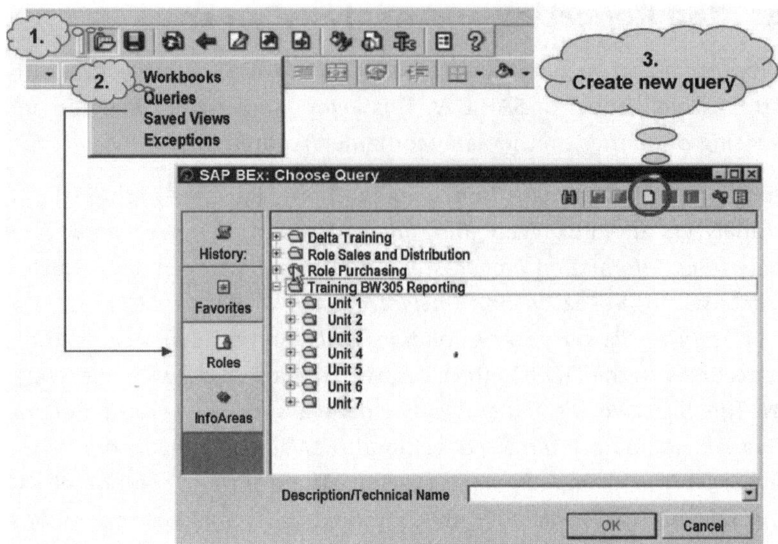

Figure 4.5 SAP BW Macro in Excel or SAP BEx Dialog

Structure of the BEx query designer

After you select the InfoProvider, the opening screen of the BEx Query Designer appears, as shown in Figure 4.6. The screen contains six zones:

- The first zone contains the worklist, all the characteristics (grouped by dimensions), key figures, and globally defined elements (structures, calculated and limited key figures, and so on) available for defining the report (see zones 2–5).
- The appearance of the report columns and rows is set in zones 2 and 3. If you want a material-based overview of prices and sales quantities, you could use the "material" characteristic in the row definition and the key figures "price" and "sales quantity" in the column definition.
- Zones 4 and 5 limit the data to values and value areas. For example, if a report is to display only materials from a specific country of origin, you can limit the query to that country (such as France) in zone 4 (free characteristics) or zone 5 (global filter). The report shows the difference between the two alternatives. Limits set in zone 4 are displayed as such when the report is executed and can be deleted from the filter if needed. But a report user cannot delete the limitation in the global filter.
- Zone 6 displays a preview of the report.

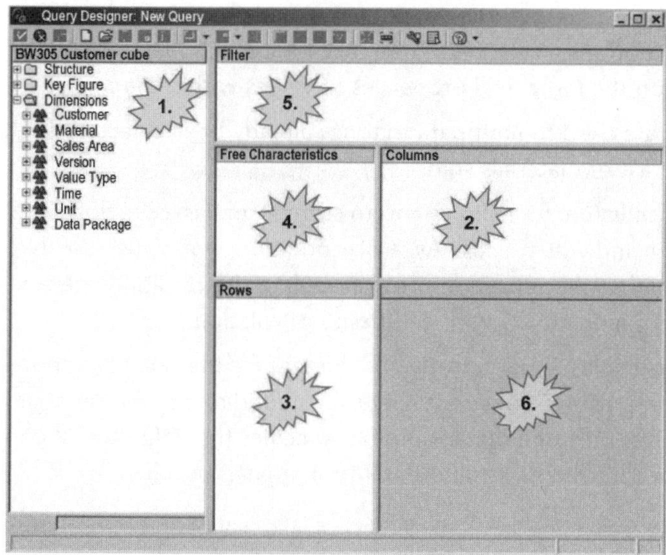

Figure 4.6 BEx Query Designer

Special aspect of query definition

Before we look at the taskbar of the BEx query designer in more detail, we should briefly note some special aspects of defining queries.

Structures are integral elements when defining queries. If a key figure is transferred from the worklist to the definition area, a structure element is automatically created for it. Structures can also be used for characteristics: they might group specific characteristic properties, for example.

Variables also play a critical role in the definition of reports because they contribute to a parameterization of reports. Variables are distinguished by their type and by their type of processing. Characteristic variables, hierarchy and hierarchy node variables, reporting variables, and so on all exist. Processing can occur with direct entry, exit processing, or by derivation from other variables or substitution paths. Depending on their type, variables can record only individual values, several individual values, or intervals. Text variables are a special type. You can use text variables for the headers of structures and populate them with values dynamically when you execute the report.

Taskbar

Figure 4.7 shows the taskbar in the BEx query designer. In addition to such standard functions as execute, open, save, and delete a query, the taskbar has the following functionalities:

- In the section on the reporting agent we already looked at the definition of **exceptions**. This definition allows conditional formatting, depending on the individual properties of values within the report.
- **Conditions** are used to limit data that has already been selected, such as a top ten list of materials sold.
- The **Define cells** function allows you to store formulas, selections, and references in individual cells. As a precondition, you must use two structures within the report. You can populate the resulting checkerboard pattern individually with cell-based calculation.
- The **Tabular display** is particularly appropriate for master data reporting. Such reporting does not involve multidimensional analyses because it uses only one dimension that specifies the definition of columns or the data-record structure. Output appears as a list.

You can use the remaining icons to call technical or validation information and to display and change the query's properties.

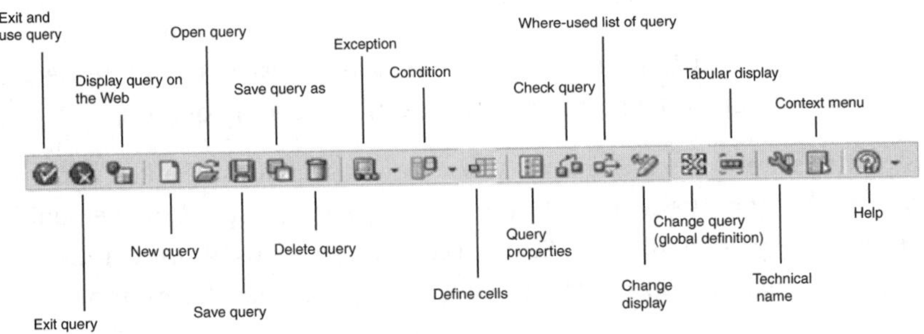

Figure 4.7 Taskbar in the BEx Query Designer

4.4.2 BEx Analyzer

Excel reports

The BEx analyzer enables you to execute BW reports in a spreadsheet—Microsoft Excel— and to use all the navigation options (filter, drilldown, and so on) that are also available on the Web. A VBA macro[1] in Excel makes this feature possible. You can use it to call standard functions, such as opening a query, saving, formatting, and so on. It also allows you to include queries in a workbook so you can set up a report folder.

1 You can use the "SAPBEX on Refresh" VBA routine to enrich workbooks with additional logic. The routine is always called when updating the data of the query involved.

Because the Excel counterpart is of less interest than the Web solution for portal integration, we will not discuss this front-end alternative in any more detail.

4.4.3 BEx Web—Analysis and Reporting on the Web

For a functional overview of the *Web Application Designer (WAD)*, the core component of BEx Web, see the next chapter, which introduces the tool based on a small example.

BEx Web features complete integration with BEx Analyzer, as seen in its functionality to download Web reports to the BEx analyzer (with the option for further navigation in an Excel environment) and automatically to recognize end devices that enable an optimal display of results, regardless of the end device involved.

5 Integrating SAP Business Information Warehouse with SAP Enterprise Portal

This chapter addresses the integration of SAP BW with SAP EP in the context of the three layers discussed in Chapter 4. Special attention is given to the reporting and analysis layer.

In Chapter 4, we presented a general overview of the data warehouse concept at SAP. In this chapter, we'll discuss the actual availability of SAP BW functionality in the portal.

Functionality scenarios

The following scenarios represent the three layers:

- **Reporting and Analysis layer**
  Availability of SAP BW Web applications in the portal, either by direct integration or via role migration. In SAP BW 3.5 and later, you can realize integration with the Knowledge Management (KM) folder.
- **Administration layer (especially Administrator Workbench (AWB))**
  Integration of BW components with the portal.
- **Extraction layer, information exchange, and exchange of events between various systems**
  A short introduction to Drag&Relate functionalities within SAP BW Web applications and with SAP R/3.

Unlike the previous chapter, which presented the layers bottom up, this chapter examines the material in a top-down sequence—from reporting to extraction.

Before you can integrate SAP BW applications with the portal, you must meet some basic technical requirements, which are discussed in the following section.

5.1 Basic Technical Requirements

SAP BW 3.0B and SAP EP 5.0 constitute the foundation for the basic technical requirements. In the next two sections, the required system settings are described. A brief integration scenario between SAP BW 3.5 and SAP EP 6.0 (SAP NetWeaver '04) is also presented according to the new philosophy of SAP NetWeaver. Technical components are no longer treated as separate entities, but as an integrated whole. This chapter concludes with a scenario based on this philosophy.

5.1.1 Requirements in the SAP BW (3.x) System

Portal plug-in

You must first make the SAP Enterprise Portal plug-in available in SAP BW. For more information, see the online documentation provided by SAP (**Business Information Warehouse · Business Explorer · Collaboration & Distribution: Integration with Enterprise Portal**) and Note 440447.

Security and single sign-on (SSO)

If you want comprehensive use of single sign-on (SSO) and start a SAP BW application within the portal, you don't need to log on to the BW again, but must install SAPSECULIB on every SAP BW application server. SAPSECULIB is a *dynamic link library* (a collection of small programs that are called by larger programs when needed) found on every application server. It offers functions for the use of digital signatures in SAP R/3 systems, for example.

You can find additional information on this topic in *Single Sign-On with SAP Logon Tickets* in the documentation of SAP EP (access from the SAP help portal at *http://help.sap.com*).

Portal certificate

You must then use Transaction STRUSTSSO2 to import the portal certificate into SAP BW. The certificate is located in file *verify.der* (in the standard directory of the J2EE server: *c:\irj\WEB-INF\plugins\portal\services\usermanagement\data*). You must also transfer the certificate into the SSOaccess control list (ACL).

You can find more detailed information in *SAP Systems for Accepting and Verifying SAP Logon Tickets*, also available in the SAP help portal.

5.1.2 Settings in Enterprise Portal (Release 5.0)

Maintenance of the systems.xml file

The *systems.xml* file stores the destinations of the SAP BW systems available in the portal. You can find the logical system name in table T000 in the SAP BW system.

Parameter

Depending on the type of connection in use, you must also maintain various parameters:

- **Application server**
  In this case, enter only the application server (technical server name) and the logical system number.

- **Load balancing with groups**
  With load balancing, you must enter the message server (**not** MSHOST), the server port, and the group.

Then complete the following steps:

1. Enter the BW system and the SAP Web Application Server (SAP Web AS) in the *systems.xml* file (as `WebAccessPoint`):

```
<WebAccessPoint category="WAS">
  <Title multilingual="true" textID="1003">
    <pcd:TitleText language="de">
      B3TCLNT800
    </pcd:TitleText>
    <pcd:TitleText language="en">
      B3TCLNT800
    </pcd:TitleText>
  </Title>
  <Description multilingual="true" textID="1005">
    <pcd:DescriptionText language="de">
      B3TCLNT800
    </pcd:DescriptionText>
    <pcd:DescriptionText language="en">
      B3TCLNT800
    </pcd:DescriptionText>
  </Description>
  <Protocol>HTTP</Protocol>
  <HostName>iwdf1622.wdf.sap-ag.de:1080</HostName>
  <Path>SAP/BW/BEx</Path>
</WebAccessPoint>
```

   If you want to be able to call Web-enabled transactions in the portal, you need access to an Internet Transaction Server (ITS). You also store this information in the *systems.xml* file.

2. Upload the *systems.xml* file into the portal and activate the file.
3. After installation of the *systems.xml* file, you must restart the JRun server. For more information, see *Defining Component Systems*, which you can access from the SAP help portal.

Maintenance of the jcoDestination.xml file

The *jcoDestination.xml* file stores much of the same information on the definition of SAP BW systems that is found in *systems.xml*; however, it uses the information for role migration. Note the following individual steps:

1. Store the destination name (`<wpl:Destination name=...>`) in the *jcoDestination.xml* file.
2. Upload the *jcoDestination.xml* file into the portal and activate it.
3. After installation of the *jcoDestination.xml* file, you must restart the JRun server. For more information, see *Defining JCo Destinations*, which you can access from the SAP help portal.

Client settings

Access to SAP EP is browser-based. Consult the documentation for a list of browsers that are compatible with SAP EP.

Parameters

Regardless of the browser you use, you must set the following parameters:

- Acceptance of cookies
- Availability of JavaScript
- Navigation in subframes across various domains (Internet Explorer)
- ActiveX controls and plug-ins (Internet Explorer)

Consult the documentation for important additional information on SAP BW Web applications, SAP BW workbooks, and so on.

5.1.3 Settings in SAP NetWeaver '04 (SAP BW 3.5/SAP EP 6.0)

Maintenance of RFC Connections

Remote Function Call

Remote function calls (RFC) involve a proprietary SAP protocol that enables calling functions over a network connection. The connection must be set up between SAP BW and SAP Enterprise Portal. SM50 is the central transaction for the display and maintenance of RFC connections.

For information on individual steps, consult the online documentation (*Integration of SAP BW 3.5 and SAP EP 6.0*). When you create the connections, it is critical that you follow the specific sequence: first from the portal (or its J2EE Engine) to the BW and then from BW to the portal. You must also select a name for the RFC connection because the name will be used for additional applications and settings—BEx query designer, BEx Web Application Designer (WAD), information broadcasting, and so on.

Maintenance of Portal Server Settings in SAP BW

You must first store the portal as the standard portal in SAP BW with table RSPOR_T_PORTAL; if this step has already been done, the system displays a warning.

Repository manager

If you want SAP Enterprise Portal to display documents and metadata stored in SAP BW, you can use the *repository manager (RM)*. RMs offer access to documents in SAP BW via knowledge management (KM). All KM functions—such as rating, full-text search, feedback, and so on—are also available for these documents.

You must maintain the following fields, especially for later information broadcasting:

- **Default**
  Identifies a portal as the standard portal in SAP BW.
- **URL prefix**
  Required for value help in BEx broadcaster.
- **KM Metad.RM prefix**
  Determines the path in KM that the RM will use to access metadata in BW.
- **KM service URL**
  Enables use of another service (when needed) for value help in KM folders. Only one service exists currently, therefore, this field must remain blank.

After the successful completion of these individual steps, the WAD menu entry **Publish** should contain an entry for **Enterprise Portal 6.0**.

Maintenance of SSO in SAP BW

Dynamic link library

You must first install SAPSECULIB on every application server (if several are being used) of the SAP BW system. You then set the profile parameters with Transaction RZ10. Consult Note 354819 and the online documentation for more information on SSO.

Exporting the BW Certificate from SAP BW

The BW certificate is a precondition for displaying portal content (roles from the portal environment, for example) in SAP BW. You can use the trust manager (Transaction STRUSTSSO2) to export the certificate that belongs to SAP BW. Use file path *<BW_SID>_certificate.crt*; *<BW_SID>* stands for the system ID of the SAP BW system. Select binary as the file format.

Importing the BW Certificate into SAP EP

You must now import the BW certificate into SAP EP. For an exact description of the individual steps, consult the SAP help portal.

Creating a BW System in SAP EP

New logical system

The next step creates the preconditions for SAP EP to display content from SAP BW. On the portal side, you must use the iView for system maintenance to create a new logical system; select *SAP_R3_LoadBalancing* as the template. You must then adjust typical system parameters, such as logon method, system type (here: BW), and so on.

Configuration of User Management in SAP EP

User management

The following settings are required to create SSO between SAP BW and SAP Enterprise Portal. You must first start the iView for configuration of user management in the portal. In the **Security Settings** tab, enter the system alias of the SAP BW system at the SAP reference system. If several ports with identical portal SIDs are attached to the SAP BW system, you must also maintain the logon ticket parameters.

Exporting the Portal Certificate from SAP EP

Certificate

After the BW system is known in the portal, you must export the portal certificate and, in the next step, import it into SAP BW. As described above, this step is required so that the portal can display SAP BW content and adhere to the naming conventions.

Importing the Portal Certificate into SAP BW

Call Transaction STRUSTSSO2 and select the **Import Certificate** option, which enables importation of the *<PORTAL_SID>_certificate.crt* file. *<PORTAL_SID>* stands for the system ID of the portal. Then, select **Certificate in ACL** to record the certificate in the SSO access control list.

Setting Up Repository Managers for BW in SAP EP

Repository manager

Start the configuration iView for KM. A new instance is required within the BW document repository. Consult the online documentation to understand the individual parameters. The same steps are also required for the BW metadata repository. You can check the settings by calling the BW documents or metadata in KM.

Maintaining User Mapping in SAP EP

User mapping occurs with the corresponding iViews in the portal: a portal user is mapped to a BW user. If you're using the SAPLOGONTICKET method, user mapping is optional; if you're using UIDPW, user mapping is mandatory.

User mapping

SAP EP 5.0 uses one-sided user mapping: from the portal into SAP BW; SAP NetWeaver '04 uses bidirectional mapping. Information broadcasting, in particular, uses bidirectionality. A description of existing special cases and the exact procedure would exceed the scope of this chapter.

Bidirectional mapping

Importing the Portal Plug-In into SAP BW

To complete integration, you must make the SAP Enterprise Portal plug-in available in the SAP BW system. Use the Transport Management System (Transaction STMS), where you can import the plug-in. For more information, see Note 655941 and the integration scenario for SAP EP 5.0 described above.

SAP Enterprise Portal plug-in

5.2 Availability of BW Web Applications in the Portal (Reporting and Analysis Layer)

Chapter 1 already indicated that the combination of and access to varied applications over one user interface can be seen as the essential advantage of the portal. The following presentation of personalization can significantly reduce the resulting demand for space for individual applications in the portal.

5.2.1 Personalization and Roles

Personalization is based on the role concept that provides the foundation for use of the LDAP server, SAP BW, and all other SAP applications. As noted in Section 2.1.4, SAP User Management has been used since SAP EP 6.0 to support enhanced functionality in the area of user management.

Roles comprise a fixed set of tasks, for example, a collection of all the activities for a purchasing agent. Users are then assigned roles that correspond to their "real" activities. In the purchasing agent example, personalization can display only a portion of the data (such as a profit center) if needed. In addition to user-specific informational content, personalization can also enable user-specific formatting—in the portal environment the term is *themes*, and themes can be stored as needed for users.

Roles

Internal and external services

Technically, roles serve to record services made available in the portal as applications. Note the distinction between internal and external services (see Section 5.2.4, particularly on handling external services for SAP EP 6.0):

- If integration of a Web application with the portal occurs directly with an iView, an internal service is involved. The iView is displayed directly in the "standard" portal page, along with many other iViews from other systems and applications.
- If integration of a Web application occurs with roles from the "source systems" (here: SAP BW), external services are involved. Unlike the situation with an internal service, the Web application is displayed in a separate page here.

The following sections describe a procedure that you can use to integrate a SAP BW Web application in your portal. But first, we'll use BEx Web application designer (WAD) to create a sample application.

5.2.2 Creating a Web Application with the WAD

The WAD is the primary tool for publishing BW reports on the Web. The range of reports extends from very simple reports (creating a report with the assistance of the Web application Wizard) to extremely complex information cockpits that not only exhaust most of the standard functionality of the WAD, but also use scripts (such as JavaScript) and markup languages (such as HTML) to provide user-friendliness to those who use the applications.

Query

The starting point for the creation of a (standard) Web template is a query or a view derived from a query. The query itself is defined for an InfoProvider and delivers an exact subset of data.

Web items

The data can be displayed in various ways: tabular form, charts, and so on. The WAD includes *Web items* that enable the simple display of data, and the navigation and selection of data. The process of linking Web items to a query is called *data binding*.

Creating a Web template

In rough terms, the process of creating a Web template can be seen as follows (see Figure 5.1):

1. Start the WAD and use Drag&Drop to integrate all the relevant Web items from the list of available Web items into a new template (layout mode).

2. You can use or incorporate an HTML table to place Web items both horizontally and vertically.
3. In the **Web item properties**, you assign the items to the foundational query (data binding). You can also store item and template-specific properties (formatting, heading, context menu, and so on).

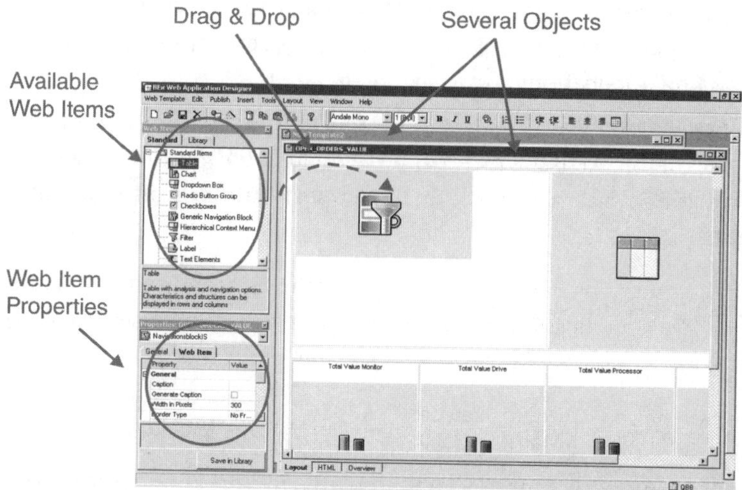

Figure 5.1 BEx Web Application Designer (WAD)

A linked query would then appear as illustrated in Figure 5.2.

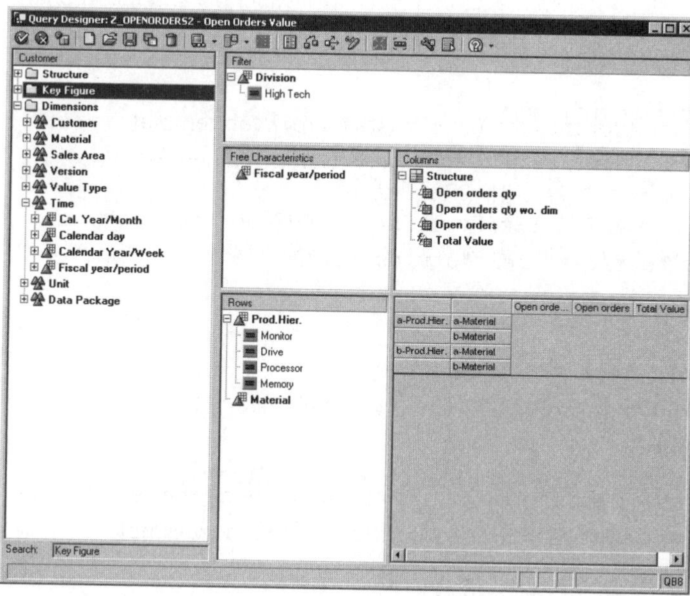

Figure 5.2 Structure of the Sample Query

The coding generated by the creation process would appear similar to the coding displayed in Listing 5.1.

```
<!-- BW data source object tags -->
<!-- Data Provider Object Tag -->
<object>
   <param name="OWNER" value="SAP_BW">
   <param name="CMD" value="SET_DATA_PROVIDER">
   <param name="NAME" value="DataProvider_1">
   <param name="QUERY" value="Z_OPENORDERS">
   <param name="INFOCUBE" value="0AFSD_C01">
   DATA_PROVIDER:            DataProvider_1
</object>

<!--Data Provider Object Tag -->

<object>
   <param name="OWNER" value="SAP_BW">
   <param name="CMD" value="SET_PROPERTIES">
   <param name="TEMPLATE_ID"
      value="Z20030620_TEMPLATE_F_BUCH">
   <param name="VARIABLE_SCREEN" value="X">
   TEMPLATE PROPERTIES
</object>
<HTML>
<HEAD>
  <META NAME="GENERATOR"
     Content="...">
  <TITLE>BW Web Application</TITLE>
  <link href= "MIME/BEx/StyleSheets/BWReports.css"
     type="text/css" rel="stylesheet">
</HEAD>
<BODY>
  <P align=center><FONT face=Verdana>
    <STRONG>Open Orders Value</STRONG>
  </FONT></P>
  <TABLE cellSpacing=1 cellPadding=1 width="75 %"
     border=0>
    <TR>
      <TD vAlign=center Align="middle">
```

```
<!--Item Object Tags -->
      <P>
        <TABLE cellSpacing=1 cellPadding=1
         width="75 %" border=0>
          <TR>
            <TD vAlign=top>
            <object>
              <param name="OWNER" value="SAP_BW">
              <param name="CMD" value="GET_ITEM">
              <param name="NAME"
                 value="Checkboxes_1">
              <param name="ITEM_CLASS"
                 value="CL_RSR_WWW_ITEM_FILTER_CHECBOX">
              <param name="DATA_PROVIDER"
                 value="DataProvider_1">
              <param name="IOBJNM" value="0MATERIAL">
              <param name="MAXVALUES" value="3">
              <param name="HORIZONTAL_ALIGNMENT"
                 value="X">
       ITEM:           Checkboxes_1
            </object>
            </TD>
            <TD vAlign=top>
            <object>
              <param name="OWNER" value="SAP_BW">
              <param name="CMD" value="GET_ITEM">
              <param name="NAME" value="Table_1">
              <param name="ITEM_CLASS"
                 value="CL_RSR_WWW_ITEM_GRID">
              <param name="DATA_PROVIDER"
                value="DataProvider_1">
       ITEM:           Table_1
            </object>
            </TD></TR></TABLE>
 </P></TD></TR>
   <TR>
     <TD vAlign=top>
       <object>
         <param name="OWNER" value="SAP_BW">
         <param name="CMD" value="GET_ITEM">
         <param name="NAME" value="Chart_1">
```

```
            <param name="ITEM_CLASS"
               value="CL_RSR_WWW_ITEM_CHART">
            <param name="DATA_PROVIDER"
             value="DataProvider_1">
            <param name="WIDTH" value="800">
          ITEM:              Chart_1
          </object>
        </TD></TR></TABLE>
</BODY>
</HTML>
```

Listing 5.1 Code of the Sample Template

Comments on the listing

The objects specific to SAP BW given above as <object> ... </object> are subdivided into template, DataProvider, and item object tags. The template and DataProvider object tags are located outside of the regular HTML coding, which is separated into header and body areas and is surrounded by an opening and closing HTML tag. These two object tags require a control command for the SAP BW and are not displayed directly. The item object tags, however, are located in the body of the template.[1]

The template object tag (exactly one object per template) stores characteristics that affect the template as a whole: the display of the variable screen, output and buffer parameters, entries in the context menu, and so on.

The DataProvider object tag assigns any Web items (table, chart, navigation block, ticker, etc.) to exactly one query or view. In principle, the number of DataProvider object tags that can occur is unlimited. The sample template, however, uses only one DataProvider.

The item object tags are the actual representation used to display data from SAP BW. The example integrates a checkbox, a table, and a graphic. The table and graphic are primarily used to display data. The context menu has options for several additional functionalities: filters, setting characteristics, etc. The check is used only to filter data or limit the values being used.

1 For more information on the exact parameterization of the template object tags and the DataProvider object tag, see the Web API reference for the Web application designer in SAP Service Marketplace.

Once created, the template appears as it does in Figure 5.3 during execution of the application. Figures 5.4 and 5.5 provide examples of additional options of the elements that the portal can display.

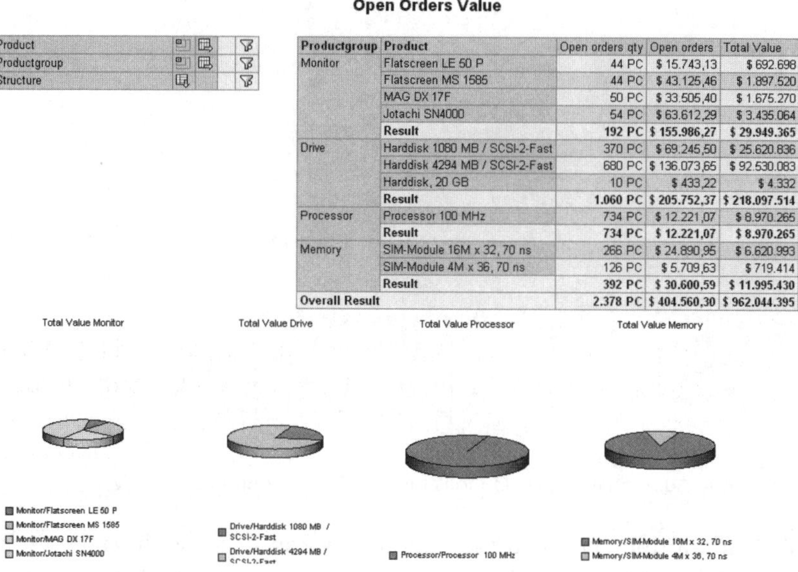

Open Orders Value

Productgroup	Product	Open orders qty	Open orders	Total Value
Monitor	Flatscreen LE 50 P	44 PC	$ 15.743,13	$ 692.698
	Flatscreen MS 1585	44 PC	$ 43.125,46	$ 1.897.520
	MAG DX 17F	50 PC	$ 33.505,40	$ 1.675.270
	Jotachi SN4000	54 PC	$ 63.612,29	$ 3.435.064
	Result	**192 PC**	**$ 155.986,27**	**$ 29.949.365**
Drive	Harddisk 1080 MB / SCSI-2-Fast	370 PC	$ 69.245,50	$ 25.620.836
	Harddisk 4294 MB / SCSI-2-Fast	680 PC	$ 136.073,65	$ 92.530.083
	Harddisk, 20 GB	10 PC	$ 433,22	$ 4.332
	Result	**1.060 PC**	**$ 205.752,37**	**$ 218.097.514**
Processor	Processor 100 MHz	734 PC	$ 12.221,07	$ 8.970.265
	Result	**734 PC**	**$ 12.221,07**	**$ 8.970.265**
Memory	SIM-Module 16M x 32, 70 ns	266 PC	$ 24.890,95	$ 6.620.993
	SIM-Module 4M x 36, 70 ns	126 PC	$ 5.709,63	$ 719.414
	Result	**392 PC**	**$ 30.600,59**	**$ 11.995.430**
Overall Result		**2.378 PC**	**$ 404.560,30**	**$ 962.044.395**

Figure 5.3 Display of the Sample Template on the Web

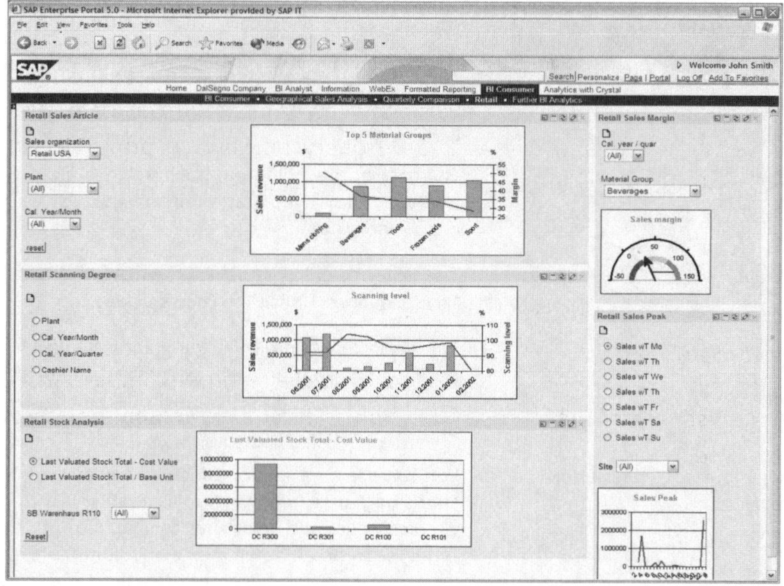

Figure 5.4 Additional Display Options for SAP BW Content in SAP EP (1)

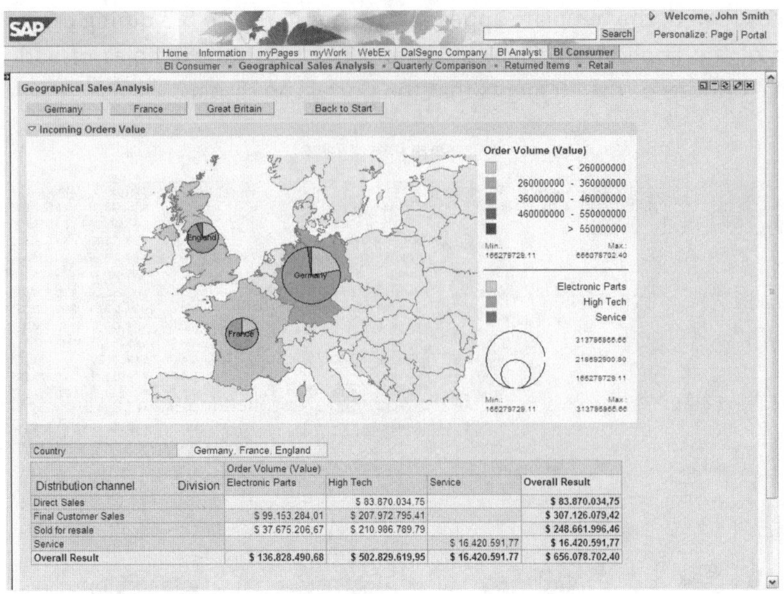

Figure 5.5 Additional Display Options for SAP BW Content in SAP EP (2)

Web-supported access

Web-supported access to the data in BW can occur with various Web items, only a few of which were used in the example. Table 5.1 provides an overview of all the standard Web items for SAP BW 3.x.

Classification	Item	Comments
Display	Table	The data of the Web item is extracted from a query. The individual cells contain links to navigation.
Display	Chart	The data of the Web item is extracted from a query and displayed graphically (chart, pie chart, and so on).
Display	Ticker	The ticker Web item enables the display of a table's data as a headline (news ticker).
Display	Map	This Web item can display geographical and business information (such as sales) as a map. A bar or pie chart represents individual key figures on the map.
Navigation/ Filters	Navigation Block	You can use a navigation block to display the status of a query's navigation as a table. It lists characteristics and structures available for filtering or to break down a row or column, etc.

Table 5.1 Overview of Web Items Available in SAP BW

Classification	Item	Comments
Navigation/ Filters	Drop-down Box	This Web item displays the characteristic values of a characteristic as a drop-down box. As soon as the user selects a characteristic value, the filter values access the assigned query.
Navigation/ Filters	Selection Button	Characteristic values are displayed as a group of selection buttons and, much like the drop-down box, are available for filtering.
Navigation/ Filters	Check Field	Corresponds to the selection button, however, this Web item allows simultaneous selection of several characteristic values.
Navigation/ Filters	Hierarchical Context Menu	A context menu is generated from the hierarchy or structure of a characteristic; users can filter with the context menu.
Navigation/ Filters	Exceptions/ Conditions	These Web items display the frame parameters that have been set: both in terms of the conditional formatting and the display of data limited by a condition. You can use the Web items to set the frame parameters to *active* or *inactive*.
Role Display	Role Menu	Depending on the setting, the role menu can display the favorites or roles of a user in a hierarchical tree. You can integrate the role menu as an iView directly in the portal. It enables user-friendly access to all the queries and Web applications that belong to a user.
Text Display	Filter	Displays the filter values as determined by navigation.
Display	Label	The label Web item enables the display of characteristics, attributes, or descriptions of structure elements. It can also reference them with a link to the related property.
Display	Text Element	Shows general information on the related query: the person who created or modified it and so on.
Other	Ad Hoc Query Designer	This Web item enables creation and modification of ad hoc queries in a Web application.
Other	Individual Document/Document List	"Individual document" helps the in-place display of documents of master data and transaction data. "Document list" displays the available documents as a list. It also enables creation of new documents and the modification and deletion of existing documents.

Table 5.1 Overview of Web Items Available in SAP BW (cont.)

Classification	Item	Comments
Other	ABC Analysis	The ABC classification Web item enables limiting objects (such as customers) based on a specific metric (such as sales) with specific classification rules.
Other	Simulation	Enables the forecasting of specific events by using services such as a decision tree, scoring, and clustering.
Other	Alert Monitor	Provides an overview of all the exceptional situations that exist in BW and that might occur because of the exceptions defined in the queries.
Additional Web items available in SAP BW 3.5		
Other	Query View Selection	Enables dynamic data binding. During reporting, you can select the views the items reference.
Other	Web Template Item	Nests Web applications.
Other	XML Items: Object Catalog and DataProvider Information	Both Web items provide specific information on the object catalog or DataProvider. They can be evaluated (with JavaScript, for example) and formatted for display.
Other	Item for Information Broadcasting	Enables integration of information broadcasting functionality within a Web application.

Table 5.1 Overview of Web Items Available in SAP BW (cont.)

We should also mention that the role menu and Ad hoc Query Designer Web items don't require data binding because they are used independently of a query or view. Also note that the Web items for navigation and filtering must be linked to a specific characteristic (use of **F4** help).

The creation process here is sufficient to build a simple Web application. We could also have used the Web Application Wizard, which is extremely well suited for creating simple Web applications, as noted above. But, because the Wizard is largely intuitive, we don't have to delve into greater detail here. Of course, you must use the WAD itself for more complex Web templates.

5.2.3 Availability of BW Web Applications in the Portal (SAP BW 3.1/SAP EP 5.0)

As noted, you have two options for making SAP BW Web applications available in SAP Enterprise Portal. Figure 5.6 summarizes both, and the sections that follow address the alternatives.

Two options for integration

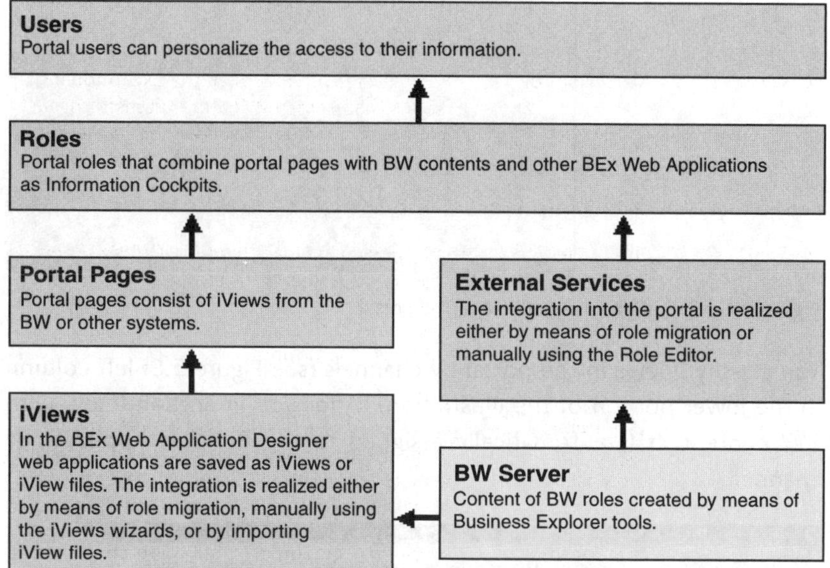

Figure 5.6 Integration of BW Applications in SAP Enterprise Portal

Direct Integration as an iView

You must first store a Web template that you have created as an iView file. You can do so in the WAD by using menu path **Publish • As iView File**. The resulting *ivu* file involves an XML file that contains its own control parameters and the technical name of the template (here: ACME_PROJECTS):

```
...
CDATA[cmd=ldoc&TEMPLATE_ID=ACME_PROJECTS]
...
```

The next step makes the file available in the portal (see Figure 5.7).

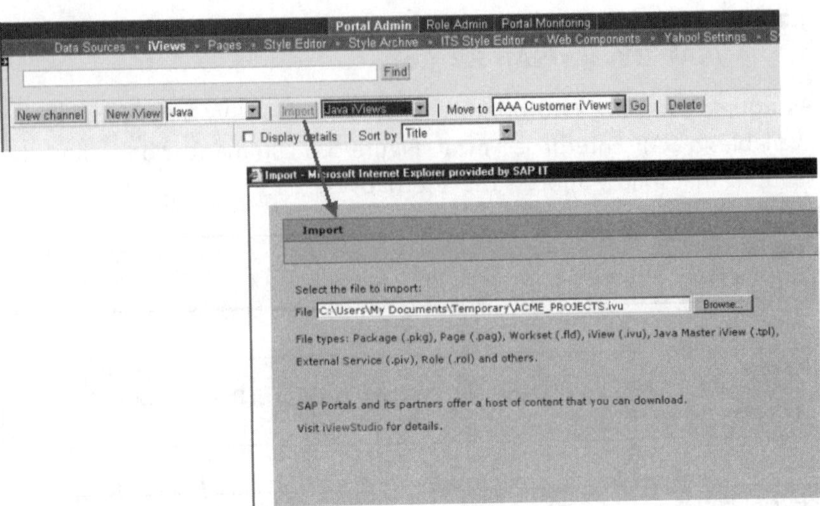

Figure 5.7 Integration of an ivu File in the Portal

Channels You classify iViews in the portal by channels (see Figure 5.8: left column in the lower portion of the illustration). After you import an iView with BW content, it is automatically assigned to the **BI Web Applications** channel.

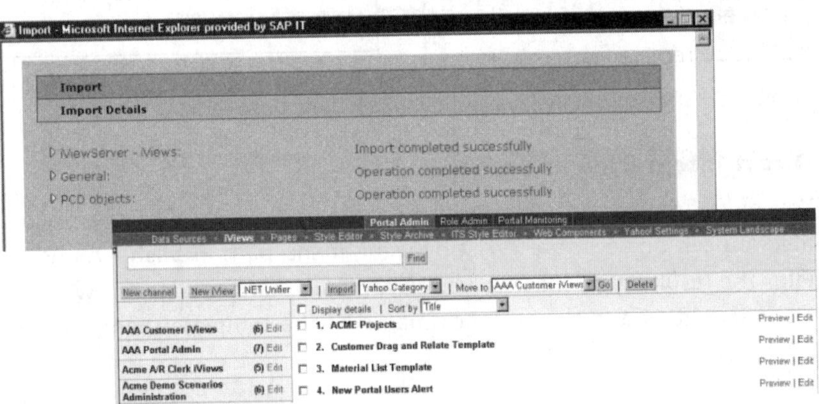

Figure 5.8 iViews and Channels

Click on **Preview** to display the integrated iViews. Click on **Edit** to modify the formatting, especially the size.

Display of the iViews Three additional steps are required before the iView can be displayed in the portal (depending on the user):

1. Creation of a new portal page (see Figure 5.9).

2. Assignment of the related iView to this page with the desired type of display (entire page, subframe, and so on; see Figure 5.9).

   You must also define an entry point; otherwise, the page cannot be displayed.

Note

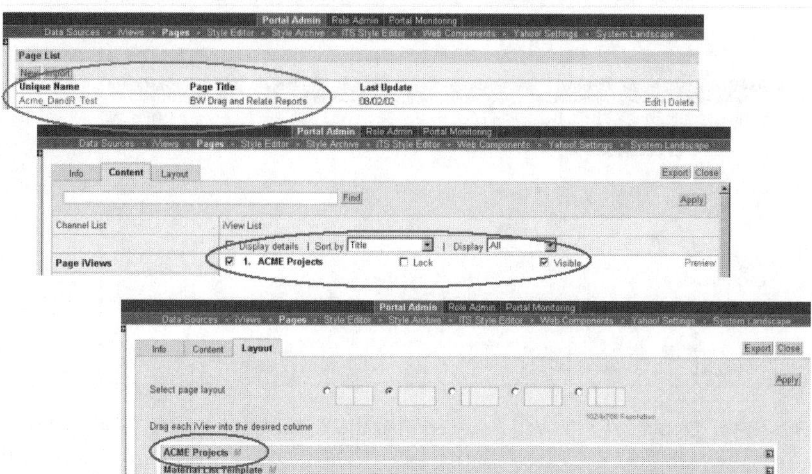

Figure 5.9 Creation of a New Portal Page and Assignment of the iViews

3. Assignment of the page to a role (see Figure 5.10).
4. If required: assignment of the corresponding role to the dedicated users (see Figure 5.10).

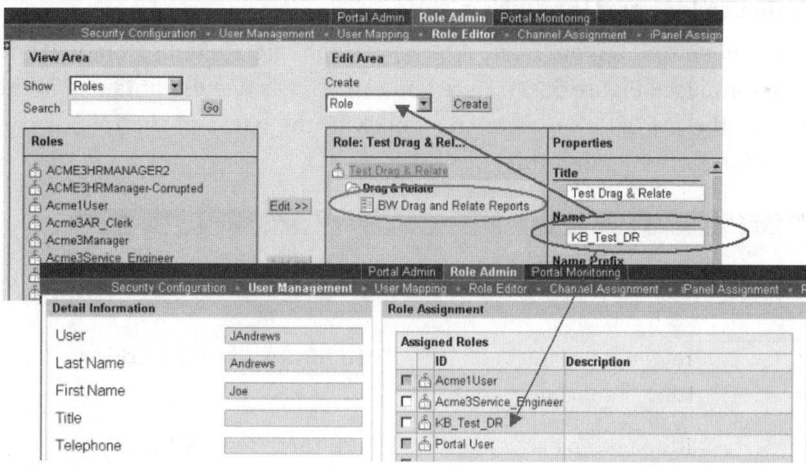

Figure 5.10 Assignment of Roles and Users

These steps complete the integration of the Web application in the portal. Figure 5.11 shows you the result. Alternatively, you can use the iView Wizard to integrate the iView directly in the portal by entering its technical name (*ivu* file). For a description of using the iView Wizard, see the online documentation. Both approaches produce the same result.

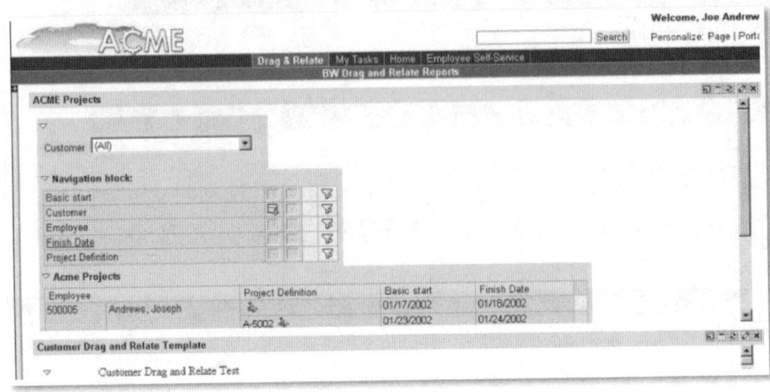

Figure 5.11 Display of a BI Web Application in the Portal

As indicated in the overview of Web items, you can also use the role menu Web item quite easily to make iViews available in the portal as a user's favorites and roles. If you later modify the underlying roles, they are available in the iView automatically, without any additional manual steps.

Indirect Integration with a Role

Role migration

If you need to integrate many iViews, you can migrate roles from BW into the portal (see Figure 5.12). Here you can use the iViews contained in the role in the portal: a separate channel (with the name of the role) is created for each migrated role.

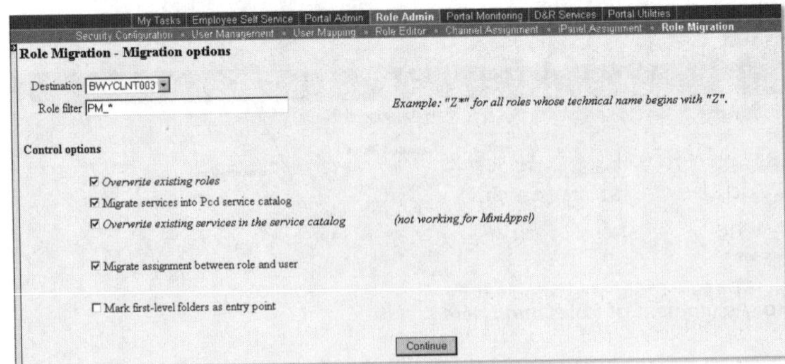

Figure 5.12 Migration of Roles into the Portal

Web applications of migrated roles can be used separately only if the application has been assigned to the role as an iView. In other cases, you can use the applications made available in role migration as external services.

5.2.4 SAP NetWeaver '04 and the Availability of BW Web Applications in the Portal (SAP BW 3.5/SAP EP 6.0)

Although end users won't detect any significant differences with more current releases (see Table 5.3, below), some differences do exist when publishing SAP BW Web applications. As before, you have two major ways to integrate a Web application into the portal as an iView or role. Current releases have significantly enhanced and simplified these options. You can also use the BEx Web Application Designer to create an iView in the portal directly. In addition to the integration of SAP BW content with iViews, you can also integrate with documents and links in KM.

BEx information broadcasting

In addition, the functionality of BEx information broadcasting provides completely new approaches to distributing BEx Web applications, (precalculated) workbooks[2], and queries. To publish BW content in the portal, you can choose among BEx Web application designer, BEx information broadcaster, and BEx query designer. You can use the portal content studio for manual integration of SAP BW content. See Figure 5.13 for an overview of analyzer components of SAP BW and alternatives for publication with information broadcasting in SAP EP.

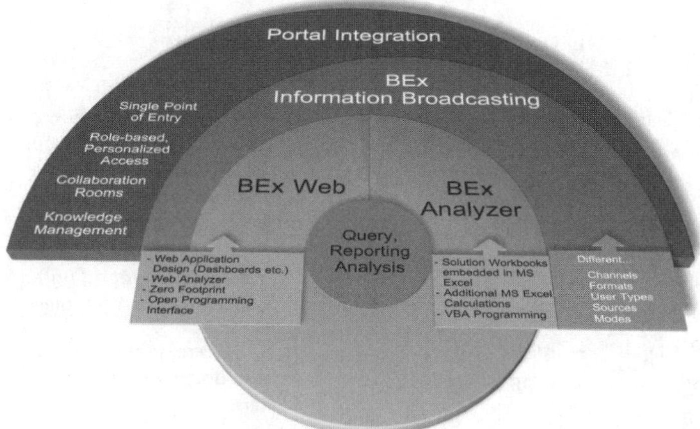

Figure 5.13 Information Broadcasting Layers between SAP EP and SAP BW

2 BEx workbooks are opened in a seperate window with Microsoft Excel; it is technically impossible to open them within a browser window.

"Expanded" system landscape

The simplification of publishing content results primarily from the "expanded" system landscape related to SAP BW 3.5 and SAP EP 6.0. Older releases had only *one* connection from the portal to the BW system, but the new release offers a *dual* connection: from BW into the portal and from the portal into BW. This strong integration of systems means that BW can now access portal content; for example, BEx Web application designer features access to assigned portal roles, folders, and documents from KM and additional objects. BW content is available in the portal without any intervening steps. The publication process is significantly simplified: you simply need to store the role that you want.

Portal content catalog

Additional simplification results from the standardization of iViews, external services, and pages in the *portal content catalog (PCC)*. The PCC enables simple, common maintenance of all portal content objects in a hierarchy and transport of content objects between portals. Because, since SAP EP 6.0, iViews can cover an entire page and exist without a "separate page," external services have become obsolete. Therefore, the previous specification is no longer relevant.

Later, related themes can be maintained for iViews, which significantly simplifies navigation in the portal. This feature involves certain assumptions for navigation, similar to Drag&Relate.

Both of the following tables show the alternatives for the integration and presentation of SAP BW content in SAP EP with the use of SAP NetWeaver '04.

Integration Tool	Type of Display of BEx Web Applications	Comments
BEx Web Application Designer	▶ iView ▶ With portal roles ▶ Links	Direct creation of iViews and documents in the portal. The following layers are available and can store Web applications: My Portfolio, CM repository view, collaboration room, portal content, and portal roles
BEx Query Designer	▶ iView ▶ With portal roles	Direct creation of iViews and documents in the portal.

Table 5.2 Clarification of Integration Points for Content from SAP BW 3.5 with SAP EP 6.0

Integration Tool	Type of Display of BEx Web Applications	Comments
Portal Content Studio	▶ iView (primarily to display documents and links) ▶ Workbooks ▶ (Layouts of) portal pages ▶ Portal roles ▶ Worksets	When creating workbooks as iViews, the system, transaction code, and application parameter must be stored. The portal catalog is used. You can also set the portal cache for an iView (see Note 690222).
BEx Broadcaster (subcomponent in the WAD)	▶ Documents (in KM) ▶ Links (in KM) ▶ Precalculation and distribution of Web applications, queries, and workbooks	Creation of documents (precalculated Web applications in BEx, for example), links in KM, and visualization with BEx portfolio (BW-specific formatting in KM and special layout for the KM navigation iView). Additional option for subscriptions.
Knowledge Management	▶ Integration of BEx Web applications as documents and links ▶ Integration of BW documents and metadata	Use of collaboration. Enabled with document rating, feedback, and personal notes.

Table 5.2 Clarification of Integration Points for Content from SAP BW 3.5 with SAP EP 6.0 (cont.)

Access (Z) and Display Components (D)	Type of Information Property	Comment
Initial Navigation Bar (Z)		Contains all of a user's initial folders and portal roles.
Navigation Panel (instead of iPanel) (Z)	▶ Drag&Relate target objects ▶ Assigned BW roles (with the Web item role menu) ▶ Any iViews and dynamic navigation ▶ Themes in use	Helps detailed navigation. A role is available automatically, depending on the depth of the layer.

Table 5.3 Clarification of Display Options in SAP EP 6.0 for Content from SAP BW 3.5

Access (Z) and Display Components (D)	Type of Information Property	Comment
iView BEx Portfolio and. KM Navigation iView	Display of documents and links	The KM navigation iView supports collaboration. Navigation occurs via the content area.
Content area (D)	▶ BEx Web application as iView ▶ Precalculated BEx Web application as a document in KM ▶ BEx Web application as a link in KM ▶ BW workbooks ▶ BW documents	

Table 5.3 Clarification of Display Options in SAP EP 6.0 for Content from SAP BW 3.5 (cont.)

Comments The presentation options available in SAP EP make the older visualization instrument for Web applications, *BEx Browser*, superfluous.

In SAP EP 6.0, the iView ID assigned when creating an iView must be unique in the folder that stores the iView. SAP EP 5.0 absolutely required maintaining cross-portal uniqueness of the iView ID.

5.3 Integration of BW Components in the Portal (Administration Layer)

In the previous section, we looked at possible ways in which to display targeted information from BW in SAP EP, particularly for end users. However, as we have seen, the using BW (and its three-layer model) requires as much administrative effort (data modeling, extraction, and loading; report creation; and so on) as a few central transactions (Administrator Workbench, AWB) and applications (WAD, BEx analyzer, and BEx query designer) involve.

Administrator Workbench In accordance with the application-related single-point-of-access paradigm, administrators must also be able to experience the paradigm. But because of the comprehensive functionality of the AWB, each client must still have an installation of SAP GUI for Windows 6.20, which shouldn't be a problem because of the manageable size of the target group of users. Much like the migration of roles, the AWB is integrated into the portal as an external service. It can then be displayed in a browser window as a Web-enabled transaction, without any additional logon (provided SSO is installed).

Integration involves the following five steps:

Integration with the portal

1. Start the External Service Wizard in the portal and then select the **New Service** option.
2. Select the corresponding BW system.
3. Set the correct application type (SAP transaction).
4. Select **WinGUI** as the type of GUI to be used.
5. Enter the transaction code (RSA1) for the AWB.

Integration of the applications from the BW environment listed above is done via an external service. The following therefore provides no additional details.

The AWB can integrate with SAP NetWeaver '04 by using the portal content studio as an SAP transaction iView. Access occurs over a Windows GUI, which presumes a local or client-side GUI installation.

5.4 Information Exchange Among Various Systems: Unification and Drag&Relate (Extraction Layer)

An intuitive procedure to capture valuable, additional information enhances the integrative design of the portal. The procedure involves use of the unification environment and is called *hyperrelational navigation functionality*. As part of a comprehensive design, the procedure combines the available data with additional data (internal or external to the company) and thus increases its informative character.

Drag&Relate

Targeted exchange of various objects among the applications connected to the portal forms the core component of the procedure. The exchange transfers objects from a sender to a receiver application with the mouse, and is called *Drag&Relate (D&R)*. But don't confuse D&R with the functionality of the *report-to-report interface (RRI)*. In detail, D&R works as follows:

A business object that requires additional information, such as a material number—0MATERIAL—is selected with the mouse and dragged to a receiver application within the portal iPanel or in the navigation panel of SAP EP 6.0 (see Section 5.4.3). For example, doing so could display information on the material master in the SAP R/3 source system. Navigation is enabled by a 1:1 key relationship between the BW InfoObject and the corresponding *business object repository (BOR)* object in the SAP R/3 system. It's important to remember that not all InfoObjects can be assigned to BOR objects and assignment involves a considerable manual effort. Various scenarios result, depending on whether the object keys of the corresponding objects agree or are at least are partially contained in another key, or whether the two keys differ fundamentally.

The RRI simultaneously contains several InfoObjects and selection parameters within the transferred parameters. It should always be used when all the context information must be transferred. This process is not limited to BW systems only, and the RRI can use D&R between BW systems and any SAP system, an SAP R/3 transaction, a program, and URLs.

Therefore, you should use D&R when 1:1 object assignments exist for which the corresponding objects have the identical key. Doing so, however, involves some technical requirements.

5.4.1 Technical Requirements and Customizing for D&R

Basic settings

You must provide the following configurations:

- At least SAP EP 5.0 with SAPNetWeaver '04 and SAP BW 3.xB
- BW Unifier (subcomponent of SAP Enterprise Portal)
- Single sign-on
- Activation of a unifier for SAP BW

You must also ensure that BW and the portal are connected to each other, that the roles in BW have been maintained correctly, and that an InfoProvider is selected for each D&R.

Cross-system field mapping

A two-dimensional matrix is built from the InfoProvider by replicating the metadata of the InfoProvider in the BW unifier. Figure 5.14 illustrates the matrix.

BW Web applications

If you want to use a BW Web application for a D&R in the portal, you must also make the following settings:

- Activate the D&R links (under **Properties**) in the related query (under **Query Properties**).
- Parameterization of the Web application URL (*&show_dr_links=X*).

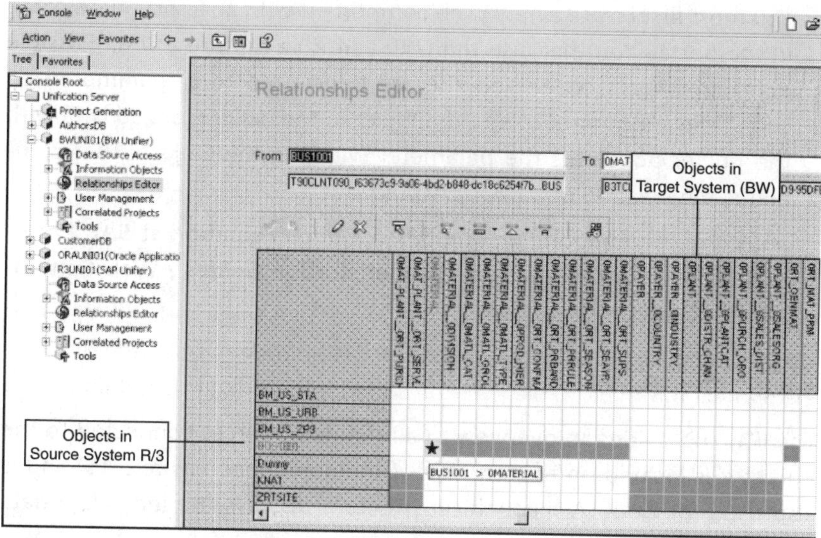

Figure 5.14 Cross-System Correlation Matrix

5.4.2 D&R Scenarios

The following three scenarios come particularly to mind for the use of D&R:

- **Within the mySAP landscape: internal to an application**
  Starting from a BW iView, the information is requested from another BW iView in the identical system. The correlation matrix would not be required here.

  In principle, it makes no difference if you use a query or a Web template.

- **Within the mySAP landscape: cross-application**
  Note that every link between a business object in the source and target system must be maintained with an entry in the correlation matrix. For D&R between a BW and an SAP R/3 system, you must also note that you can use only characteristics with assigned BOR object types.

  Many central InfoObjects are supported: see the online documentation for an overview.

- **Outside the mySAP landscape**
  If a D&R-enabled URL is located within the iPanel or the navigation panel in SAP EP 6.0 (*http://www.yahoo.com*, for example), you can call cross-application information. For example, you can display background information on a specific customer.

You must first create a new Web component with an appropriate name in the portal. You then use the URL editor to capture a URL. Possible entry arguments on a Web site are transferred to a "parameterized URL." The assignment of an InfoObject to the parameterized URL with the unifier populates the parameter with the InfoObject. That completes the creation of a D&R-enabled URL.

For more information, see the SAP EP documentation at **SAP Enterprise Portal Documentation · Administration Guides · Web Components**.

5.4.3 The iPanel

The iPanel provides an overview of all the data sources connected to the portal: it is located on the left side of the portal (see Figure 5.15) and is also used for D&R. A hierarchical structure displays the individual data sources and systems.

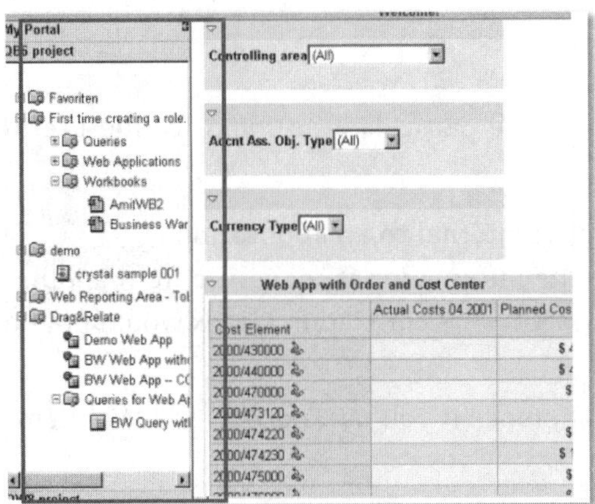

Figure 5.15 The iPanel in the Portal

As noted above, the navigation panel replaces the iPanel in SAP EP 6.0.

5.4.4 D&R Example

In the BW Web application shown in Figure 5.16, a list of the top customers (with sales revenues, sales costs, and absolute and percentage-based overhead) is displayed.

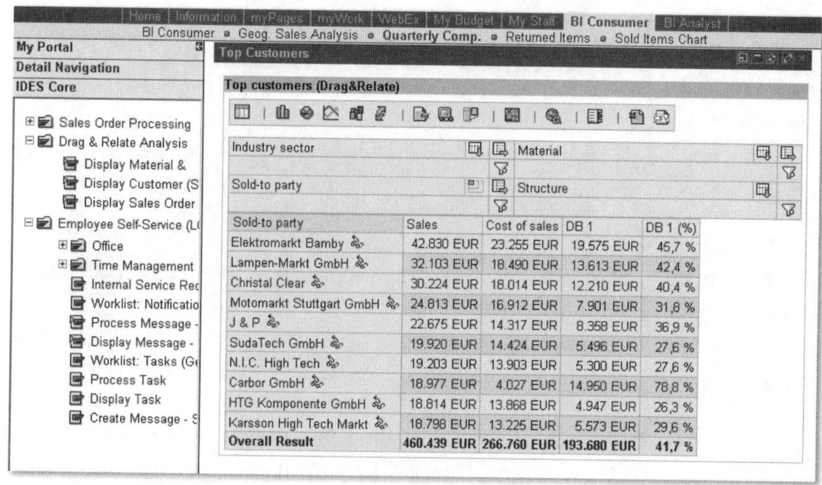

Sold-to party	Sales	Cost of sales	DB 1	DB 1 (%)
Elektromarkt Bamby	42.830 EUR	23.255 EUR	19.575 EUR	45,7 %
Lampen-Markt GmbH	32.103 EUR	18.490 EUR	13.613 EUR	42,4 %
Christal Clear	30.224 EUR	18.014 EUR	12.210 EUR	40,4 %
Motomarkt Stuttgart GmbH	24.813 EUR	16.912 EUR	7.901 EUR	31,8 %
J & P	22.675 EUR	14.317 EUR	8.358 EUR	36,9 %
SudaTech GmbH	19.920 EUR	14.424 EUR	5.496 EUR	27,6 %
N.I.C. High Tech	19.203 EUR	13.903 EUR	5.300 EUR	27,6 %
Carbor GmbH	18.977 EUR	4.027 EUR	14.950 EUR	78,8 %
HTG Komponente GmbH	18.814 EUR	13.868 EUR	4.947 EUR	26,3 %
Karsson High Tech Markt	18.798 EUR	13.225 EUR	5.573 EUR	29,6 %
Overall Result	**460.439 EUR**	**266.760 EUR**	**193.680 EUR**	**41,7 %**

Figure 5.16 Sample Report on the Top Ten Customers in the Portal

We can use the D&R links, noted with an eyeglasses icon, to obtain more detailed information on customers (see Figure 5.17). The link jumps to the SAP R/3 system (see Figure 5.18).

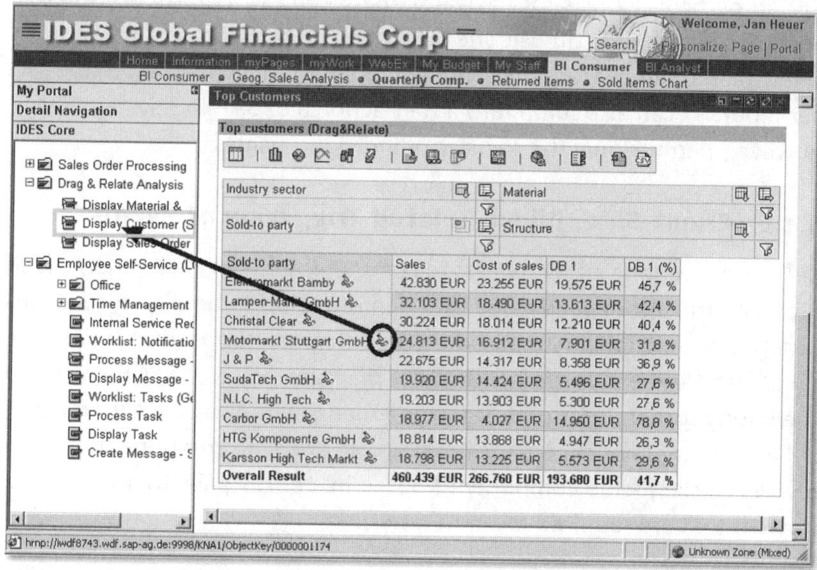

Figure 5.17 Drag&Relate from the Display of Top Customers and the BW Report

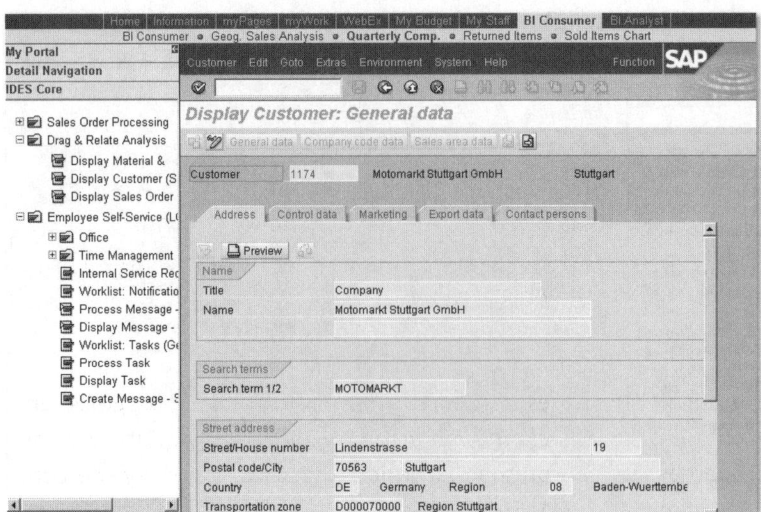

Figure 5.18 Detailed Information on Customers in an SAP R/3 System

5.4.5 D&R and the Multidimensionality of BW

RRI

SAP BW is characterized by its multidimensionality with reporting. The RRI, in particular, exists for navigation between BW reports. As noted in Section 5.4, the RRI can use one navigation step to record a list of characteristic properties from the sending report and transfer them to the target report. It can also jump into a transactional or SAP R/3 system. D&R, however, permits only the transfer of individual values.

5.4.6 Client-Side, iView-Related Triggering of Events

Client-side eventing

Client-side eventing allows iViews to communicate with each other, which increases the informative value of the information to be displayed. Technically, this functionality is based on the *enterprise portal client framework (EPCF)* and the *enterprise portal client manager (EPCM)*. EPCF enhances the information output of portal components with JavaScript functionality. It also simplifies client-side programming of Web components. EPCM involves a client-side component housed in a portal page that makes the services that are required for EPCF available.

Client-side triggering of events refers to communication among various iViews and to communication between an iView and the portal. For example, if the "BW iView" sender generates an event based on a selection in a drop-down box, the receiver "iView" records the event and processes it so that certain attributes within the related Web application change their current status based on the *command URL*.

6 mySAP Customer Relationship Management and SAP Enterprise Portal

CRM directs the processes within a company to provide sufficient customer orientation at optimal cost. However, a company must also know the value of its customers, which requires an exact analysis.

This chapter first provides a general overview of the basics, goals, and vocabulary of *customer relationship management (CRM)* and its SAP-specific properties. It then presents a project scenario to display the combined use of mySAP CRM, SAP BW, and SAP EP. The scenario covers only the functional issues; Chapter 5 examined the technical foundation of this relationship among the SAP components.

6.1 Basics of Customer Orientation

6.1.1 The Term CRM

Definition

CRM consists of three individual terms: *customer*, *relationship*, and *management*. The term customer refers to the retention of existing customers and the development of potential relationships with (new) customers. Individual maintenance of these associations, aimed at meeting the needs of customers, is expressed by the term *relationship*. The third part of CRM, *management*, underscores the limitless and continuous coordination of all activities required for customers.

In other words, "CRM comprises a company-wide orientation of company processes to the habits, needs, and value of individual customers and the building of long-term relationships. This approach ensures the success of a company and enhances its competitive advantage."[1]

6.1.2 Functional Areas of CRM

CRM distinguishes three functional areas, *operative*, *analytical*, and *collaborative*, as illustrated in Figure 6.1.

1 Translation of: Sven H. Gericke, *Customer Relationship Management in der Assekuranz unter besonderer Berücksichtigung neuer Verfahren und moderner Informationstechnologie*. Karlsruhe: Verlag Versicherungswirtschaft, 2001.

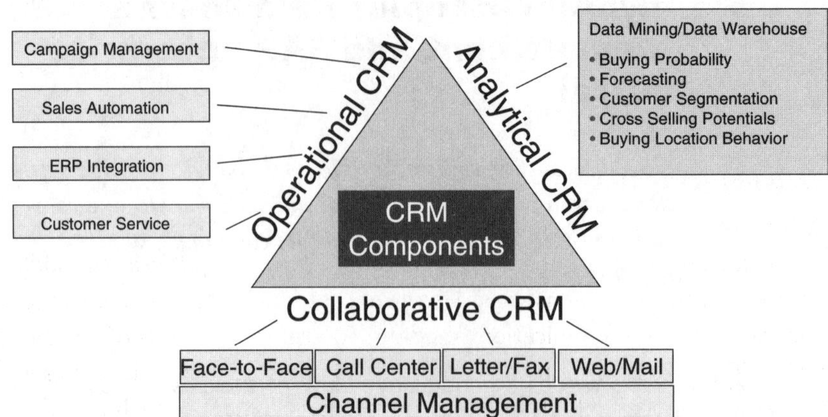

Figure 6.1 Functional Areas of CRM

Operative CRM

Operative CRM helps perform tasks related to contact with customers and administration. A customer service representative comes into contact with customers in this area—with the assistance of CRM front-office systems. Front-office applications optimize the dialog between customers and companies and the required business processes.

Back office

CRM back-office systems handle all processes that occur behind the scenes, including the internal processing of orders or returns. The CRM back office is also an interface to front-office systems and to *enterprise resource planning (ERP)* systems. The integration of CRM front-office and back-office systems is another integral component of operative CRM: the fulfillment of administrative tasks.

Analytical CRM

Analytical CRM provides a detailed study and evaluation of the data on customers and sales partners captured in operative CRM. It's critical to use the knowledge gained from that information to optimize individual CRM measures. So that the entire process of capturing and evaluating information and of optimizing activities and measures can function without frictional losses, the operative and analytical CRM solutions must enjoy seamless integration. A "feedback chain" aims at technical implementation of this process.

Data Warehouse

A *data warehouse* handles the storage and analysis of data (see Chapter 4 and Chapter 5). It's important that the information provided by the operative CRM system can be evaluated at certain times and for specific customers. The data requires an appropriate level of granularity. Via sophisticated business-management methodologies and data-mining techniques,[2] this data enables an operative CRM system to optimize its system-integrated processes.

Collaborative CRM

Collaborative CRM provides customers with various communications interfaces and contact channels. Customers can then choose the ideal access channel for themselves. However, the quality of service cannot depend on the communications medium. Therefore, the goal of collaborative CRM is to provide reliable information and a consistent level of service across all channels. The enterprise portal is also a key technology in this context: the functionality of personalization can create an interface to the company that is tailored to individual customers.

6.1.3 Other Important CRM Terms

The following explains some additional and important terms that you will encounter when dealing with CRM.

- **Closed loop marketing**
  This term is a synonym for *feedback chain*, a closed loop of rules from operative and analytical CRM. Contact with a customer (operative CRM) first results in information that is passed to analytical CRM. This information serves as the basis for evaluations and analyses. It provides new knowledge that then flows back into operative CRM, where it can be used for sales and marketing campaigns.
- **Computer Telephony Integration (CTI)**
  CTI involves the integration of traditional telecommunications with data processing: integration at the computer workstation, for example. Actually, partially and completely integrated solutions are separated from each other. For example, the simplest solution consists of a computer setting up and closing down a connection that supports only a completely integrated solution. Such a solution might relay a customer's telephone number to a specific employee. The display of this customer data on the screen of an employee's PC ensures optimal preparation for a call on the customer.

---

2 Data mining is the process of discovering new significant relationships, patterns, and trends by analyzing large data sets via pattern recognition and statistical and mathematical methods.

- **Customer Interaction Software (CIS)**
  CIS is a collective term for software used for the interaction between sellers and customers, primarily in call centers and on the Internet. CIS often combines and aligns various communications channels to customers.
- **Customer Service System (CSS)**
  A system to control and support service. In addition to assigning orders for customer service, a CSS usually contains a help desk to answer customers' most frequent questions.
- **Database marketing**
  Database marketing provides a precondition for realizing campaigns or actions with selected customers. Here you would use a collection of address data that you can delineate and classify according to several qualification characteristics. Actual contact occurs with the usual instruments of direct marketing.
- **Geographical Information Systems (GIS)**
  GIS visualizes data in a two-dimensional display on a digital map. SAP BW covers the functionality of a GIS with *BEx map*—see Section 6.3 for a more detailed explanation of GIS and the role it plays in ABC analyses.
- **Interactive Selling System (ISS)**
  An ISS helps to process sales conversations. Possible properties include electronic catalogs and (product) configuration systems that have become popular.
- **Campaign management**
  Campaigns serve to develop the "accessibility" of a selected group of customers. The coordination of campaigns assumes the use of a system for campaign management. These systems plan, control, and monitor campaigns, even when they occur across several communications channels (multichannel campaigns).
- **One-to-one marketing**
  The personal sales call occupies the foreground of one-to-one marketing. This form of marketing can meet the needs of a customer in a very individualized manner.

Figure 6.1 summarizes the functional subareas of CRM along with many of the terms related to it. In the following sections, we look at the SAP-specific design of a CRM system.

Functional areas

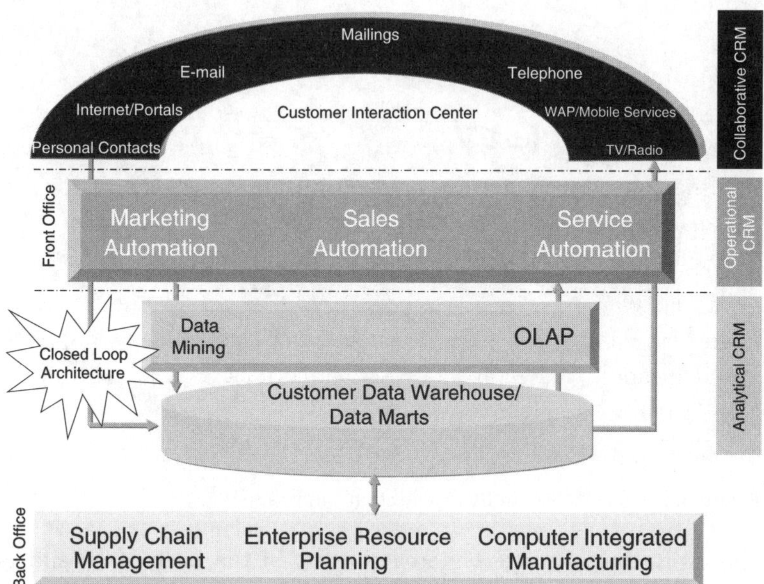

Figure 6.2 Components of a CRM System

6.2 mySAP CRM (Release 4.0)

Because of the technical complexity of an SAP CRM system, the following section can address only part of the overall architecture in detail.

Business packages

See the previous sections for information on connecting a CRM system to SAP EP. Much like the integration of an SAP BW system, this connection requires the setup of an RFC connection between the systems. Business packages handle the actual integration of the contents of an SAP CRM system; the business packages consist of a collection of roles. Here, too, the integration of roles occurs similarly to the procedure used with SAP BW. See the online documentation for detailed information and the collective note for business packages from SAP EP 6.0 SP1 onward (see Note 642775).

6.2.1 Architectural Overview

Figure 6.3 provides an overview of the functional areas of a CRM system discussed above in relation to central SAP NetWeaver components—SAP EP and SAP BW.

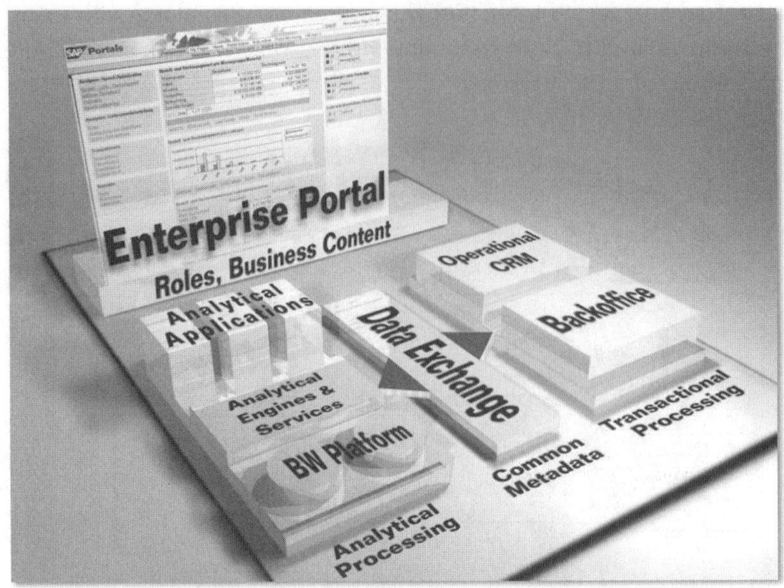

Figure 6.3 Place of CRM in the Application Landscape

Transactional processing

The *transactional processing* area consists of the back office and operational CRM. SAP BW stands across from this area; it is used for specific analyses and evaluations and thus ultimately functions as the basis for analytical CRM. Bidirectional data or information exchange exists between both applications: it ensures that the information captured in SAP BW flows back into CRM. SAP EP serves as the central access tool for users.

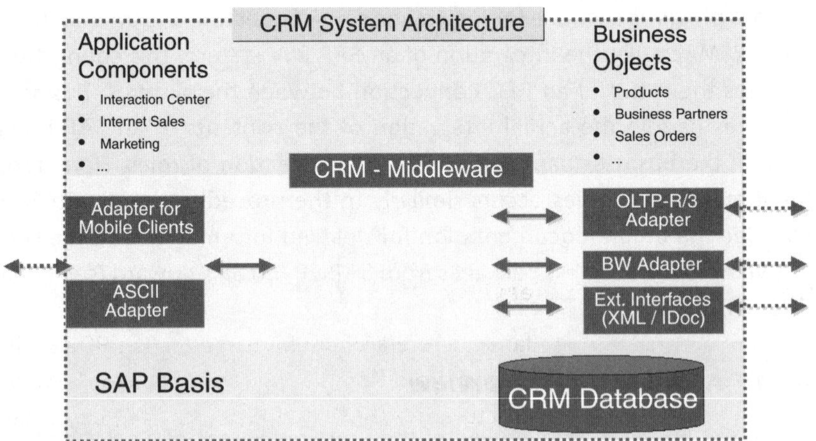

Figure 6.4 CRM Architecture

In more detail, Figure 6.4 illustrates the subcomponents of a CRM system. Similar to the architecture of SAP BW, three layers are differentiated here (although in terms of technology and contents, the layers have nothing in common): CRM system architecture with various application components and business objects, CRM middleware with interfaces and adapters to external applications and end devices, and SAP Basis. Figure 6.5 provides even more detail: some of the subcomponents shown in this figure have already been treated in this chapter, some in other chapters.

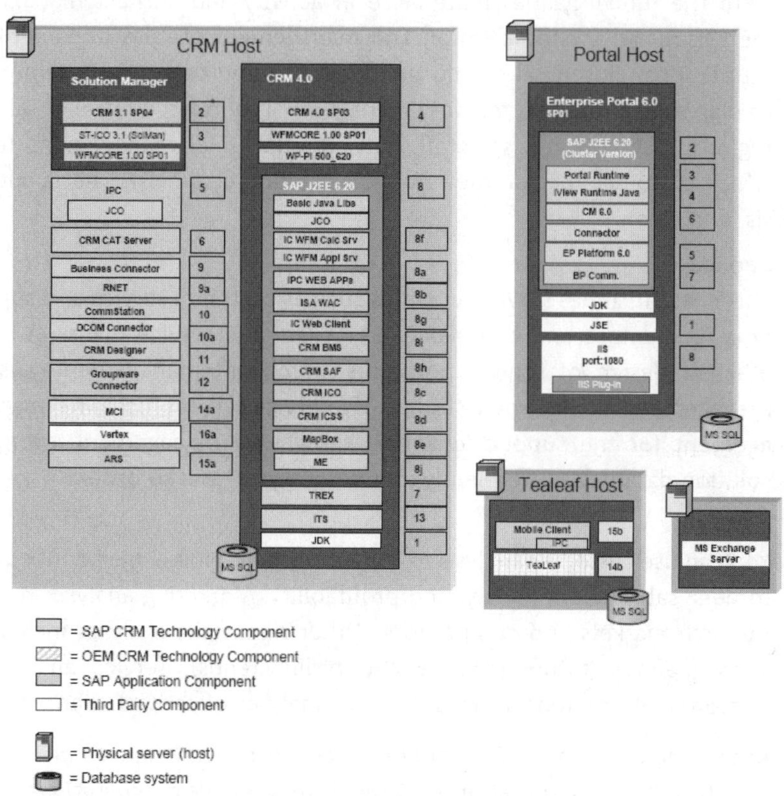

Figure 6.5 Architecture of a CRM System (The consecutive numbers correspond to the installation sequence.)

6.2.2 Functional Overview

Modular structure

mySAP CRM has a modular structure and contains more than 90 usable business scenarios that extend from "marketing planning" to "service order management." To structure the CRM solution from SAP, customer relationship management or the customer interaction cycle is divided into four phases:

- **Marketing**
  This phase helps improve the effectiveness of marketing activities. The available functionality contains marketing and campaign planning, trade promotion management for successful placement of products on the market, campaign management and automation, selection of target groups to segment customers according to specific criteria, lead management, and so on.
- **Sales and distribution**
  Here the functionalities materialize in activity and contact management, support for the creation and management of sales documents (quotations, closed sales, and processing), opportunity management to plan sales strategies, territory management for exact control of sales regions that you can select flexibly, multichannel management (in which customers decide their own distribution channels), sales analysis, and so on.
- **Service**
  This phase includes service activities such as customer service and support (guarantees and complaints, for example), service planning for efficient design of service processes, complaint management, case management for electronic storage of a service call, multichannel management for the support channel, knowledge management with a solution database of frequently asked questions, and so on.
- **Analysis**
  You can use customer analysis to gain important knowledge about customers: satisfaction, loyalty, and profitability. Marketing analyses help research markets and competitors. Other significant analyses include sales analyses (future revenue and profit trends), service analyses (research into reasons for returns), and analyses of contact channels.

Field applications

Internal employees have permanent access to relevant customer data. Similar to the core application of CRM Enterprise, *field applications* are subdivided into four phases. Sales staff and service workers can use an "offline environment" to access and update customer relationship data with their notebook computers or PDAs.

These phases can also use e-commerce and Web-enabled applications. The goal of a customer/interaction center is to enable customers to contact the company via the communication channel they find most appropriate and thereby offer them efficient and consistent service. Besides several other enhancements in mySAP CRM 4.0, we must also mention multi-channel management, which, as a new subapplication, enables cross-company collaboration with marketing, sales, and service partners.

Before we can discuss the integration scenario for analytical CRM, we must look at the technological platform of mySAP CRM 4.0.

6.2.3 Integration with SAP NetWeaver

As noted in the previous chapters and as we'll discuss in more detail in Chapter 12, the goal of providing a seamless flow of information—one that extends beyond the confines of a company—is the integration of software solutions.

Realization of integration layers

The critical aspect of the philosophy behind SAP NetWeaver is the integration of people (*people integration*), information (*information integration*), and the integration of business processes (*process integration*) that is also experienced within mySAP CRM 4.0. The following sections cannot, however, address additional system levels, such as the application platform or life cycle management.

- **User interaction**
  The portal-based user interface of mySAP CRM rests on reusable interaction patterns and supports various user roles. User roles are structured on tasks and industries and create the central object for integrating the contents of mySAP CRM into the portal. Access can occur with various end devices, ranging from a standard PC, to tablet PCs, and to a handheld computer. Additional interaction channels also exist: telephone, fax, email, page, SMS, and so on.
- **Information management**
  The management and evaluation of documents occurs at this level. Note the distinction between *structured* and *unstructured* documents. Content and knowledge management store unstructured information; a data warehouse contains structured information. The (active) distribution of this information over *BackWeb* makes it available at all times, even to mobile users of mySAP CRM.
- **Process integration**
  mySAP CRM offers tailored options for seamless support of business processes. In particular, collaborative, cross-company processes (such as mySAP CRM channel management for collaboration with sales partners) represent a special challenge. Groupware integration allows for the mutual exchange with familiar mail applications. Comprehensive workflows are also supported.

6.3 Integration Scenario: mySAP CRM and SAP EP

The following integration scenario from analytical CRM can be understood as a project solution that exceeds some of the standard functionality of mySAP CRM 4.0. The scenario provides an overview—in the sense of the closed-loop design—of how information is captured from operative CRM, evaluated in SAP BW, and then flows back into operative CRM to optimize processes. It combines the use of mySAP CRM, SAP BW, and SAP EP.

Top-down design

The scenario uses 13 steps to clarify a top-down design. It begins with a marketing manager who analyzes and highlights critical key figures captured with data mining. This case involves declining sales figures for some *A* customers (as part of an *ABC analysis*)—potentially high-profit customers—the cause of which has not yet been determined. It also studies why some potential *A* customers did not actually become *A* customers. The knowledge gained from the analyses serves as input for the marketing manager.

1. The scenario begins with a map of the United Sates (see Figure 6.6) that illustrates *A* customers (light gray), potential *A* customers (dark grey), and their revenues. The marketing manager notes a significant deviation between A and potential A customers in some states.
2. The marketing manager selects a state (Illinois), and based on Figure 6.7, determines that the number of *A* customers is significantly lower than the number of potential *A* customers. The manager also notes that the number of potential *B* and *C* customers is too low. The manager first decides to find out the cause of the gap between A and potential A customers.

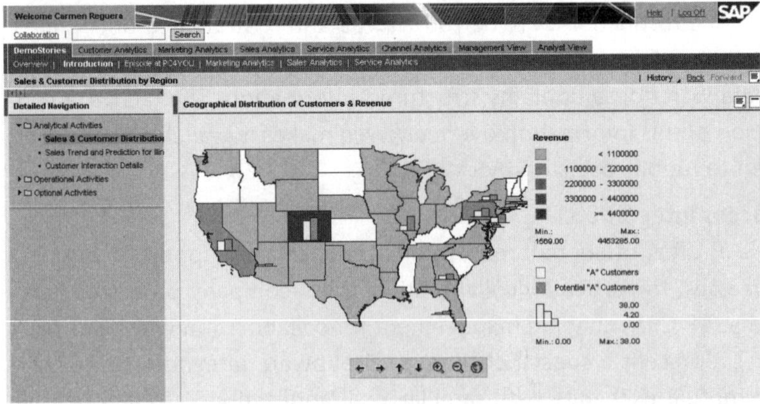

Figure 6.6 Distribution of Sales and Customers in a Region

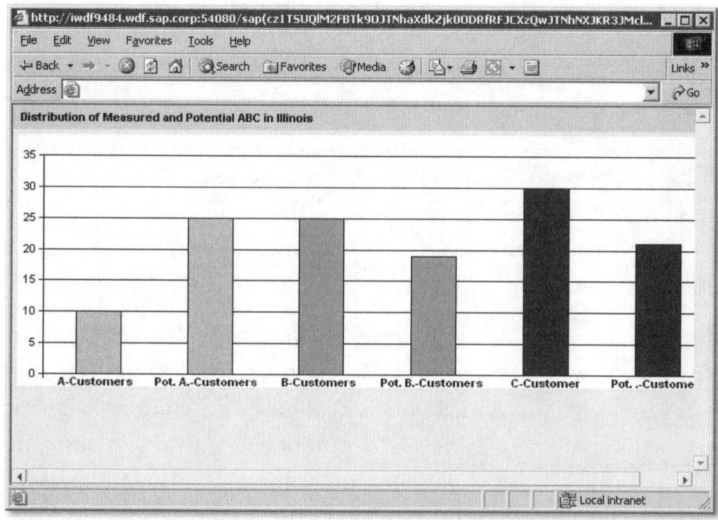

Figure 6.7 Overview of A, B, and C Customers in Illinois

3. The manager uses detailed navigation with a detailed report that shows customer trends over time (see Figure 6.8). The report shows a continual downward trend of sales among A customers.

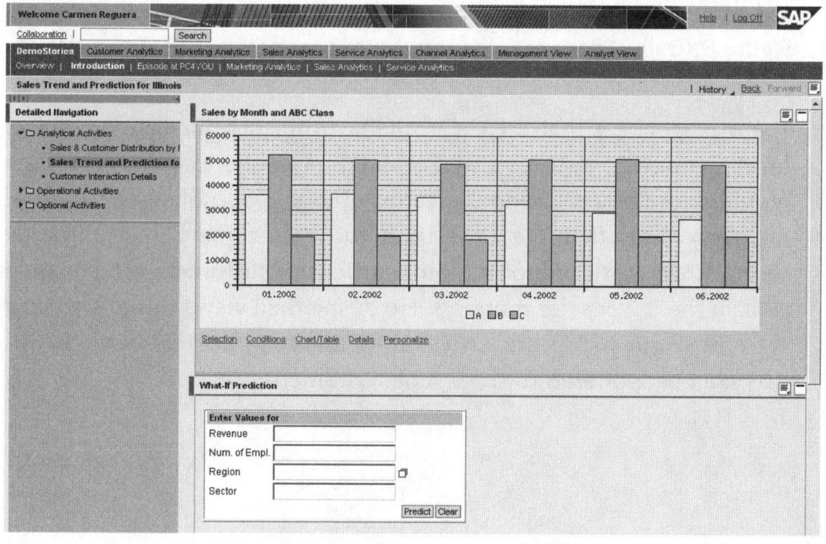

Figure 6.8 Sales Trend and Prediction in Illinois

4. To better understand the profile of *A* customers, the marketing manager performs a *what-if prediction*, a simulated forecast under specific parameters (see Figure 6.9).

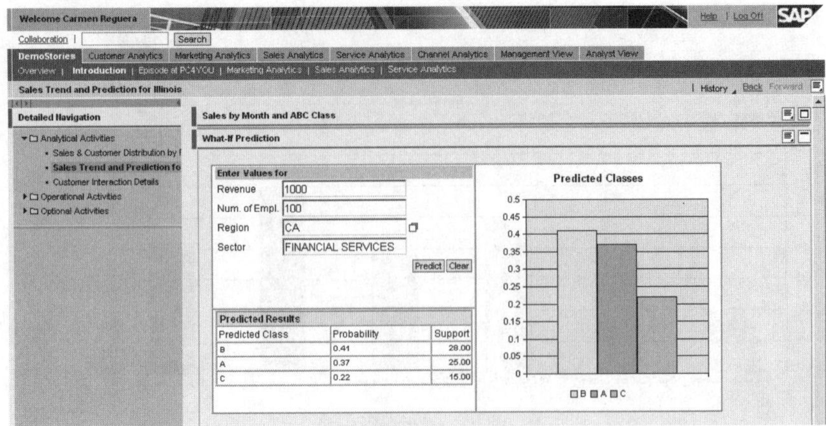

Figure 6.9 What-If Prediction

5. To obtain a better understanding of the worsening sales figures, the manager decides to navigate deeper into the data. To do so, he or she studies statistics on the following communications channels:
   - Call center
   - Direct sales
   - Internet

   Figure 6.10 illustrates the distribution of channels by customer classification over time.
6. The manager sees that the CIC is the favorite communication channel for *A* customers. Based on that finding, he or she examines the time required for the CIC channel in terms of each group of customers. The manager notes that the time used for *A* customers is significantly shorter than that used for the other groups of customers, which could explain the lower sales numbers. He or she then views the *cross-selling rules* (see Figure 6.11), and arrives at the alarming fact that wrong products are being offered to the wrong customers.

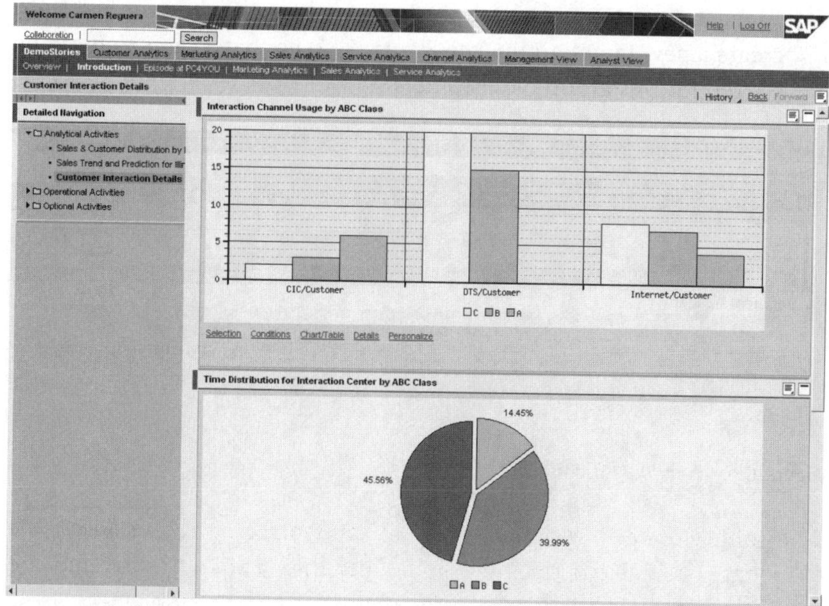

Figure 6.10 Communication Channel and Customer Group (including the time used)

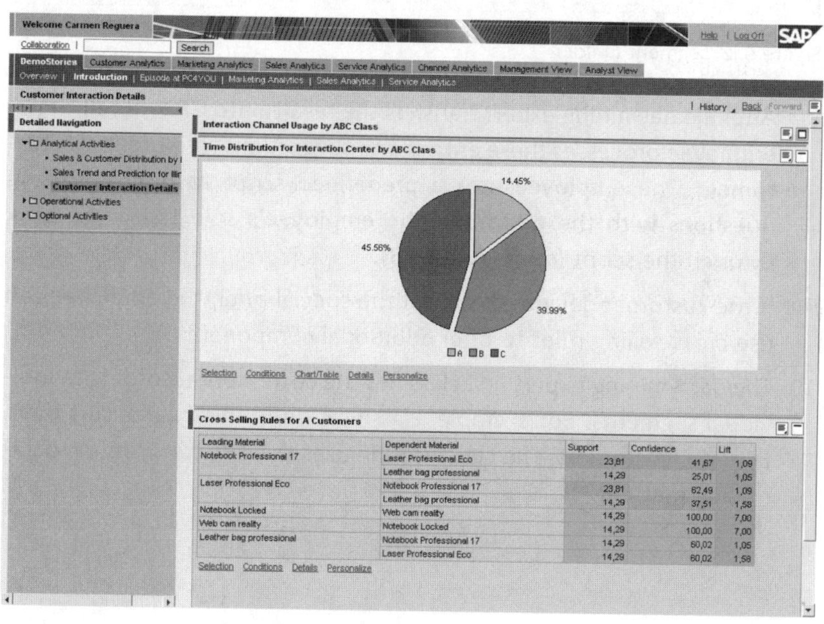

Figure 6.11 Cross-Selling Rules

7. To reach A customers better, the manager uses the *segment builder* to create a new target group (see Figure 6.12) so that a campaign can be started for this group of customers.

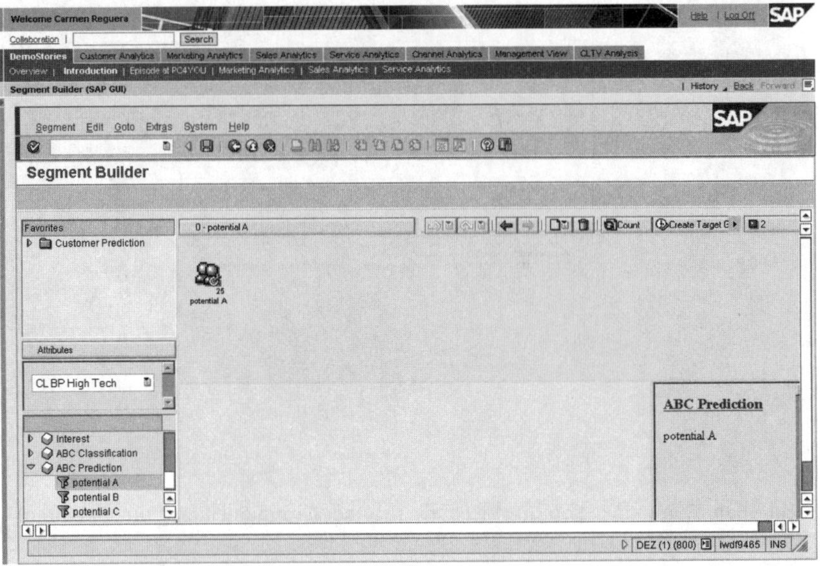

Figure 6.12 Segment Builder

8. After a data-mining expert transfers the results into CRM, a call center employee processes these entries and suggestions for potential *A* customers. The employee uses a predefined script to discuss various questions with the customer: the employee's sole task is to work through the script (see Figure 6.13).
9. If the customer decides to accept the special offer, the employee can use cross-selling rules to offer additional components.
10. The data-mining expert first classifies the customers according to individual segments. For example, classification in this case occurs by A, B, and C customers. The classification uses the *ABC classification* data-mining method.

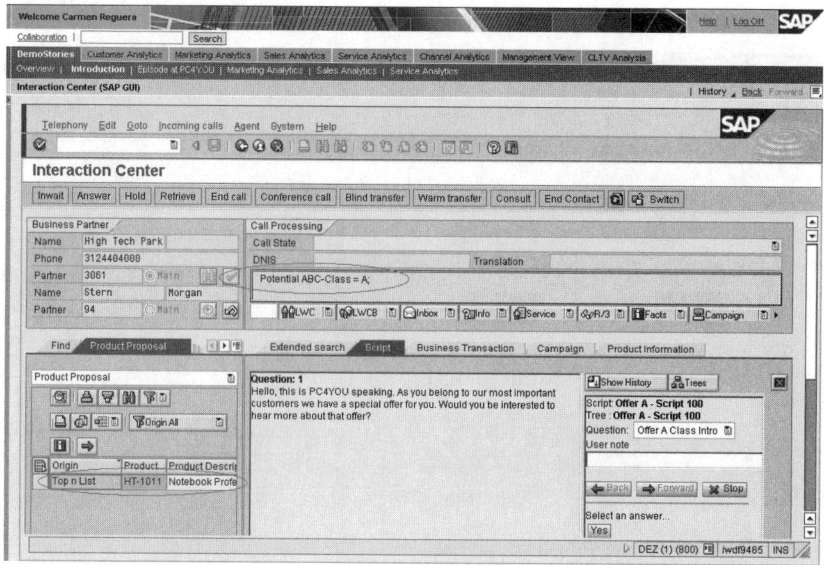

Figure 6.13 Call Center

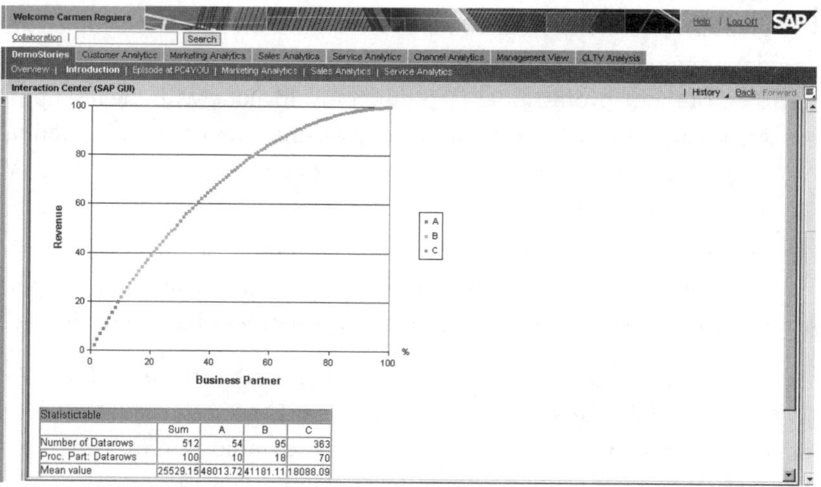

	Sum	A	B	C
Number of Datarows	512	54	95	363
Proc. Part: Datarows	100	10	18	70
Mean value	25529.15	48013.72	41181.11	18088.09

Figure 6.14 Data Mining Workbench: View of Results

11. The data mining expert must identify potential *A* customers according to the results of the data mining workbench. Potential *A* customers have the same profile as pure *A* customers, so that you can simply derive the group of potential *A* customers with the results of the ABC classification and demographic transaction data (see Figure 6.15).

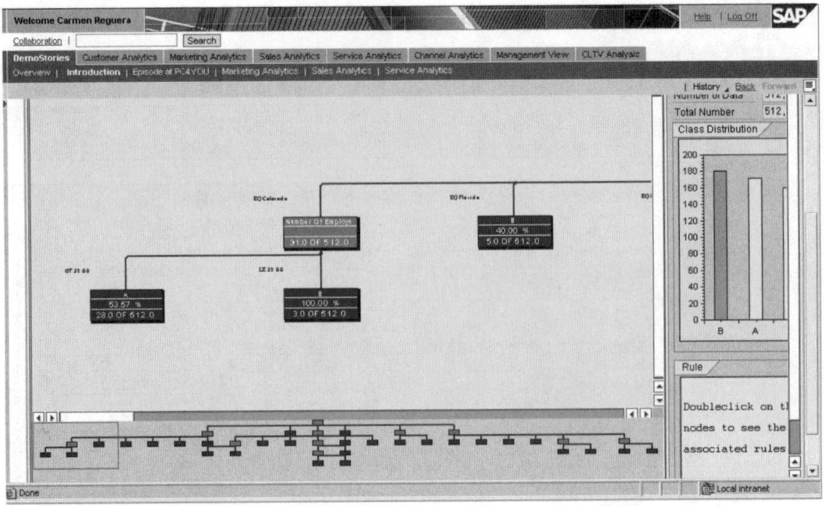

Figure 6.15 Decision Tree

12. To update the cross-selling rules, the data mining expert starts an association analysis, which also helps determine the products of greatest interest to *A* customers (see Figure 6.16). For example, the data mining expert recognizes that with a probability of about 23%, the notebook professional 17 product is sold along with the laser professional Eco printer. Additional analysis produces a list of potential suggestions for *A* customers. The rules can be transferred to the CRM system in the next step.
13. That closes the "circle" of information. The tool used here is the *analytical process designer* shown in Figure 6.17. The data mining expert can then make the results available in the segment builder or the CIC.

As the example makes clear, the components used in mySAP CRM, SAP BW, and SAP EP access each other seamlessly. Exactly this uninterrupted flow of information is the foundation for the identification of highly specific details and the capture of long-term competitive advantages.

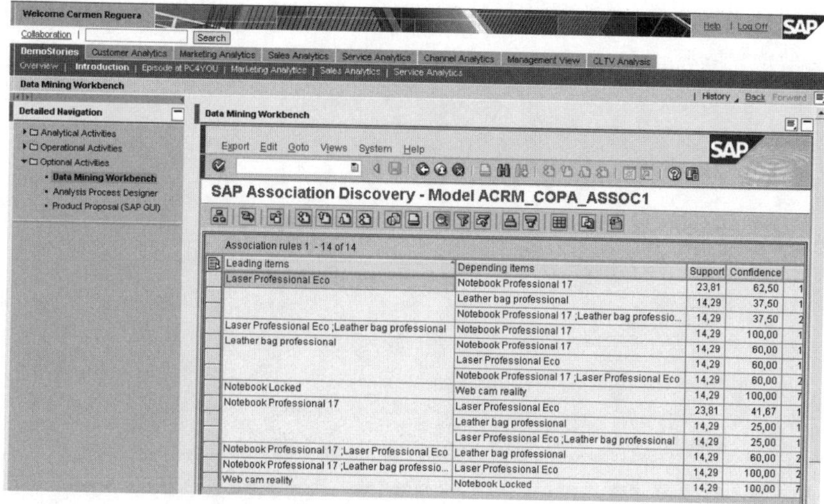

Figure 6.16 Result of the Association Analysis

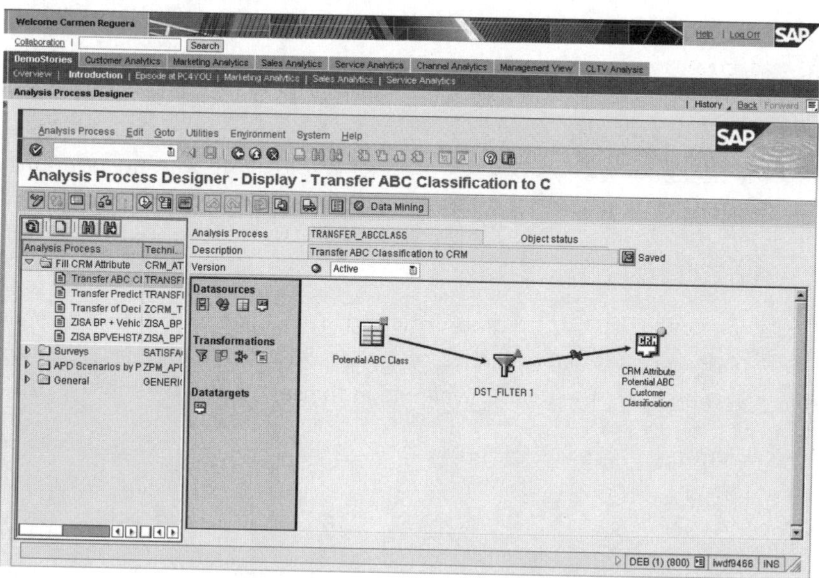

Figure 6.17 Analytical Process Designed

7 Unifiers

The ability to link applications from various manufacturers seamlessly has always been a goal. Today, the exchange of data between applications is possible. But linking one application to another with Drag&Drop—thereby ensuring that the other application understands the information (Drag&Relate)—is relatively new.

SAP Enterprise Portal offers more than the integration of data from various sources and manufacturers. It also facilitates interaction and collaboration among these applications. In this manner, various applications integrated in and referenced by SAP EP can communicate and exchange information. However, applications cannot yet perform this task on their own. Components of SAP EP make the data understandable to each application and then make it available in the required format. The components that perform this task—and others—are the *unifiers* and the *unification servers*.

7.1 Unifiers and the Unification Server

The *unification server* is a component of SAP EP that allows companies to access systems and then enables these systems to interact. In short, it enables two similar or different systems to understand each other. The following example clarifies such an understanding.

Example

Imagine that a company uses SAP Business Information Warehouse (SAP BW), SAP Advanced Planner and Optimizer (SAP APO), SAP Materials Management (SAP MM), SAP Controlling (CO), and SAP Financial Accounting (FI). The HR department uses software from Baan while an Oracle database is used to store addresses. Additionally, a Siebel CRM system is in use. So far, the interplay among the applications has been extremely complex. The SAP systems could transmit data among themselves and understand each other easily. But data from the Oracle database had to be transferred to SAP R/3 manually with copy and paste. For a customer number from the Siebel CRM system, users had to find the correct description (the counterpart) in the R/3 system before they could call the transaction. For an analysis in SAP BW, users had to search for an employee's personnel number or cost center in the Baan system and transfer the data to the SAP system before they could trigger the analysis.

This example highlights the complex, error-prone, and repetitious tasks of employees in many departments. SAP Enterprise Portal and its unification server can help. A single back-end engine creates unification between enterprise applications and database applications. Data from the most varied of sources is linked at the metalevel of the database on this unified basis. The components that extract data from applications and databases and understand the logic behind the data are the so-called *unifiers*.

How unifiers work

As indicated in the previous example, if a customer number (KDNR, for example) is taken from the Siebel CRM system and transferred into SAP BW, the latter won't know the meaning of the number or field name at first. In SAP BW, the customer number is called CUSTOMER. However, if a unifier for Siebel and a unifier for SAP are used and both reside on the unification server, SAP BW can understand both the customer number and the business logic behind the Siebel data and also generate an easy to understand format for this information. SAP BW will start the report or application with the converted customer number parameter (KDNR) from the Siebel system and display it with the appropriate presentation elements. It can do so because the Siebel unifier understands the Siebel logic and the SAP unifier understands the SAP logic. The unification server links the logic of both sides at the database level and thus connects both sides.

Figure 7.1 shows the unification server with the various unifiers. The database unifier can address Oracle, DB2, SQL7, SQL 2000, Sybase, Informix, and Access databases. Application unifiers are available for SAP R/3, SAP BW (with SAP EP 5.0 SP5), and Oracle. A separate unification server (BDN) is available for Baan and can be ordered from Baan. The SAP unifier for SAP R/3 and the SAP unifier for SAP BW are part of the standard license for SAP EP. Use of the database unifier requires the *unification for EP* license.

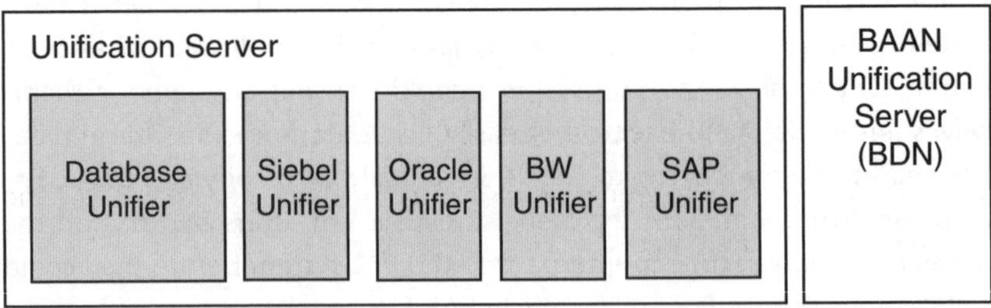

Figure 7.1 Unifiers and the Unification Server

7.2 Unification Server

The unification server is the basis for the unifiers (see Figure 7.2 for an overview).

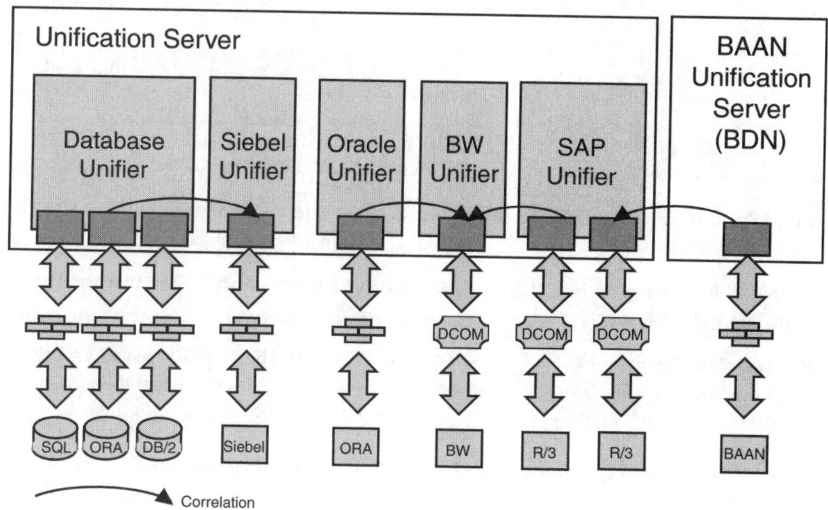

Figure 7.2 Overview of the Unification Server

The requirements for use of the unification server include the following:

- SAP Enterprise Portal SP4 > Patch 2
- Microsoft Windows Server 2000 SP2
- Microsoft FrontPage 2000 Server Extensions
- Microsoft SQL Server 2000 SP2
- Microsoft InterDev 6.0 SP4 (for iView modification)
- Microsoft Internet Explorer > 5.01 (SP1 for clients and SP2 for the server)
- MSXML 4.0

7.3 SAP Unifier for SAP R/3 and SAP BW

Requirements

Table 7.1 shows the requirements to use the SAP unifier for SAP R/3 and SAP BW.

SAP Unifier for SAP R/3	SAP Unifier for SAP BW
▶ Unification Server Version 5.0 SP4 Patch 3	▶ Unification Server Version 5.0 SP4 Patch 3
▶ SAP Enterprise Portal 5.0, at least SP4 Patch 2	▶ SAP Enterprise Portal 5.0, at least SP4 Patch 2
▶ SAP R/3 Release >= 4.0B	▶ SAP BW 3.0A with SP7 or BW 3.0B
▶ MS SQL Server 2000 SP2	▶ MS SQL Server 2000 SP2
▶ DCOM Version >= 4.6D	▶ DCOM Version >= 4.6D
▶ SAP R/3 must be configured for Drag&Relate and SSO	▶ BW must be configured for Drag&Relate and SSO
▶ WP Plug-In must be installed on SAP R/3 (for BOR Import)	▶ WP Plug-In must be installed on the BW system
▶ Web GUI: ITS or Win GUI: The SAP frontend must be installed on the client	▶ Win GUI: The SAP frontend (with the BW add-on) must be installed on the client (only to deploy queries)

Table 7.1 Technical Requirements for the SAP R/3 and SAP BW Unifiers

The Drag&Relate example provided at the end of Chapter 5 (see Figure 5.17) showed how to move the entry for *Motomarkt Stuttgart GmbH* or the sunglasses icon next to it into the iPanel entry for *Motomarkt Stuttgart GmbH* with **Drag&Relate Analysis · Display Customer**. It also showed the display of the customer data for *Motomarkt Stuttgart GmbH* in the SAP system—on the right side in the content area.

Transferring data with Drag&Relate

This scenario shows how easily you can transfer data from one system to another. Users don't have to remember the customer number or use copy and paste to transfer it from one system to another: the customer number is stored with the customer name—transparent to the user. Breaking down the customer name into the customer number and calling the transaction in the SAP system occur in the background. The transaction in the SAP system is simultaneously populated with the customer number, and the system then displays the customer data. The advantages of Drag&Relate—and the unifier—are obvious: reliable information is transferred, errors during entry are avoided, and the overall processing time for the user is significantly reduced.

Installation and configuration

To use the SAP unifiers (SAP R/3 and SAP BW), you must first install the SAP DCOM connector and the unification server. The particular SAP unifier is installed on that foundation. You must also maintain the *systems.xml* file for SAP BW and SAP R/3. Chapter 5 examined the configuration of the system files. The system names must agree with the logical system names of SAP BW and SAP R/3 (MANCLNT907, for example). In addition to system specifications for SAP's Internet Transaction Server (ITS) or the SAP Web Application Server (Web AS) connection data, you must specify the unification server and port number

Note

The preceding material does not apply to SAP Enterprise Portal 6.0. Unification projects are controlled in SAP EP 6.0 with the portal content directory and are no longer integrated into the portal as a data source. The unification server no longer accesses user management in the portal (Lightweight Directory Access Portal, LDAP) directly; the portal itself controls user access to resources.

Listing 7.1 shows the entries in the *systems.xml* file (in addition to system integration) needed to use the unifiers.

```
<WebAccessPoints>
   <WebAccessPoint category="WAS">
      ...
   </WebAccessPoint>
   <WebAccessPoint category="DRS">
      <Protocol>HRNP</Protocol>
         <HostName>hostname:port</HostName>
   </WebAccessPoint>
</WebAccessPoints>
```

Listing 7.1 Excerpt from the systems.xml File

For each new project, you must create a new database instance on the SQL server before generating the project.

Creating a project

To create a project, start the unification server. You should see an entry for the project generator (SAP unifier) and a project generator entry for the database (see Figure 7.3).

For an SAP unifier project, double-click on the **Project Generator (SAP unifier)**. You'll be prompted to enter the server, the database you just created, the name of the SAP R/3 system, and the user for the SAP R/3 system. The project is then generated. You must configure user management for each project. To do so, you can access the data on the portal server, such as the LDAP server settings, and copy and paste it here.

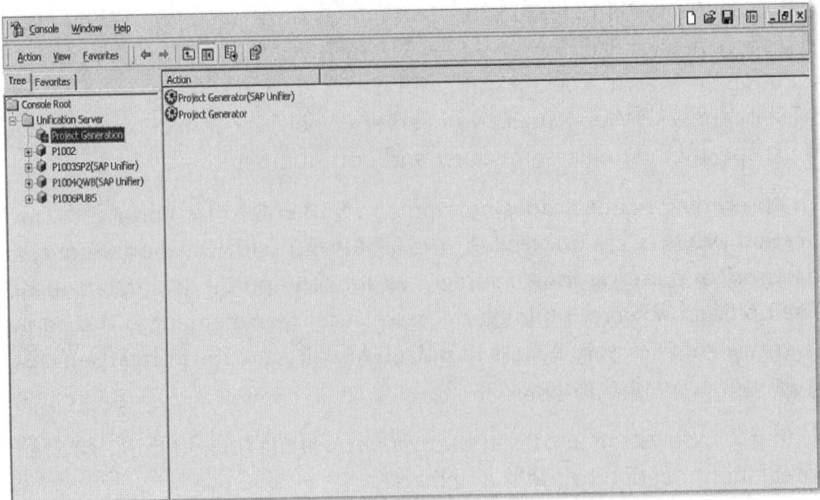

Figure 7.3 Unification Server with Entries for the Database and the SAP Unifier

Correlator wizard You must then start the *correlator wizard* and configure it for the relationships among the projects. For example: the OBJECTKEY field of table OSOLD_TO is linked to the OBJECTKEY field of table KNA1. OBJECTKEY represents the *bridge* between the two projects. You can use the relationship editor to view or edit the relationships.

7.4 Database Unifier

The *database unifier* is delivered with the unification server. It offers the same functionality as other unifiers, but does so based on database tables and relations rather than business objects or BW InfoCubes. For that reason, the relationships here are one level deeper—at the database table level instead of business logic.

Installation Currently, the unification server and the unifier are available only for Windows and the MS SQL server. Installation is simple and intuitive. You can decide whether you want to install the unification server on the same computer as the portal or on another, separate computer. If you plan to use unification intensively, we recommend that you install the server on a separate computer. Ensure that you recheck the system requirements and the required software before the installation. The *FrontPage server extensions* are elementary for Drag&Relate. It's easy to forget to install them or verify whether they're installed when errors occur. Therefore, make sure your computer meets the hardware and software technical requirements for installation of the unification server.

7.4.1 Project Generation

Once you have completed the installation, you can start generating a project. Every unification project (and the SAP unifiers associated with the project) requires a separate database. First create a new database. Follow menu path **Start · Programs · Microsoft SQL-Server · Enterprise Manager** to start the enterprise manager of the MS SQL server. Position the pointer on **Databases** and right-click to display the context menu. Select **New Database** and assign a database name, such as "MyFirstUnificationProject." Select **OK**. The database is created. You can now close the enterprise manager. Start the unifier management console via menu path **Start · Unification Server · Unifier Management Console**. Enter an administrator ID and password (admin/admin for the initial start). Select **Unification Server · Project Generation** and then **Project Generator** in the right pane. Select **Create project with content** (see Figure 7.4). Then, click **Next** and then, **Finish**.

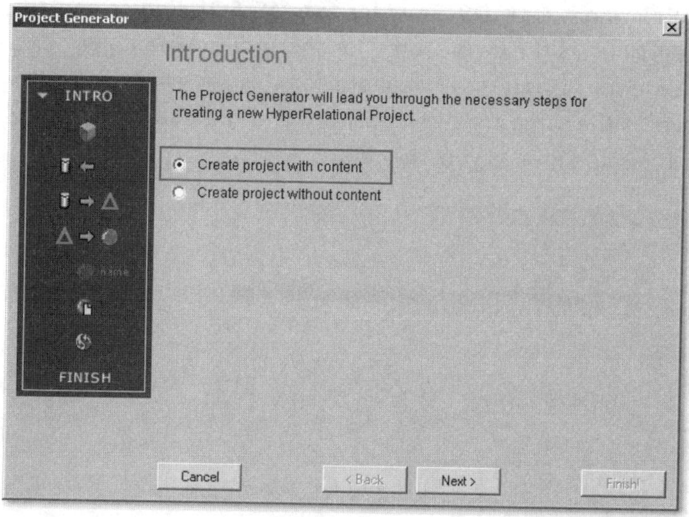

Figure 7.4 Creating a Project with Content

Authorizations

You are now prompted to enter the project name, the unifier project server, the port under which the project will run, the database server, the user and password, and the repository database (see Figure 7.5). Make sure that the user you enter for the database has the appropriate authorizations for it. If the user doesn't, you won't be allowed to select the database that you just created or will be refused access. If you need to modify the authorizations, you can do so in the enterprise manager of the MS SQL server.

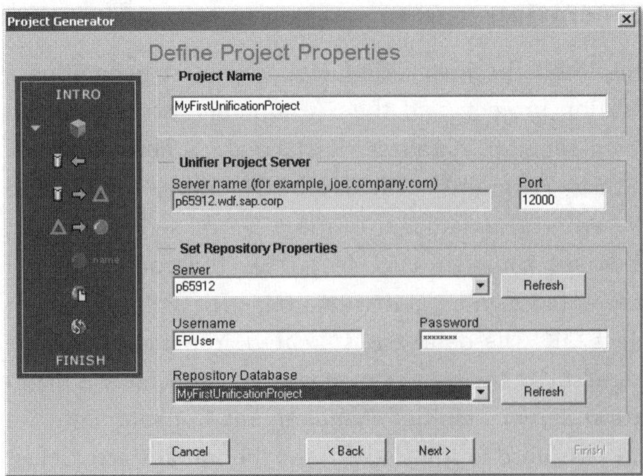

Figure 7.5 Project Settings

Because you are accessing an MS SQL database, in the next screen you select **HyperRelational OLE DB Provider for MS SQL Server** and the server that functions as the data source for the project (see Figure 7.6). You must then enter a user and password for this server. Because the database server is the same for the repository and the data source, you should enter the same user as you did before.

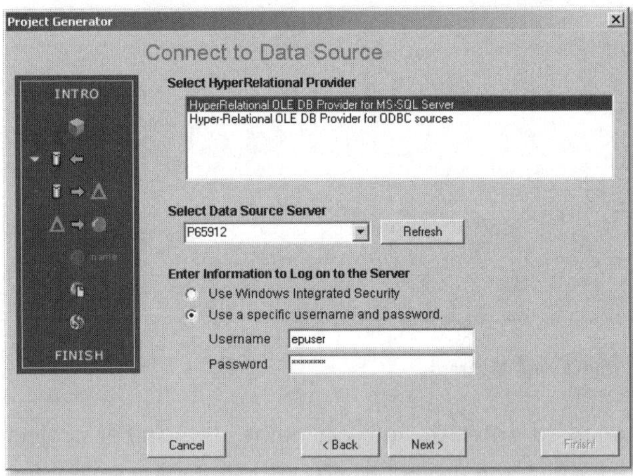

Figure 7.6 Establishing the Connection to the Data Source

Data objects You now need the data objects that you'll use for the unifier project. For example, you can now select the Northwind database and all its tables by selecting **Northwind · dbo · TABLE** and then select **Add** to insert it into the right pane.

Now perform the same procedure for the presentation objects. You might have a smaller number of presentation objects because you might not want to display all the data that you will be working with. Templates are created only for the objects selected here.

Presentation objects

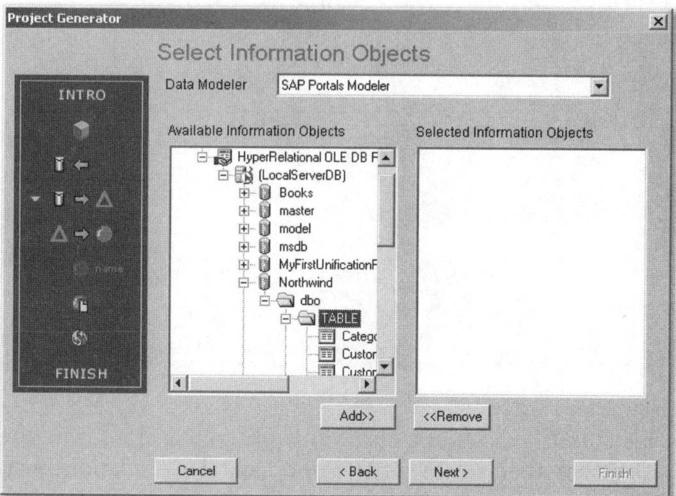

Figure 7.7 Selecting Data Objects

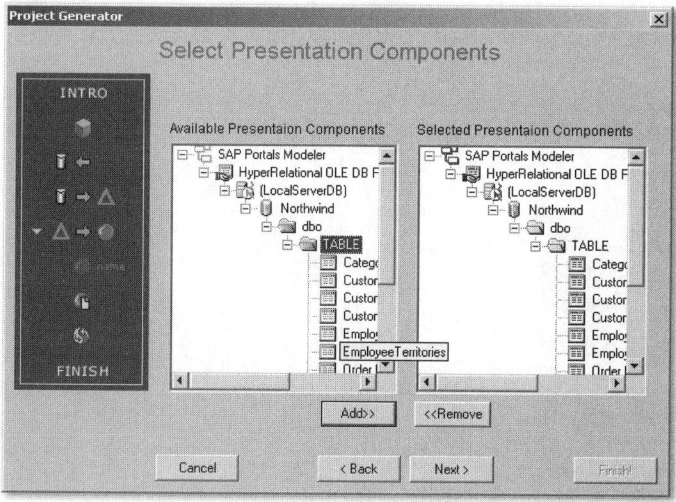

Figure 7.8 Presentation Components

Then select all the metatemplates that you want to use: Add, Find, Export in Excel, List Display, Update, and View, for example.

Metatemplates

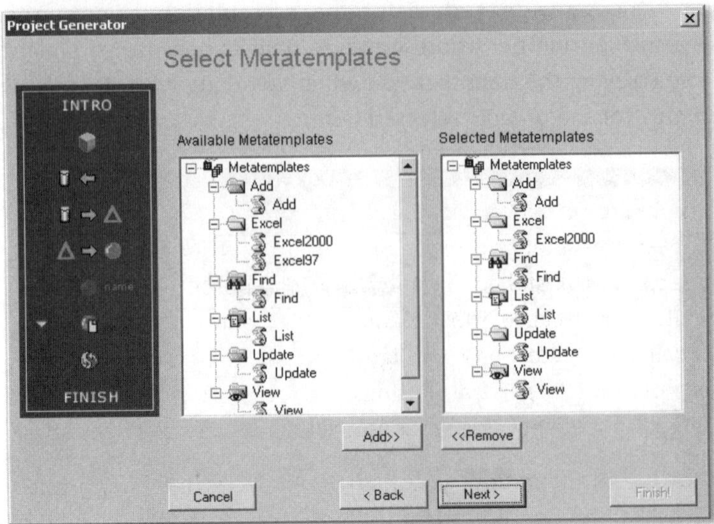

Figure 7.9 Metatemplates

Importing relationships

You are now asked whether you want to import database relationships. Select the default (recommended) option; otherwise, you'll have to set the relationships manually at some point later on. The generator performs this work for you. Confirm the next screen and allow the project to be generated. The progress display shows you the status of the process (see Figure 7.10).

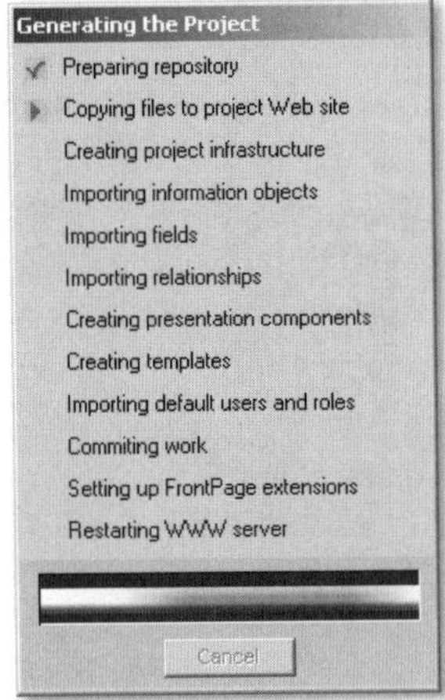

Figure 7.10 Progress Display During Project Generation

7.4.2 User Management

If your project was generated successfully, it is available in the unification management console, where you can set authorizations and access rights, display components, and much more. Use **<Project_name> · User Management · Security & Configuration** to make settings for user management. This procedure is similar to the one for portal settings; you can use the same entries here that you used for the portal. If the portal and the unification server are installed on the same computer, the entries are already maintained because the default configuration of the portal is used. If you want to create a new configuration, you can modify the other settings, except for the general settings. You cannot do so with the default configuration. Check the settings and update them as needed.

According to this configuration, you have access to all users and roles, such as the LDAP directory service. You can now grant portal user roles or individual users access to database tables. You might have to start the MS IIS and the J2EE Engine.

7.4.3 iPanel Assignment

Select **<Project_name> · User Management · iPanel Editor**. You can now select the users and roles for which you want to grant access to individual tables (see Figure 7.11). Use the **Components** tab to drag the tables with Drag&Drop into the iPanel of the user or role. You can use the context menu to show or hide entries. Doing so is a good idea when you want to allow a user access to the same table multiple times with several roles. You can avoid double entries with **Hide**.

Selecting objects

You can now select individual tables, search for entries, display all entries, or move values of a row from one table to another with Drag&Relate. If a relationship exists, the corresponding data is displayed. As much as possible, you should select only those objects that you really need for project generation—information and presentation objects. Large databases can involve large volumes of data and therefore the project generation can be very time-consuming. The selection of all tables creates a template for each table.

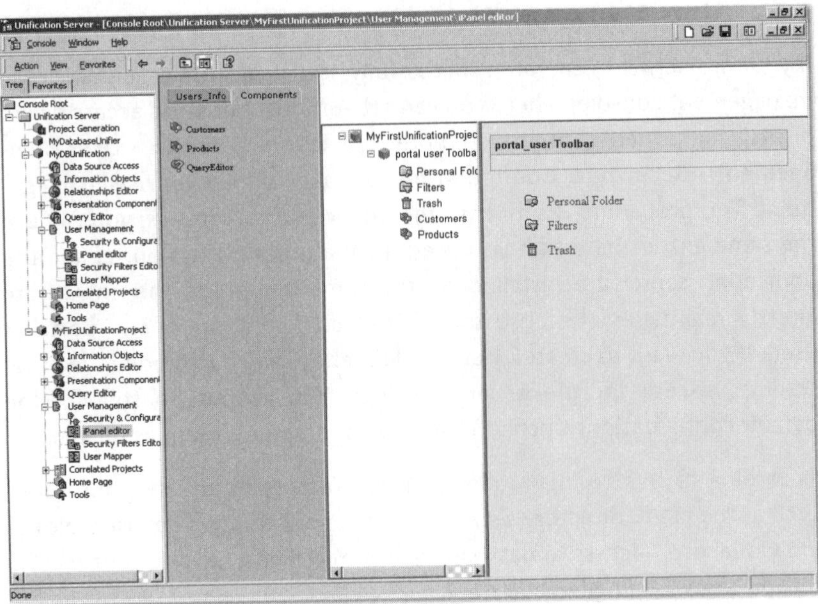

Figure 7.11 Assignment of Authorizations for Individual Tables in the iPanel

7.4.4 Editing Relationships

If you make the appropriate selections when installing it, the database unifier has accepted the relationships from the database. It also attempted to create relationships for relationships that don't exist between the entities. If the relationships don't meet your requirements, you can edit them. To do so, select the **Relationships Editor** in your project. It displays all the relationships among the individual entities (see Figure 7.12). To understand the meaning of the various colors, select the **color key**.

Editing relationships

Double-click on a file to edit the relationships by assigning various weights for specific relationships. If several paths or relationships between objects are created, you can assign *weights* to indicate your preferences for finding appropriate objects (the *shortest path*).

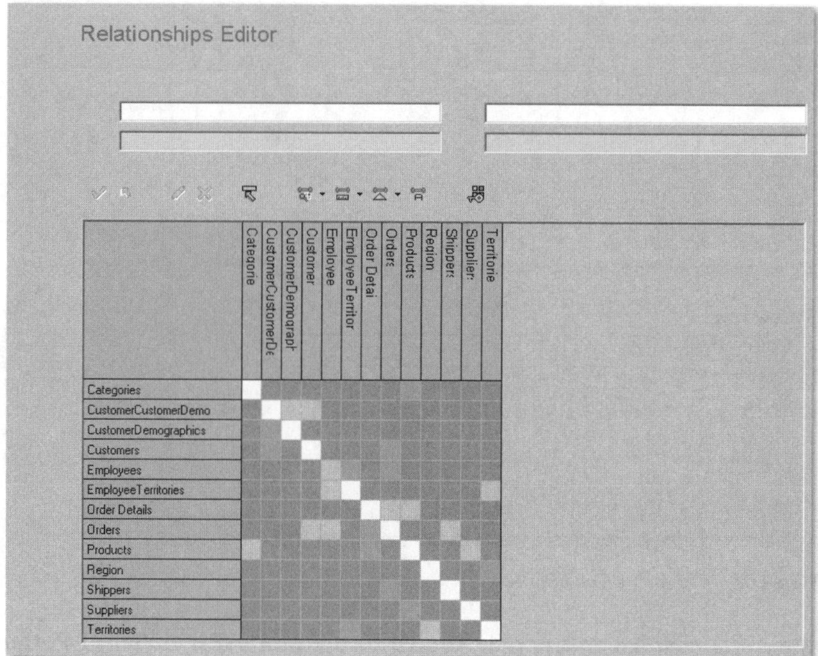

Figure 7.12 Relationships Editor

7.4.5 Integration of the Unifier with the Portal

You have now created a database unification project. User management is configured and you have assigned tables to users and roles. So far, you have been able to access your project only via the unification management console. To integrate the project with the portal, you must perform the following steps.

Creating a data source

Start your portal and log on with administrator rights. To access the unification project, you must first create a data source (see Figure 7.13). Select **System Configuration • Data Sources • New**. Enter a name, a description of the URL you want to use to address the unification project (the computer on which the unification server is running), and the port that you have assigned. You can take this information from the project settings in the **Unification Management Console**.

Keep the remaining settings as they are. They involve a unifier project and the user information should be used to log on. The Authentication Method is **Basic**, but the Authorization Level is **Automatic Synchronization**. Click on **Add** to create the data source.

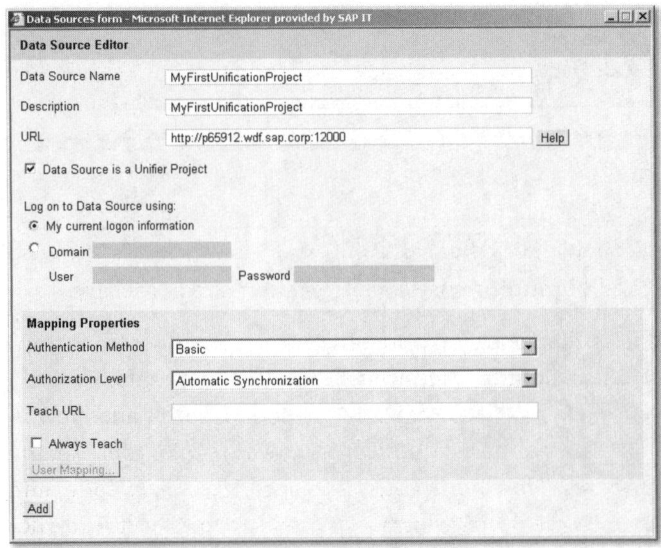

Figure 7.13 Creating a Data Source

iPanel Assignment

You must now assign the data source to the user's iPanel. Select **Portal Admin • iPanel Assignment.** Select the *portal_user* role to which you want to assign the unification project. The data sources are displayed. Check the appropriate data source and save your settings. Now close your browser and open it again. Log on as a portal user (not as admin/admin). The iPanel with the unification project is displayed. You can now select any data records and use Drag&Relate to move them into the iPanel.

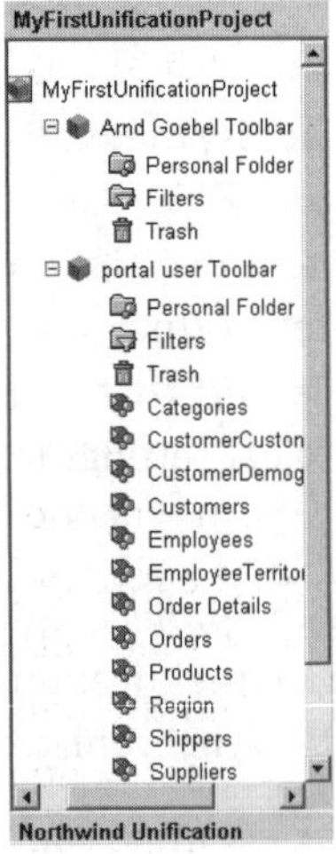

Figure 7.14 The Unification Project in the iPanel of the Portal

7.5 Internet Components

In addition to the unifiers, you have other options to realize Drag&Relate. Internet components enable the movement of information data from a unifier project into the form of an Internet site. You'll see an example of this in Chapter 8: package tracking for FedEx is defined as an iView, not as an Internet component. You could create an Internet component instead of the FedEx iView, which would allow pulling a tracking number from an SAP R/3 system and outputting the storage location of the package.

Example

We'll use another example to introduce Internet components. In top-level navigation, select **Content Admin · Internet components**. Create a new Internet component, such as **Map 24**. Select **URL editor** and **New**. A browser window opens; enter URL *http://www.us.map24.com/* in the window. Enter "Address" for the street, "Citycode" for the zip code, and "City" for the city into the Map24 form. Then select **Go**. Select **Add URL** in the address bar of the portal; **URL added** confirms the action. Now select **Close**. Enter an additional URL in the small portal window, the one you want to use as the standard URL: *http://www.us.map24.com/*. The Internet component is added to the iPanel later on. The standard URL is displayed when the user selects the entry. The other URL, the one that records parameters, is used when an entry is drawn over it with Drag&Relate.

Adjusting parameters

The parameters you entered in the form of Map24 are now being stored as fixed values. They will later be transferred as parameters of the table cell you indicate with Drag&Relate. To enable this function, select the URL with the parameters and then **Edit**. You now see the static parameters as currently set. In the second column, (Address, Citycode, and City) place a number (#) sign both in front of and behind each entry, so that Address becomes #Address#, Citycode becomes #Citycode#, and City becomes #City#. Now you must map the application's parameters to these parameters. Select the **Parameter** tab and select the data source that is to provide the data. You then select the unification project you have created. The main object is the **Customers** table. For Address, select the **Customers** table and the **Address** field. Proceed in the same manner for Citycode and City. Save your entries. You must also assign the Internet components to the iPanel. To assign roles, proceed here as you did with the unification project treated above. You can drag entries from the unification project displayed in the table to the Internet components. Map24 will then display the map of the appropriate address from your unification project in a Java applet in the portal.

You are now familiar with the usual unifiers and know the basics of how they function. However, due to the constraints of this section, we can present you with only the most important features. SAP offers special courses on unification and unifiers so that you can enhance your knowledge.

7.6 Enhancement for SAP Enterprise Portal 6.0

Unification technology has been enhanced in SAP Enterprise Portal 6.0. SAP Enterprise Portal 5.0 unifiers were linked directly to SAP EP 6.0 and their functionality expanded to support new processes in SAP EP 6.0, such as the user management engine and the portal content directory.

The user interface was also improved. SAP is currently working on the re-implementation of unifiers in Java. This effort will be completed when SAP NetWeaver '04 becomes generally available.

Figures 7.15 and 7.16 show the integration of unifiers in SAP Enterprise Portal 6.0.

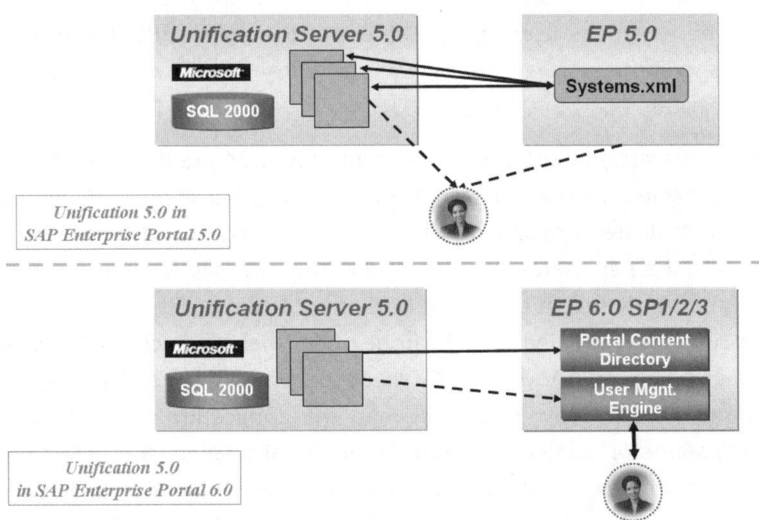

Figure 7.15 Modifications for Unification from SAP EP 5.0 to SAP EP 6.0

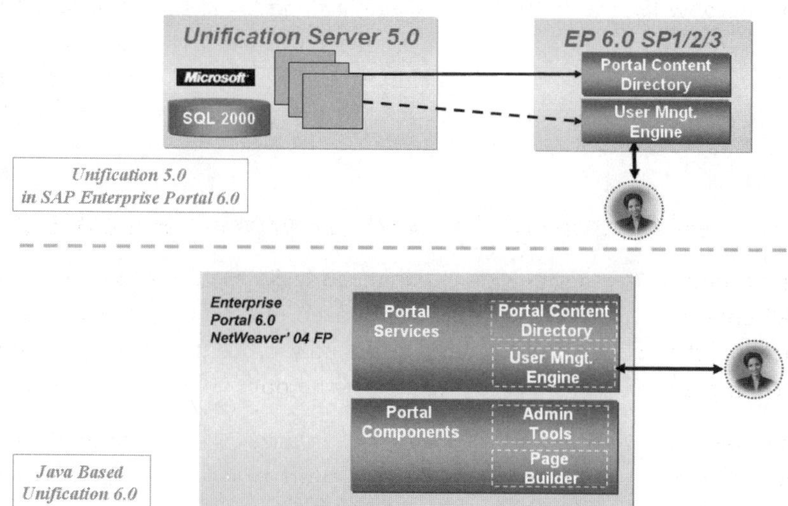

Figure 7.16 Modifications for Unification in SAP EP 6.0 (partly in planning)

8 iViews

iViews are an integral component of SAP Enterprise Portal. They contain applications and information that portal users need for their daily work.

SAP Enterprise Portal offers a wealth of functionalities that can integrate applications and display all types of information. In particular, applications can interact and communicate with each other. Simple user interaction executes transactions and updates the display in the portal. It gives portal users a hands-on ability to work with programs from various sources and makes working with the components completely transparent to the user. It now makes no difference whether an enterprise resource planning (ERP) system from SAP or a database from Oracle work behind an application. What's important is that the applications can communicate and create a completely transparent and seamless chain of worksteps.

Uniform interface

The greatest advantage of the portal is that it has only one interface that integrates all these applications. Users no longer have to deal with various menus or screens: all components look alike. The portal can have a uniform interface because it isn't required to integrate an application's complete frontend (SAP, Siebel, or Oracle). It only has to provide the most important excerpts or views of the required information. However, you can, of course, choose to integrate the complete GUI if necessary. But this approach is usually adopted only when no tailored version exists for a specific group of users (purchasing, for example), or an end user must function as a power user and access every single menu of a dynpro.

Whether it's a question of integrating views or a complete application, both scenarios involve integrating components in the portal. In the language of portals, the components are called *iViews*. iViews do more than just display information. They enable users to query information from the most varied sources according to their own search criteria, or establish settings in back-end systems that are linked to the iViews. The full range of iViews extends from the simple display of a Web site to the complex integration of an ERP system.

Example

Consider the following example. You create an order in SAP's Supplier Relationship Management's Enterprise Buyer Professional (SRM/EBP). The order triggers a purchase request in the backend (in SAP R/3). The purchasing agent must now find an appropriate vendor and the product at the most attractive price. A material master might have to be created in the backend. If a bottleneck develops at the manufacturer, you're sure to call the purchasing agent eventually to ask why the product you ordered has not yet arrived.

Even this scenario makes it clear that a given process must access several different systems. Until now, the purchasing agent has had to deal with an SRM/EBP system with a Web frontend, an SAP GUI with access to the backend, several of the vendor's Web pages, and probably even the Web site of the transportation provider. Working with all these sources required having to toggle between various windows. The purchasing agent had to note the shopping cart number from one system—or even copy and paste the number so that the next system could process it—and then switch to yet another system.

Clearly, these activities are very time-consuming. That's where SAP Enterprise Portal can help. Its configuration for frequently used system and Web pages means that you never have to switch from one application window to another. You can access the material master, SRM/EBP, and the Web sites of the vendor and the transportation provider easily with the iPanel. You can use Drag&Relate to exchange information among applications. When applications exchange information, the purchasing agent sees the order in SAP Enterprise Buyer and the purchase request in the backend. The agent can easily call and create materials in the backend and then move to the vendor's Web site to select materials. When an order and an order confirmation already exist, the purchasing agent can enter the tracking number of the package at the transport provider's Internet site to determine whether the shipment is already on its way.

Figure 8.1 shows an example from FedEx. Drag&Relate has not yet been configured here. This iView is based on a page created with the iView catcher. Drag&Relate can be implemented with an Internet component that can receive data from an application or a database via a unifier.

Single sign-on

The big advantage here—over the simple display of information—is that portal users are authenticated automatically. They can access protected information without having to re-authenticate themselves. The technology used here is called single sign-on (SSO). Users' authentications are transferred in encrypted form with each query; other portals trust the querying portal and the users. It's easy to see how much time you can save with this functionality. Passwords are no longer forgotten; the information that the applications exchange is reliable; and the danger of copying incorrect data is reduced, or, in some cases, almost completely eradicated.

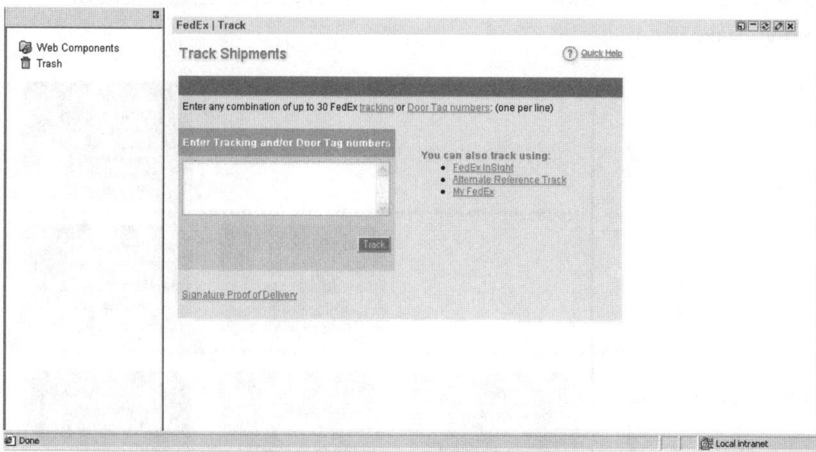

Figure 8.1 Tracking a Package with a Tracking Number

iView categories

iViews can be categorized. You can first differentiate iViews in terms of development languages. The term was originally developed by TopTier, a company whose development paralleled Microsoft. Consequently, most iViews were written in Visual Basic Script and then implemented as Active Server Pages (ASP) for the Internet. A specific dialect, which is now called SAPPortals XML, was also used. The dialect receives instructions that the portal processor interprets and then renders them accordingly. The dialect can be combined with Visual Basic Script as desired to allow dynamic queries.

An iView can also be created with Java—the powerful Internet language. Note another distinction between simple Java servlets and the more demanding Java Server Pages (JSPs) with Java beans. You can also create an iView with the iView Catcher, a tool delivered with the portal (SAP EP 5.0 only). You can use the tool to display sections of Web sites from the Internet, such as a column, in the portal.

You can also draw a distinction between ready-made iViews and those you create yourself. The iViewStudio (*http://www.iviewstudio.com*) offers portal operators many ready-made iViews delivered in business packages. The packages were created in view of a meaningful aggregation of services for specific groups of users. iViews are summarized in worksets, which, in turn, are summarized in business packages. Depending on the assigned role, users can access specific pages that contain iViews from business packages, or iViews summarized in worksets that are themselves summarized in business packages. Figure 8.2 shows the types of iViews, differentiated according to programming language, specialization, and individualization.

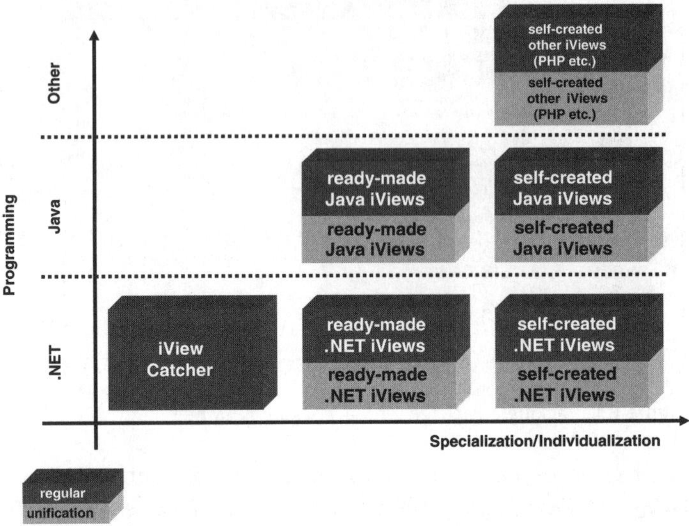

Figure 8.2 Differentiation of iViews

iViewStudio With the iViewStudio (see Figure 8.3), SAP offers several ready-made business packages with iViews for the portal. This material allows quick and user-friendly integration of information, applications, and services in SAP EP.

In addition to ready-made content, the iViewStudio also provides you with tools that you need to create your own portal applications. After an introduction to the role concept and navigation in SAP Enterprise Portal, the following sections look at the differentiation of ready-made and self-created iViews. You'll become familiar with tools that you can use to create your own iViews and with the programming languages that you can use for development.

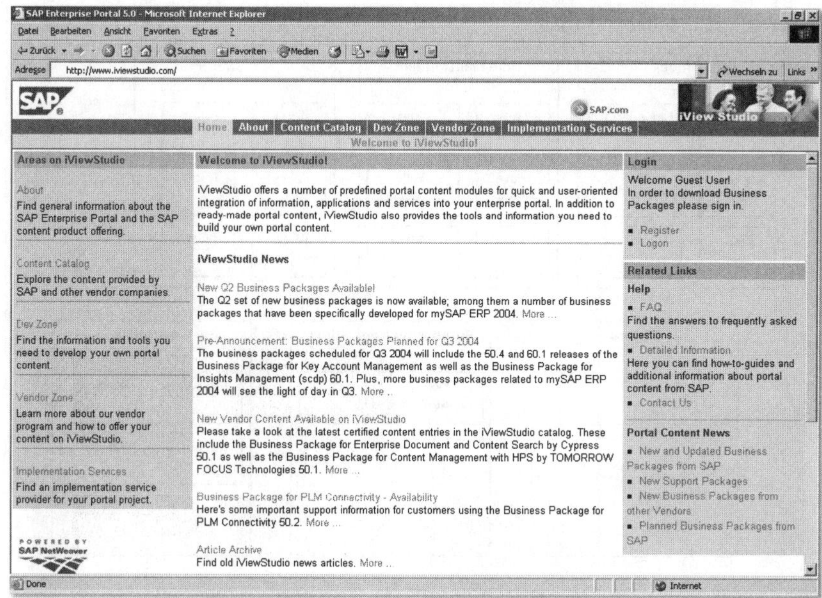

Figure 8.3 iViewStudio

8.1 Roles and Navigation in the Portal

Packages

In the following sections the term *packages* is often used. Packages are a collection of logically-related directories, also called folders or worksets, which are contained in iViews. An example clarifies this hierarchy best. A business package for the purchasing department can also contain subgroups (folders or worksets) for subordinate departments like order processing, order requests, and invoice verification. The worksets or folders logically belong to purchasing. But because not all groups of purchasing employees process all the procedures, we recommend that you subdivide the business process into smaller units. These folders or worksets can now be assigned to individual iViews. Figure 8.4 shows an example of a fictitious business package for purchasing. The package is not based on the SAP business package for purchasing; instead, it was created specifically for this example.

Limited view

Employees who have access to only one folder or one workset cannot access the entire *purchasing* business package: they have a limited view of the business package. These iViews are the smallest element of the portal. They form a meaningful unit only when they are summarized or combined into folders, worksets, or business packages, unless, of course, they fulfill individual tasks.

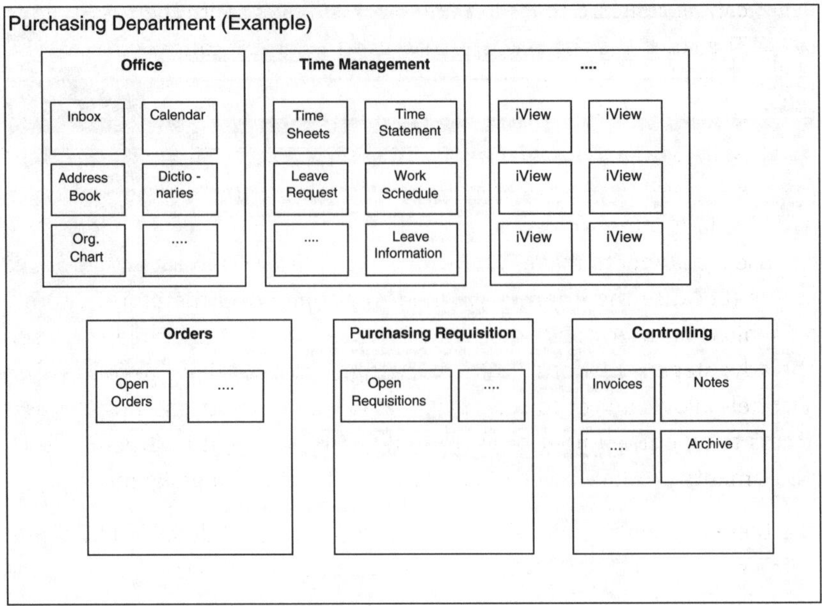

Figure 8.4 Example of a Business Package

Figure 8.5 clarifies the relationship between the terms page, folder, work-set, channel, role, and external service. As you know from Chapter 3, you can integrate Yahoo! categories into the portal. iViews, external services, and Yahoo! categories access different data sources. Yahoo! categories and iViews can be combined on a page, but an external service, which is based on a Java iView, requires a full page for display.

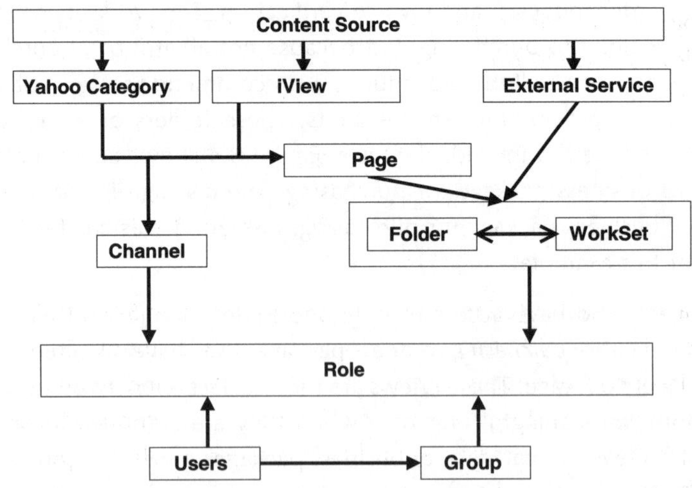

Figure 8.5 Portal Navigation and Role Hierarchy in SAP EP 5.0

Assignment options

Pages can be assigned to folders and worksets, which are then assigned to roles. The roles are then assigned to users or user groups. You can also assign individual iViews or Yahoo! categories to a channel and then assign the channel to a role. It's easy to understand that you have several options to assign iViews, Yahoo! categories, pages, folders, worksets, channels, or external services to users or groups of users with roles. Pages and channels offer various views of different combinations of iViews. You can use a channel to make iViews for which a user does not actually have access (because the iView is assigned to a folder and therefore to a role for which the user does not have authorization) that is visible to a user. The advantage is obvious. The smart assignment of iViews to folders and channels allows a user to see individual iViews without granting the user access to an entire folder or a workset. Similar to a matrix structure, such assignments produce a vertical and horizontal chart of assignments.

The hierarchy within roles enables both top-level and detailed navigation in the portal. Folders and worksets that belong to the highest level of role are called *entry points* of top-level navigation in the portal. Users can navigate in the portal with the entry points. The folders and worksets contain pages and external services (in SAP EP 5.0). Pages are components that can incorporate iViews. External services, such as SAP transactions, require either a full page or a new window to be displayed.

If you compare SAP EP 5.0 with SAP EP 6.0, you'll see that the assignment structure of objects is simpler in SAP EP 6.0, which no longer has external services and channels. One role can contain additional roles, worksets, pages, and iViews. One workset can contain additional worksets, pages, and iViews; a page can contain additional pages and iViews. An iView, however, cannot contain any other object: it represents the smallest unit in the portal.

Figure 8.6 shows an overview of portal navigation in SAP EP 6.0. Note that the folders don't represent the Portal Content Directory (PCD) object. Folders can be generated within a role or a workset to define a hierarchical structure of objects.

A delta link is generated for every object assignment in SAP EP 6.0. Every object in the PCD can be copied to one or more locations. Copying can occur in one of two ways: copy and paste, or copy and paste as a delta link. A simple copy does not restrict or limit the connection to the original object; a copy as a delta link retains the connection. When copying, users must have at least read authorization for the object. But, in any case, an object can only be copied, even as a delta link: it cannot be edited. Only the copy itself can be edited locally.

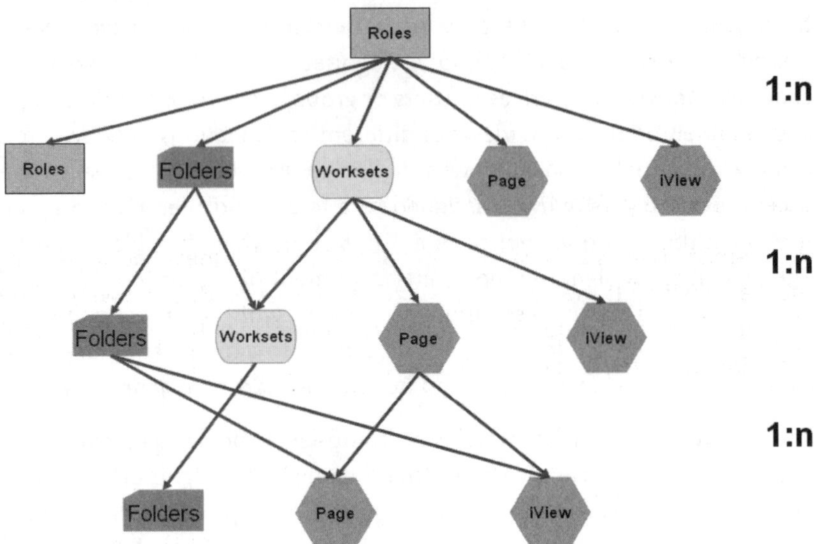

Figure 8.6 Portal Navigation and Role Hierarchy in SAP EP 6.0

Table 8.1 shows an overview of the terms discussed.

Content Component	Function
iView	Represents the smallest portal component for the display of information that might allow user interaction.
Master iView	Represents the standard metadata of the portal components.
Page	Incorporates and displays iViews.
Folder	Incorporates pages and external services.
Workset	Similar to folders, but designed only for grouping and creating hierarchies.
Channel (SAP EP 5.0)	Incorporates iViews and Yahoo! categories; allows partitioned access to business packages (e.g., to individual iViews and not to an entire package).

Table 8.1 Overview of Portal Components with Content

Content Component	Function
Role	Collection of information and services.
External Service (SAP EP 5.0)	Based on master iViews that display SAP transactions, Internet sites, or SAP BW applications. They populate the entire content area (a full page).

Table 8.1 Overview of Portal Components with Content (cont.)

8.2 Ready-Made iViews

Ready-made iViews are available for various uses. Business packages summarize most of these iViews. As shown in Figure 8.7, iViews can be divided into three groups: content for general users of the portal, content for a line manager, and content for a specialist.

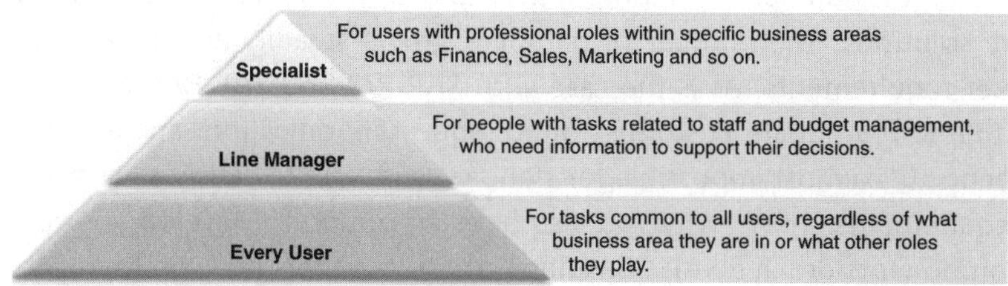

Figure 8.7 Categorization of Business Packages

Packages that all portal users can use, regardless of their role and function within a company, include the *portal user package*. It allows portal users quick and comfortable access to some fundamental services, such as the display of outstanding tasks, sending and receiving email, access to the employee address book, and access to personal or company information. Additional packages offer services to integrate *collaboration tools* that allow you to collaborate with coworkers on documents, drawings, and so on. These packages can integrate Microsoft Outlook as well as document and project management tools. Employee Self-Services (ESS) are also important: they enable users to submit requests for vacations or change their address or bank information. Other business packages are available for a line manager, a specialist, shipping agents, members of the board of directors, executive assistants to the board of directors or managers, managers, the company physician, quality managers, human resources personnel, employees in production planning and assembly, logistics specialists, property managers, marketing personnel, purchasing agents, service personnel, and many others.

Certified content The iViewStudio divides the content and certification into three groups: content from SAP; external, certified content; and external, non-certified content. SAP partners can publish their own content and submit if for certification if they want. The iViewStudio enables users to search by function as well as by all industries—from the automobile industry to energy and telecommunications. Additional areas can also be classified within these industries and then assigned according to the position or role of a user. It enables searching by partner products and a free search by keyword to find the appropriate package. Users can download the free packages from the iViewStudio and add them to the portal with the import function. Cost-bearing packages are invoiced as appropriate. The packages also require a backend with additional functionalities that, of course, can be accessed only when such a system or application component (SAP BW, MM, PP, FI, CO, and so on) is being used.

The largest number of offerings is available for the standard area of industry solutions. The number of packages grows steadily and covers most user requirements. As is the case with SAP R/2 and SAP R/3, and many other SAP products, customers often request modifications and enhancements; it's almost impossible for standard software to satisfy all customer requirements. That's why you also have an option to develop your own components or have SAP Consulting or SAP partners develop them.

8.3 Self-Created iViews

The area of self-created iViews is quite comprehensive. Therefore, the following sections provide only a general overview of how you can create your own iViews. Chapter 9 addresses the development of iViews with the Java programming language.

You can create iViews in various ways. With the *iView Catcher*, you can display excerpts from Web sites in the portal. You can also create *.NET iViews*, or *Java iViews*. The type of iView and the manner of its creation determine how it will run in the portal. We examine these considerations in more detail in the following sections.

8.3.1 iView Catcher

The iView Catcher of SAP Enterprise Portal allows the integration of excerpts from Internet sites. Select **Content Admin · iViews** to arrive at the list of iViews and channels. Here you can select the creation of an iView with the iView Catcher. Select **iView catcher** and **New iView**. You'll arrive at the editor for a new catcher iView. Enter the URL at **Browse** and select **Go** (see Figure 8.8). The iView is displayed. You can use **Capture** to mark areas that you want to integrate into the portal. To do so, select a new frame. Save the frame; after confirmation of the copyright notice, the iView is saved.

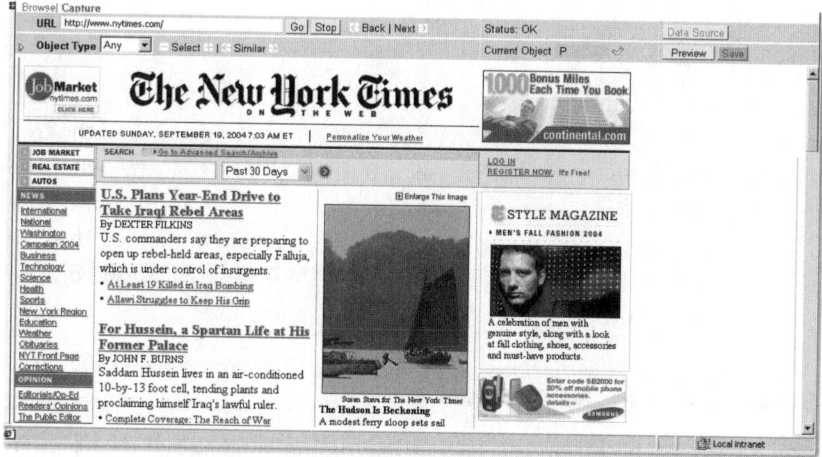

Figure 8.8 Selecting a Frame from an Internet Page in the iView Catcher

Note that the contents of the new iView can change or the frame you selected might not exist after a while because the Web site has changed. Because the iView Catcher stores only the relative links and cannot check the content, there's no guarantee that the contents will remain for very long.

Figure 8.9 illustrates a possible result. The left side of the figure shows information from *The New York Times* (*http://www.nytimes.com*); the right side displays package tracking from the FedEx example at the beginning of this chapter. The iView Catcher created both views and integrated them into the page.

Note

The iView Catcher is not available with SAP EP 6.0.

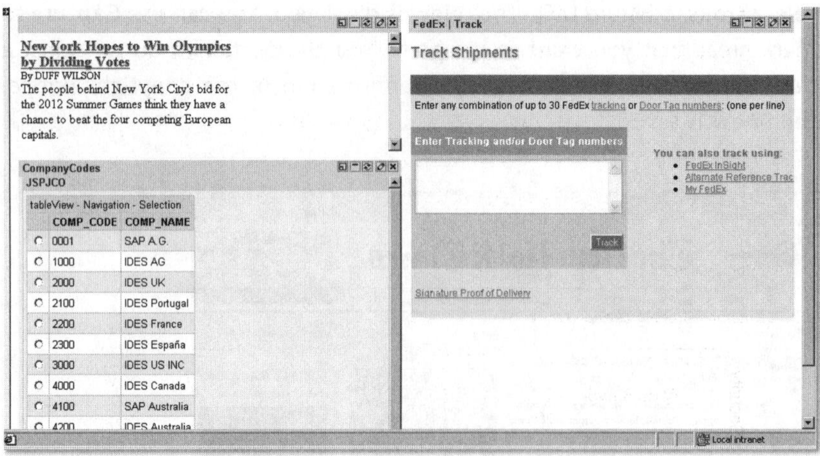

Figure 8.9 Two iViews Integrated with the iView Catcher

8.3.2 Java and .NET iViews

Java iViews are based on the Java programming language; they are interpreted and executed at runtime by the iView runtime for Java. You can create Microsoft .NET iViews directly from SAP EP 5.0. As noted, the functionality of the standard components is often insufficient, which means that you have to create your own iViews. .NET iViews can be based on XML, ASP, or Java-coded applications. To do so, you use the proprietary SAPPortals XML dialect. The .NET iView runtime interprets and executes a .NET iView at runtime.

SAP Enterprise Portal 6.0 supports .NET iViews only when a Windows server is available or when a UNIX installation includes an additional Windows server with Microsoft Internet Information Services (IIS). Only Java iViews are used under UNIX.

To understand better how iViews run and are interpreted, we must reexamine the system landscape and architecture illustrated in Figure 8.10, as addressed in Chapter 2.

Portal architecture

Figure 8.10 provides a technical display of the architecture of SAP Enterprise Portal and its individual components. SAP EP is divided into the following three areas: the portal client, which uses the services of the portal; the company's actual enterprise portal solution; and the information sources. The BI platform is not part of the portal, but can be easily integrated with it. First, the illustration shows that almost all information sources can be integrated into the portal, as long as they support a standard format (XML, HTML, SOAP, and so on) or a general interface. Information sources include documents, SAP applications such as SAP R/2 and SAP R/3, the entire SAP NetWeaver platform, mySAP Business Suite components (SAP SRM, SAP BW, SAP APO, SAP CRM, etc.), third-party products (Siebel, Baan, PeopleSoft, Oracle, databases, etc.), Web services, Yahoo! services, and any chosen content from the Internet.

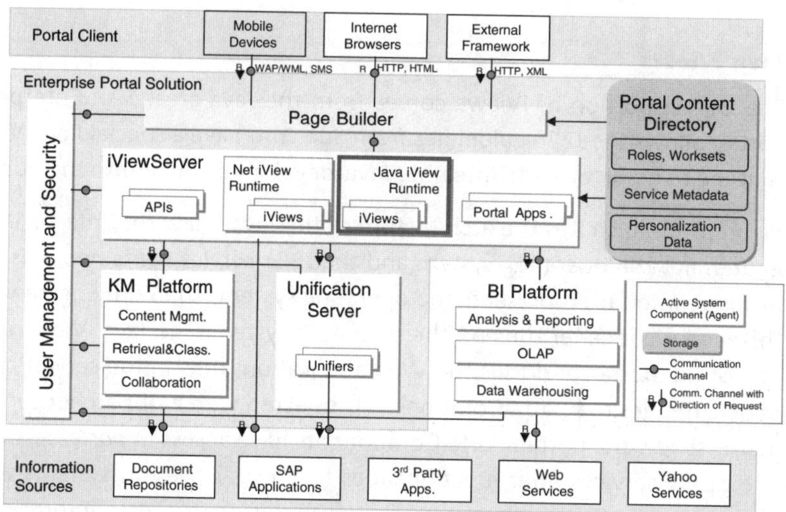

Figure 8.10 Portal Architecture

Portal client

The level of the portal client shows that information from the portal can be displayed in any browser, mobile device, or on an external framework. Communication with the browser occurs exclusively over the HTTP via HTML and XML. Communication with mobile devices occurs over the *wireless application protocol (WAP)* via *wireless markup language (WML)* and *short message service* (SMS).

Now, let's look at the center area (the Enterprise Portal Solution) of the illustration, the outlined "black box" of SAP Enterprise Portal, in more detail. The portal solution consists of several components: the page builder, the portal content directory (database and file system), the KM platform, the unification server, user management and security.

Unification

The unification server enables you to transfer information from one application to another using Drag&Relate. The applications use information objects to exchange information. Whether the SAP or third-party applications operate behind the objects is immaterial. Several unifiers are available: the unification server, which affects unification at the database level;

a unifier for SAP R/3; a unifier for SAP BW; and a unifier for Baan (see also Chapter 7).

The illustration of the portal architecture shows the iView runtime within SAP Enterprise Portal. If you look at the iView server block more closely, you'll see that it contains two other blocks: the .NET iView runtime and the Java iView runtime.

Java iViews

The largest portion of iViews comes from the Java area. SAP Enterprise Portal follows the J2EE guidelines from Sun. You have a special Java iView runtime to use in order to integrate Java-developed iViews into the portal.

Java iView runtime

Figure 8.11 illustrates the architecture of the Java iView runtime, as integrated into the operating system and the J2EE servlet container. This all-inclusive interface represents the operating system. The J2EE Engine with the servlet container runs on the operating system. The Java iView runtime of the portal, and thus the Web application, runs in the servlet container. The desired PortalComponent is selected with a dispatcher servlet addressed by the portal. PortalComponents have access to *portal services*. The portal services offer functionalities to access back-end systems with connectors (SAP Java connector, for example) or to access information from the LDAP directory with user management. Additional functionalities enable the *sharing* or exchanging of information with other Web applications.

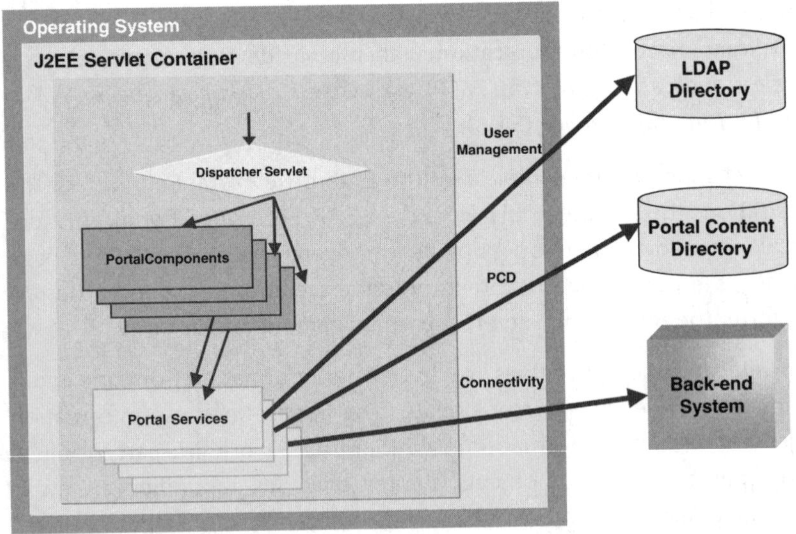

Figure 8.11 Architecture of the Java iView Runtime

The following section looks at the terms *PortalComponents*, *master iViews*, and *portal services*.

PortalComponents and master iViews

In the Java iView runtime, PortalComponents are executable units that implement user dialogs. They consist of the implementation (IPortalComponent, the native Java servlet, or the native Java server page), the profile for configuration and personalization, and resources (images, static HTML pages, scripts, applets, and so on).

When a PortalComponent is uploaded into the portal, a master iView is created in the *portal content directory (PCD)* to represent the standard metadata of the PortalComponent. You can create multiple Java iViews or external services with differing parameterization based on this master iView and then execute them on the iView server.

Initially, development of an iView in the portal requires that you create the Java source text in an editor or with an Integrated Development Environment (IDE). All the required resources and the profile files with the compiled Java source text, the Java class files, are summarized in a file. The compressed file must have *.par* as its suffix. The *par* file is then uploaded into the portal and a master iView is created in the PCD. You can now create Java iView or external services based on this master iView.

The task of a PortalComponent is to offer users the functionality necessary to access information sources of any type, which is why the PortalComponent requires additional functionalities to determine whether a user has authorization to access the information. Middleware is also required in order to create a connection to the data source; and it must be able to format the data it captures in a legible form.

Portal services

Portal services perform exactly these tasks. They offer the Java iView runtime those functionalities that the PortalComponents and other portal services require. Ready-made portal services are available, but you can also create your own. The traditional portal services already built into the portal include:

- User management
- JCo service for connections to SAP R/3
- System landscape service
- HTMLB service

To clearly separate PortalComponents from portal services, the Java iView runtime implements its own class loaders. By default, PortalComponents and portal services have access to only the portal API and its own classes. However, PortalComponents can share classes with other components by declaring a *sharing reference*. Portal services and components can access service APIs by declaring a *service reference*.

The portal development kit (PDK) from SAP, based on the J2EE Engine, provides a good test environment for SAP Enterprise Portal. With the OpenTools available for the Borland JBuilder and Eclipse for the PDK of SAP EP 5.0, you have an adequate development environment for PortalComponents. For the PDK of SAP EP 6.0, the OpenTools are available only for Eclipse.

Sample Java-iView

Listing 8.1 shows a simple example of a Java iView component.

```
package myFirstPortalComponent;
import com.sapportals.portal.prt.component.*;
public class Hello extends AbstractPortalComponent {
   protected void doContent(
      IportalComponentRequest request,
      IPortalComponentResponse response) {
      response.write("Hello World!");
   }
}
```

Listing 8.1 Sample Java iView Component

If you're already familiar with the Java programming language, you'll quickly see that the technique used on portal components is Java servlets. They receive a request from the portal and can "package" a response for the user. If you're not familiar with Java, you'll find a concise introduction to Java in Chapter 9, which includes a general overview of Java technologies and an introduction to Java iView development. For more information, we recommend the sources listed in this book's bibliography.

.NET iViews

SAPPortals XML

The .NET iView runtime is made by TopTier and enables the integration of iViews that are based on .NET technology and that use SAPPortals XML. This dialect (noted above) can be enhanced with Visual Basic script. Doing so makes the .NET iViews somewhat more dynamic and separates the data from the design. For example, the .NET portion of the content is queried from a database but the XML portion handles the display of data in the portal according to the specifications given by the user. The user can utilize SAPPortals XML to determine what information should be displayed in a header line and in the individual fields of a table. Summation lines, navigation buttons, and other details can also be determined. You should recall that .NET iViews cannot be executed under UNIX: they require a separate Windows server with Microsoft IIS.

Listing 8.2 shows a simple use of .NET iViews. If you want to use the sample, save the following lines as an XML file under *\Inetpub\wwwroot\SAP-Portal*.

```
<busdoc>
   SAPPortals XML Example
   <dataset>
      <constructor language="HyperRelational">
         <properties>
            <name>mymatrix</name>
         </properties>
         <return>
         <HRRow id="matrix" position="0" dispRows="5">
            <HRField>
               <aliasName>column1</aliasName>
               <label>EmployeeID</label>
               <type>number</type>
            </HRField>
            <HRField>
               <aliasName>column2</aliasName>
               <label>FirstName</label>
               <type>string</type>
            </HRField>
            <HRField>
               <aliasName>column3</aliasName>
               <label>LastName</label>
               <type>string</type>
            </HRField>
         </HRRow>
         <controlStrip type="SAPPortal" counter="yes"
            firstRec="yes" lastRec="yes" prevRec="yes"
            nextRec="yes" position="right"/>
         </return>
      </constructor>
      <tuple>
         <old>
```

```
          <mymatrix>
             <column1>1</column1>
             <column2>Hans</column2>
             <column3>Mueller</column3>
          </mymatrix>
       </old>
    </tuple>
    <tuple>
       <old>
          <mymatrix>
             <column1>2</column1>
             <—additional entries follow here -->
          </mymatrix>
       </old>
    </tuple>
  </dataset>
</busdoc>
```

Listing 8.2 Example of a .NET iView

After successful integration, this simple .NET application is displayed in the portal as shown in Figure 8.12.

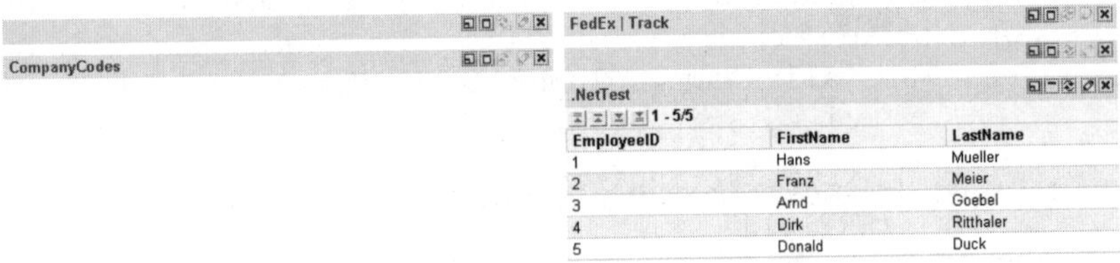

CompanyCodes

FedEx | Track

.NetTest

1 - 5/5

EmployeeID	FirstName	LastName
1	Hans	Mueller
2	Franz	Meier
3	Arnd	Goebel
4	Dirk	Ritthaler
5	Donald	Duck

Figure 8.12 NET iView in the Portal

Note that you can enhance the source test in Visual Basic script to include any instructions you want, such as dynamic queries of an SAP system. Because of their limitations, .NET iViews are rarely used, particularly for SAP applications.

9 Java iView Development

This chapter introduces you to the Java programming language and Java technologies. It also provides valuable information on the development of Java iViews for SAP Enterprise Portal.

The previous chapters provided you with an overview of the architecture of SAP Enterprise Portal, system requirements, and individual components. You know how iViews are integrated into the portal, what roles they play, and that various technologies exist to develop and use iViews. You also have a general understanding of Java iView technology.

The following sections introduce the Java programming language, Java Internet technologies, and the development of your own Java iViews.

9.1 Java, Java Servlets, and Java Server Pages

Java has not only changed the Web; it has fundamentally changed programming for Web applications—in fact, it's revolutionized it. Originally used to make the Web more dynamic, Java has developed into a serious programming language. But, what characterizes Java? With C, C++, Delphi, and many other familiar languages already in existence, why was it necessary to develop another programming language ?

9.1.1 Java Is More Than an Island

Platform independence

Java applications have found extensive use because they can be executed on various platforms. The primary goal of the development of Java was to openly support computer architectures worldwide and to reach as many end users as possible.

In addition to its characteristics of platform-independence and usability for the Web, Java was also designed to meet additional requirements. Support of a graphical user interface, network abilities, and the realization of distributed applications and processes also played a decisive role in the development of this new language.

Object orientation

And, of course, Java had to meet all the other requirements of a modern programming language—it had to be understandable, easy to learn, and enable object-oriented programming.

The existence of Java can be traced back to the following three factors:

1. First, it became clear that all the languages prior to Java could not ensure the simple distribution of the applications created with them. Although some tried to create a model with C++, they soon learned that it could meet the requirements of simplicity and security only with great difficulty.
2. The second factor that contributed to the launching of Java involved a decision to initiate a project named *OAK*. OAK covered a broad spectrum of IT technologies: it developed not only a programming language, but also an operating system and a development environment, including a complete hardware platform (with special chips). Copyright law required use of a different name, however, so Java was chosen as a replacement for OAK.
3. Hence, the technical and naming requirements for a Web-enabled programming language were established and Java more than met these requirements But, Java was ahead of its time. It took almost another two years until the global advance of the Internet created enough of a user base to use the language comprehensively. The exponential growth of the Web therefore represents a third and central factor that contributed to the sudden growth in popularity of the Java programming language.

Development forced by the Web

Before we look at the technologies in the Java environment, particularly for the somewhat complex issue of client/server programming, let's examine some special features of object-oriented programming.

9.1.2 Java as a Representative Object-Oriented Programming Language

Until recently, procedural programming was the leading methodology for programming. As object-oriented programming sought to map an abstract image in a system with objects, procedural programming split complex tasks into several subunits that were then implemented by using so-called *methods*.

Classes and Objects

If you look closely at your environment, you will notice that you're confronted with a large number of *objects*, many of which depend on each other or interact with each other. Examples include buildings, vending machines, cars, and many others.

To comprehend the complexity of the environment, we combine similar objects and think of them abstractly as classes of objects. The same process takes place in object-oriented programming: a program uses the definition of a class to determine the appearance (functionality, characteristics, and so on) that an object (*instance* of the corresponding class) will have when the program runs.

Classes help abstraction

Let's consider the following objects: a transit vending machine, a debit card, and public transportation. The first interaction occurs between the debit card object and the vending machine: a new object, the fare card, results from this interaction. And the fare card then interacts with public transportation.

Compared to procedural programming, the use of classes and objects offers an advantage: it provides a clear description when a program is created. This advantage increases the importance of the term "software architecture." Object-oriented, descriptive languages (all before Unified Modeling Language, UML) guarantee a very clear description of classes and objects, including their interaction. Various types of diagrams exist in this context: class, object, interaction, collaboration, and others.

Inheritance

Common properties

Classes define the properties for objects, or, in other words, the objects of a common class share specific properties. This situation implies that the more detailed or precise the definitions of a class, the fewer the objects that must be assigned to the class because of identical properties. The more abstract a class, the more objects it can include.

In reality, many objects with many properties exist that differ from each other only slightly. Figure 9.1 illustrates such an example.

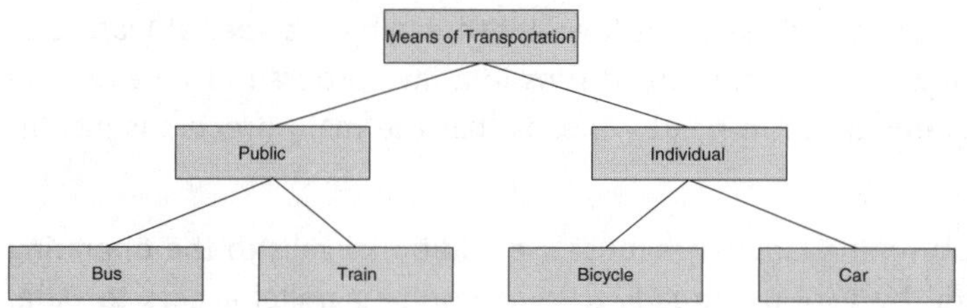

Figure 9.1 Sample Class Hierarchy

Superclasses and Subclasses

As the example makes clear, a general means of transportation, a *superclass*, includes various properties and attributes that the subordinate classes can also use (manufacturer, operational performance, highest speed, and so on). These properties are also made available to the derived classes, the *subclasses*. For example, "public" and "private" are examples of completely abstract classes because they cannot map a specific instance (real properties).

The advantage of this concept is that the developer must implement only the differences between the subclasses and the superclasses. This technique supports the reusability of programming code.

Encapsulation and Information Hiding

Encapsulation also supports this approach. In fact, encapsulation means that the individual elements of an object are hidden from the outside. The goal of this procedure is to make only the required data and methods that are directly relevant to the object visible as an interface.

Reuse

On the one hand, this concept has a clear advantage for the reuse of a class. If programmers want to reuse a class that they haven't created, they don't have to understand all the details of its implementation. On the other hand, the compiler guarantees appropriate support: it prohibits the manipulation of internal data.

Polymorphism

Overwriting methods

Polymorphism is an essential property within inheritance. It refers to overwriting methods that are inherited by a subclass from a superclass and that are overwritten within the subclass. At runtime, the object class is determined. The class is used to search for the hierarchy of the class until a method with the identical signature is found.

Consequently, you can execute various actions with a method.

Synchronization

Multithreading

Direct and user-friendly support for multithreading is a special feature of Java. Typically, only a main thread runs in a Java program. However, the use of programs that run nearby means that the main process is insufficient.

Other programming languages must use additional calls to the operating system made by various threads to synchronize parallel access to data. This condition does not exist in Java. The keyword, `synchronized`, can ensure that other threads don't influence a required access to part of the working memory. On its own, Java tries to request a block for an associated object. If it cannot do so at a particular moment, the system goes into wait status. Note that all threads access the same address space.

9.1.3 Applets, Applications, and a First Small Java Program

The following sections are meant to whet your appetite for working with Java. Important key technologies in the Java environment are examined without delving into gross detail.

Differing program structure

The development of Java programs distinguishes between *applets* and *applications*. But what's the exact difference? Unlike applications, which function independently, an applet involves a special program that is embedded in Web pages. The applet takes over at least part of the control in a Web page and therefore makes the page more dynamic or interactive. Technically, the primary difference between the two types of programs is the fundamental different setup of program structures, although applets also have only limited access to system resources.

Listing 9.1 shows the simplest structure of a Java application:

```
class MyFirstProg
{
  public static void main( String args[] )
  {
  // Program start
  // Instructions
  // Program end
  }
}
```

Listing 9.1 Sample Structure of a Java Application

Main method

Every Java program is an element of a class, described here as `MyFirstProg`. Within Java applications—not in applets—the `main` method plays a critical role because it can be seen as an entry point. In other words, `main` is executed as the first method when a Java application starts.

Modifier

Additional arguments are placed in front of this method. The additional arguments are called *modifiers*. Here, `static` means that the method can be used without an object; `public` is used in the context of encapsulation, which aims at a clear separation between interface and implementation. `public` means that the method is not subject to access limitations and can thus be accessed from every other part of the coding. `void` simply indicates that a method rather than a function is involved, so that no values are returned.

Arrays The sample text for the body of the method (between the curly brackets {}) contains only comments. One item that demands attention is the `String args` expression within the definition of the method. It first defines an array, a specific data type that summarizes several value properties into one component. Access occurs with a whole-number index. The `main` method requires the array because additional parameters might be entered when the program is called: they are called with the array.

As noted, the goal of an applet differs from that of an application. The difference is seen in the basic structure of the program. Unlike the case with applications, the operating system is not responsible for the execution of an applet—the browser in which the applet was started is.

Listing 9.2 shows an applet with a simple structure:

```
import java.awt.*;
import java.net.URL;
public class play_sound extends java.applet.Applet
{
      URL                 addr;
      String              name;
     //Initialization of the applet

      public void init()
      {
           //Data is taken from the applet tag of the
           //underlying HTML file
           addr = newURL (getParameter ("URL"));
           name = getParameter ("File_name");
      }

      public void start()
      {
           play (url, name);
      }

      public void stop()
      {
           //Not used here
      }
}
```

Listing 9.2 Sample Structure of a Java Applet

Some differences from the previous program are directly related to the applet type of program.

The following expression is particularly important:

```
extends java.applet.Applet.
```

Derivation

This expression involves a specific aspect of object-oriented programming. The play_sound class being implemented is derived from the java.applet.Applet class. But what's the point of using a derivation?

One of the central principles of object-oriented programming is the reuse of code. The reuse of standard classes from a class library (as in this case) or from self-created classes in Java is enabled by referencing: derivation from a class with the keyword extends. With this feature, you can reuse the properties (methods, functions, variables, and so on) or superordinate classes.

By definition, all applets are derived from the java.applet.Applet class. Note that the source code does not contain the main entry method. Instead, the code uses init, start, and stop.

When a Java program is called, an object or an instance is first mapped from a class. You can imagine this process as follows: the class defines the "gene" or logical property, and the object represents the "organism" or actual property. Objects are generated or born when a program starts and die when the program ends. Depending on the current "stage" of an object's life, the methods noted above are run for each object or instance.

The individual methods have the following characteristics:

Methods

The init method is called by the browser as soon as the applet starts. Several objects that cooperate with each other are created here, variables are initialized, and graphics and fonts are loaded. It also queries two parameters that are stored in the related HTML page in an applet tag. In a simple case, the applet tag can appear as follows:

```
<APPLET CODE="play_sound.class">
</APPLET>
<PARAM NAME="addr"
       VALUE="http://...">
<PARAM NAME="name"
       VALUE="...">
```

`start` is called right after `init` and runs whenever the page that contains the applet is reread. It behaves differently than the `stop` method, which is called whenever you leave the page that contains the applet.[1]

The example uses the `start` method to call the `play` method, a component of the `java.applet.Applet` class. The URL and filename previously read in the `init` parameter are transferred here. You can use both variables across all methods because the variables are defined outside of the methods.

Class libraries

Now let's look at the `import java.awt.*;` and `import java.net.URL;` statements. They capture classes of other packages, so that the programmer can access comprehensive "class bundles" (`awt` is used to model the graphical user interface) that run during translation of the source text into byte code by the Java compiler. An `import` statement consists of the keyword `import` and the package name.

Table 9.1 contains an overview of important, basic class packages:

Package	Content
java.awt	Classes for graphics, texts, windows, and GUIs
java.beans	Classes for subject components
java.io	Classes for all types of input and output
java.lang	Classes for basic functions in Java
java.math	Classes for mathematical methods
java.net	Classes for network functions
java.util	Classes with usable data types

Table 9.1 Important, Basic Class Packages in Java

9.1.4 Java and Network Programming

As noted, Java is characterized by its problem-free use of networks, particularly the Internet, which implies communication between various computers.

Note the distinction between systems that offer a service and systems that call service-providing systems. Systems that act as service providers

1 In addition to the three methods presented above, two other methods exist: `destroy` and `paint`. `destroy` is called after `stop` and executes before the applet object is deleted. `paint` is executed when a new graphic component signals that it must be redrawn because the content it displays has changed.

and, for example, accept and process requests "from outside," are called *servers*. Systems that call a service are called *clients*. Obviously, you do not have to install only one server on a computer. Depending on the complexity of the services involved, in most cases you can offer services on several servers, each of which offers various services. Port numbers are used to distinguish various servers. Messages are exchanged between client and server systems based on various protocols.

Simplified Network Layer Model

The most familiar protocol, used on the Internet, is *Hypertext Transfer Protocol (HTTP)*. Other important protocols include *File Transfer Protocol (FTP)*, which was developed to exchange files, and the *Simple Mail Transfer Protocol (SMTP)*, used for email.

All these protocols are assigned in the simplified network layer model and are based on its three underlying layers (see Figure 9.2).

Physical layer

The *physical layer* or *bit transfer layer* refers directly to the hardware used to transfer data. In particular, the hardware involves the network layer cards, including the connection cables (or satellites). In this layer, it's important that all the electronic, mechanical, and optical parameters meet the specifications given in standardization norms.

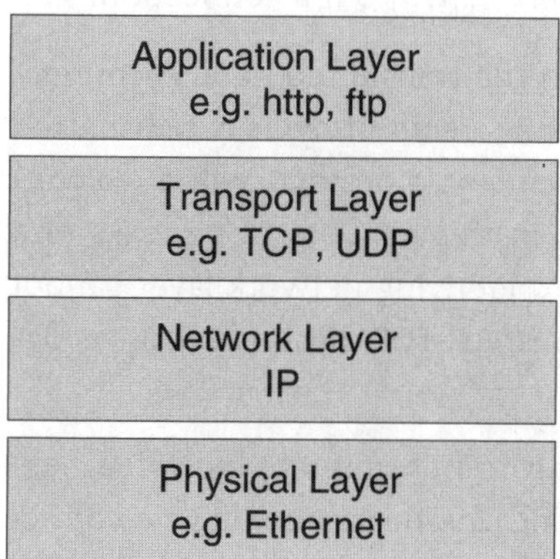

Figure 9.2 Simplified Network Layer Model

Pragmatically, this layer ensures the correct transmission of individual bits—that a zero sent as a zero and that a one sent as a one are received as a zero and a one by the recipient.

Network layer

The *network layer* or *relay layer* accepts packets from subordinate layers and transmits them to the correct network address. This protocol uses numerical addresses that currently have a length of four bytes. If several options exist to transmit the data, the layer determines the most effective way and thus ensures that the data arrives at the correct location. One familiar protocol used in this layer is the *Internet Protocol (IP)*.

Transport layer

Once the data has reached its intended destination, the sequence of packets might be incorrect or one or more packets might have been lost or damaged. That's why the *transport layer* exists. The primary task of this layer is to guarantee that packets contain no errors, that all packets arrive, and that the original sequence is maintained. *Transmission Control Protocol (TCP)* and *User Datagram Protocol (UDP)* are the traditional representatives of this layer. The network layer and the transport layer are often combined, so that many Internet users are familiar with the term TCP/IP.

Application layer

The highest level is the *application layer*, which represents a direct connection between a user and the network. It contains protocols needed for network access, some of which we noted at the start of this section.

A Short Comparison of TCP and UDP

Oriented toward a connection and without a connection

Note the distinction between connection-oriented service and services without a connection. TCP is a connection-oriented service. Before a sender and recipient can communicate with each other, a connection must be set up. It must also be deleted or broken after the communication. This process is not required for a service without a connection.

The difference is particularly apparent in the transferred data. A connection-oriented protocol must ensure that a stream of bytes is transmitted without errors from the sender to the recipient; a protocol without a connection does not provide this security. In this context, one speaks of a reliable transport of data. Because the underlying network layer cannot ensure the correctness of the data it transmits, TCP must use error-recognition and correction mechanisms.

Data packets

TCP breaks down the stream of bytes it is to transmit into individual segments and assigns each of them a header. The header contains a correction code that enables validation of the transmitted data. The individual segments are then redirected to the network layer and then fed to the network. The transport layer of the target host reassembles the segments into a coherent output stream. The client transmits a confirmation for each segment it receives. If a segment is destroyed or contains errors, an error code is transmitted to the server, which must then retransmit the segment in question. TCP also regulates the stream of data so that a slow recipient is not overwhelmed with too many messages.

UDP is the exact opposite of TCP: it's an unreliable protocol without a connection. The recipient does not confirm receipt of data. The primary advantage of UDP is its ability to transmit quickly and with little administrative effort because it does not use header data. UDP is primarily used with simple question/answer protocols and with applications that have their own error-correction mechanisms.

Implementing a TCP Connection with Java

As noted above, Java supports data transmission with TCP and UDP. As an example, the following sections demonstrate the TCP connection first from the perspective of a client and then from the perspective of a server. To avoid confusion, the following coding excerpts involve applications: for the sake of clarity, the `main()` method is not included.

```
//Client program:
import java.net.*;
import java.io.*;
public static void starteClient()
{
  try {
    // Setting up the connection to the server
    //(Server + Port number)
    Socket socket = new Socket
      (InetAddress.getLocalHost().getHostName(), 4000);

    DataInputStream in = new DataInputStream
     (socket.getInputStream());
    DataOutputStream out = new DataOutputStream
     (socket.getOutputStream());
    // ... communicate with the server here

    // End the connection to the server
    socket.close();

  } catch (Exception e) {
    System.out.println("Connection error");
    e.printStackTrace();
  }
}
```

Listing 9.3 Excerpt from a TCP Connection: Client Perspective

Client program The import statements in Listing 9.3 (and those in Listing 9.4) help integrate Java standard packages. The `java.io` package contains input and output classes in addition to interfaces for streams (and files). It is needed within the program for the input and output stream statements. The `java.net` package contains classes and interfaces to execute network operations: for sockets and URLs, for example.

The program has a very simple structure and first contains a `try ... catch` statement that is to catch exceptions while the connection is being set up and while it operates. A `socket` type object is then created: it must include arguments for the name of the server host and the appropriate port number. After the `socket` for the corresponding server exists, the program defines input and output streams that enable bidirectional communication between the client and the server. Once communication has ended, the connection must be closed (`socket.close();`)—the `close` method is used within the `socket` object.

Exceptions If a connection error or an exception occurs, a notification is output. If the connection to the host cannot be established because of resolution difficulties on the part of the domain name server, or if an error occurs during creation of the socket, an "unknown host exception" is output. But when errors related to the input and output streams occur, an IOException is triggered. Additional exceptions can be triggered because of timeouts and so on.

Server program The server program has a similar structure (see Listing 9.4); the `main()` method is omitted here as well.

```
//Server program:
import java.net.Socket;
import java.net.ServerSocket;
import java.io.*;
public static void starteServer()
{
  try {
    // Open port 4000 for communications with clients
    ServerSocket server = new ServerSocket (4000);

    while (true) {
      // Wait when a client issues a request and
      // connect
      Socket client = server.accept();
```

```
        DataInputStream in = new DataInputStream
          (client.getInputStream());
        DataOutputStream out = new DataOutputStream
          (client.getOutputStream());
        // ... Read requests from "in" and write answers
        // in "out"

        // Close connection to client
        client.close();
      }
    } catch (Exception e) {
      System.out.println ("Error in server");
      e.printStackTrace();
    }

    // End server service
    server.close();
  }
```

Listing 9.4 Excerpt from a TCP Connection: Server Perspective

For the most part, the server application corresponds to the client application, except for the following difference. Both additional packages must first be imported so that the "server socket" can be used.

During creation of the server socket object, only the port number is transferred. If a zero is entered here, a random number is generated. The random number is requested with `getLocalPort()` and can be sent to the client. The `accept()` method waits until a client wishes to establish a connection to the server. When that occurs, a socket object is made available: it can be set up much like the output and input stream in the client application.

Here too, the `client.close()` method is used to close the connection to the client. If you don't want the server to connect to any more clients, you can use the `server.close();` method.

This scenario has an amazing ability to set up a complex and reliable connection with just a few lines of code. If you tried to program a secure connection on your own, instead of using the classes given here, you'd have to produce several pages of code.

9.1.5 Java Servlets and Java Server Pages

We will now look at components that play an important role in the integration of information in the portal. The logic of the components is based on iViews that can be directly integrated into SAP Enterprise Portal.

Java Servlets

Definition and functionality

A servlet is an Internet component managed by a "container." It generates the dynamic content for a requesting client. You can create servlets with the *Java servlet development kit (JSDK)* or the *Java servlet API*.

Stated more pragmatically, a servlet is a class made available as a standard package: `javax.servlet(.*)`. Servlets run on a server; they are called by interaction with a client (such as a Web browser) with a request–response model. The request–response model is made available by a servlet container and is based on HTTP.

Servlets help answer requests from a client and integrate with a client. To do so, activities must occur on the server side, activities such as processing, verifying, and evaluating HTML forms or comprehensive, distributed Web applications.

Request–response model

The request–response model, which serves as the basis for communication between server and client when servlets are used, is borrowed from HTTP. According to the model, a client sends a request message to the server, which reacts with a reply message. The `GET` and `POST` methods, typical of HTTP, are available on the client side to implement the corresponding request message. On the server side, a Web server (such as Apache), on which an add-on (the servlet engine in the case of Apache JServ) is installed, accepts the request. The servlet engine takes over processing and generates a specific response to the client's request.

The data required to generate the reply message was delivered along with the client's request. The data contains the client's IP address, specific session data, user authentication, and so on. In addition to providing *directives* (see below), the servlet engine also offers options to execute Java servlets to set up pages with dynamic content.

Context

Java servlets can be classified as those that primarily focus on flow logic or fixed program structures and those that are primarily used to generate content, forms, and interaction in general. All servlets require a context for execution: the servlet engine provides the context. The context is the interface between the servlet server and the *servlet container*. A servlet container offers all the interfaces required to execute one or more servlets.

Servlets and the containers (including their context) needed to execute servlets offer additional service functions. The functions include features for secure data transmission, URL rewriting (linking a URL with session-dependent data, such as form data), *session tracking*, managing pools (for the reuse of database connections between queries), and so on.

Session tracking enables efficient use and scalability of system resources, especially when compared with query-oriented technologies, such as the *common gateway interface* (CGI). Because the coding of the servlet is already present in byte code, it performs much better than script-oriented languages.

Example

The sample servlet in Listing 9.5 refers to the source text from Listing 9.4, which demonstrated a TCP connection between server and client. The server component is now covered by the use of a servlet.

```
import javax.servlet.*;
import javax.servlet.http.*;
import java.io.*;
public class Servlet extends HttpServlet
{

  // Called by the server after the servlet
  // has been loaded in response to a request.

    public void init (ServletConfig config)
    throws ServletException
  {
    super.init (config);

    try {
      // Initialization work
    } catch (Exception e) {
      System.out.println ("Error in Servlet.init()");
      throw new ServletException();
    }
  }

   public void destroy()
  {
```

```
    // Cleanup
  }

  // doGet is called when a request
  // uses the "GET" method

  public void doGet (HttpServletRequest req,
    HttpServletResponse res)
    throws IOException, ServletException
  {
    doPost (req, res);  // simply redirect to
    // doPost
  }

  // doPost is called when a request
  // uses the "POST" method

  public void doPost(HttpServletRequest req,
   HttpServletResponse res)
    throws IOException, ServletException
  {
    try {
      res.setContentType ("text/html");
      PrintWriter writer = res.getWriter();

      // Reading the form fields ...
      String value = req.getParameter ("field name");

      // ...and writing the HTML page in "writer"

    } catch (Exception ex) {
      System.out.println ("Error in doPost");
      ex.printStackTrace();
    }
  }

} // class Servlet
```

Listing 9.5 Sample Java Servlet

Servlet classes are contained in the `javax.servlet` and `javax.servlet.http` packages. They are unavailable in the standard JDK and must be installed if necessary. Both applets and servlets are Internet components: Applets are run in the client browser and servlets are started by a Web server. However, in terms of the standard methods that both make available, they have a great deal in common. The following three methods exist for servlets:

- The `init()` method runs when the servlet is to be started based on the first request. As is also the case with applets, this method can be overwritten when additional initializations are needed.
- The `service()` method runs when the servlet is called yet again: a separate thread controls each additional call.
- `destroy()` is executed when the servlet is to be removed.

Generally, a servlet is implemented as a subclass of the abstract `HttpServlet` class. By default, the service method is set up so that it implicitly checks whether a client-side request is performed with `doGet` or `doPost`, which explains why the service method doesn't necessarily have to be overwritten. In Listing 9.5, the `doGet` method branches directly to `doPost`.

The first parameter, `req`, enables direct access to the incoming request; `res` contains the consequential result.

Then, a MIME type is set on the `res` object—HTML format is selected because an HTML page is to be returned. In addition, another output stream is defined and a field read from `req`, which can then be evaluated to determine the result. Even when other properties are involved with this type of exception, the basic exception-handling that occurs is similar to the examples given above.

Servlets and script languages

The presentation given above shows that the use of servlets offers decisive advantages over the use of script language and that servlets can be implemented without any problems. However, servlets also have a significant disadvantage regarding the display of the results. They don't adequately consider a syntactic and semantic separation of code and content, therefore, we recommend that you become familiar with Java server pages (JSPs).

Java Server Pages (JSPs)

Java server pages (JSPs) and their supplemental taglibs represent an enhancement of servlets and the servlet API. The separation of code and presentation makes it easier to deal with various data sources, especially when dynamic content is involved.

In particular, servlets use several sequential `println()` statements to return results. Naturally, such a procedure is prone to errors. It is also very difficult to separate information and visualization: just think of the maintenance required for the coding. For example, even if the presentation of the data alone varies but the program's flow logic remains the same, comprehensive changes to the servlet coding are a necessary evil. Also, typically, the roles of content programmer and designer aren't merged into one position.

Instead of outputting specific Java code to an HTML page (as is the case with servlets), JSPs involve HTML pages enriched with some Java code (see Listing 9.6).

```
<html>
<head></head>
<body>
This is completely normal text in HTML format.
// A JSP expression has the following form:
<%= new java.util.Date() %>.
</body>
</html>
```

Listing 9.6 Example of a Java Server Page

JSPs therefore enable the simple adjustment of content and presentation.

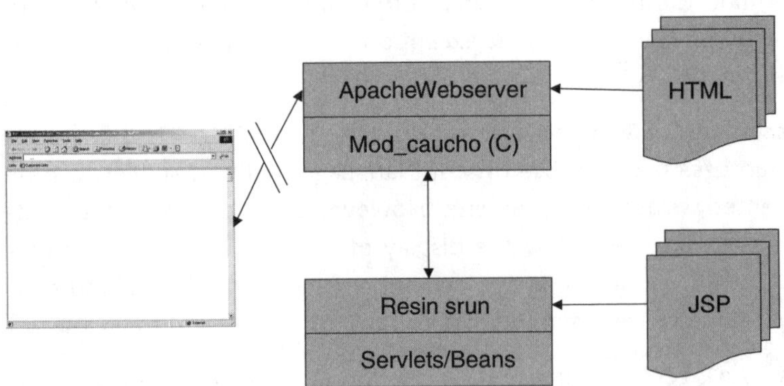

Figure 9.3 Processing of Java Server Pages

In technical terms, the use of a JSP engine transforms JSP pages into servlets and returns the resulting page as HTML.

Figure 9.3 illustrates the different handling of a purely static HTML page and a JSP. Pure HTML files are redirected directly to the client, but JSPs first use Resin[2] to call a JSP servlet engine. Resin then translates the JSP pages into a servlet and delivers the response.

When a servlet is called, a series of predefined variables is generated. The following table summarizes the variables:

Variable	Function
request	Enables access to the request parameter, the request type, and the request header.
response	Returns data to the client.
out	The PrintWriter sends data to the client. You can change the size of the buffer using the `page` directive (`buffer` attribute).
session	Helps define a connection uniquely: HTTP is stateless. This variable is always generated, except if you use the `page` directive (`session` attribute) and turn it around. The variable requests information on the current session, particularly information about the user.
application	The variable for the `ServletContext` object: it contains persistent data and can be accessed by all servlets.
config	This variable contains the `ServletConfig` object for the page.
pageContext	The variable for the `PageContext` object: Java beans should be stored in this object to ensure access with the `getAttribute` method at any time during the request.
page	The `page` object is a reference to the servlet object that processes the request. The server software determines the class to which it belongs.

Table 9.2 Predefined Variables When Calling a Servlet

When setting up JSPs, various script elements are distinguished for statements, scriptlets, and declarations. However, all of them start with a <% tag and end with a %> tag.

Declaration

A declaration can appear as follows:

```
<%! double db; %>
```

The example given in Listing 9.6 contains a statement. The appearance of scriptlets is similar to that of statements, but with an equal (=) sign; they record pure Java coding.

2 Like Tomcat, Resin is a JSP servlet engine. It is manufactured by Caucho Technology, Inc. For more information, visit *http://www.caucho.com*.

Directives You can also use *directives* (see Table 9.3) to provide the related container with context parameters that indicate how a JSP page is to be processed.

Directive	Use
page	The page directive controls imports of individual classes.
include	The include directive enables the insertion of files into the servlet when they are translated. It is placed where the file is to be inserted.
taglib	The taglib directive can be used to define your own markup tags.

Table 9.3 JSP Directives

Table 9.4 provides an overview of the language elements used with JSPs:

Language Element	Meaning
<!–SGML comment (HTML, XML) -->	The comment remains in the HTML output file that is generated.
<!-- SGML comment: <%=statement%> -->	The statement is evaluated before being included in the HTML comment.
<%-- JSP comment --%>	The HTML file that is generated no longer contains the comment.

<%!
// Definition
final String s = "Test";
 	
public String getTest()
{
return s;
}
%>
	Declares attributes, constants, and methods.

<%= statement %>	Placeholder for a statement.
<% // Scriptlet (Java code) %>	A code fragment of the script language in use (in the case of JSP Java). Example: <% out.println(new java.util.Date(). toString()); %>

Table 9.4 Language Elements with the Use of JSPs

<table>
<tr><th>Language Element</th><th>Meaning</th></tr>
<tr><td><%@ include
file="URI|Pfad"
%></td><td>Includes a file with text, HTML source text, or script source text at the point of translation (compiling).</td></tr>
<tr><td><%@ taglib
uri="DTD"
%></td><td>Defines a tag library.</td></tr>
<tr><td><%@ page
language="java"
extends="Parent class"
%></td><td>Defines attributes valid throughout the document.</td></tr>
<tr><td><jsp:useBean
id="Instance name of the Java bean"
scope="page"
[...]
beanName="Name of the bean"
>
JSP or HTML code
</jsp:useBean></td><td>Links a Java bean to the context or generates a new instance if the bean has not yet been linked.</td></tr>
</table>

Table 9.4 Language Elements with the Use of JSPs (cont.)

If you combine the concept of servlets and JSPs (including the taglibs) with Enterprise Java beans (discussed briefly below), you have a comprehensive tool for the creation of substantial, distributed Web applications.

Java Beans

The idea behind Java beans is to make reusable Java code available, which simplifies the implementation of familiar programming guidelines. The support of standard interfaces enables directional access.

Information hiding, which is a method that good programmers use to make their code more reusable, is also used consistently here, so that you don't need to know how the internal processing and programming of Java beans works.

You simply access the available `set()` and `get()`methods, or link the aforementioned JSP directives to link the Java beans to a JSP. This approach also supports transparent access to services or a database.

Characteristics All Java beans have the following characteristics:

- Every Java bean has an empty constructor.
- No variables are declared as `public` in bean classes.
- The `set` and `get` methods must be used to access persistent variables.

9.2 Servlets and PortalComponents—Introductory Example

The previous section introduced Java Internet technologies, so that you are now familiar with the basics of Java servlets. This section concentrates on the development of self-created Java iViews.

As you have seen, portal components borrow from the Sun concept of Java servlets. Some terms might be different or other methods might be used, but you can see the portal client receives a request, as is also the case with Java servlets, and that it can respond to the request. You can use the request to evaluate the transferred parameters; the response sends the requested information back to the portal client.

Library portal: example A small example should help explain things here. Imagine a university library (UL) that offers students and professors an opportunity to query the availability of books over the Internet. The request runs on the UL portal. That's where the user is given a form (in HTML, for example) to enter the search criteria for the desired books. The user then clicks a button and starts the search request. The name of the text field into which the user entered the search terms is TITLE. Behind the search button in the HTML source text, an action must be defined that executes as soon as the button is clicked. This action directs the request to our portal component. The portal component receives the parameters of the request that contain the search terms, such as the TITLE field. The portal component can then use the TITLE request parameter to evaluate the search term for the title. A connection to a database or an SAP R/3 system is then set up. The search parameters are transferred into a new request that is then sent to the database. The database waits for the response from the information source. The information source transmits the requested data to the portal component. The information is then redirected to the response object of the portal component, and then to the browser (the client), which is the frontend of the UL portal. Instead of sending blank text to the browser, the output can be formatted graphically. The user then sees the results of the request and can, if desired, create another, more detailed request.

Figure 9.4 illustrates how the initial screen of this simple request might appear on the UL portal.

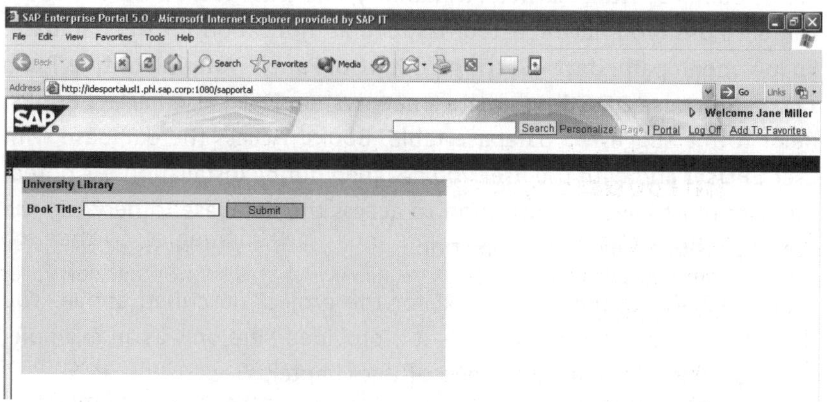

Figure 9.4 Search Screen for the UL Portal

Output

After the title of the book and the request have been transmitted with the **Submit** button, the screen should display the title it has found along with the book's ID and author. If only part of the title was entered ("Shake" rather than "Shakespeare," for example), wildcards should be used to find a meaningful title. If the user leaves the TITLE field blank, the screen should display all the titles in the database. Since our sample database contains only two entries, this is a reasonable response. Of course, you can have an empty field return a message by prompting a user for an entry.

Entry of "portal" in the screen results in output similar to that shown in Figure 9.5.

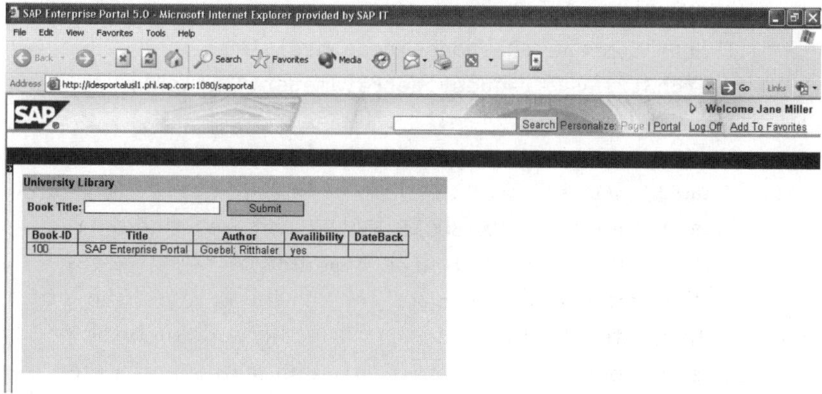

Figure 9.5 Result of a Search Request for the UL Portal

Preparation of the database

To use this example, create a new database named Books on the MS SQL database and a new table named Books. The table should include five fields: **Book ID**, **Title**, **Author**, **Availability**, and **DateBack**. Ensure that the database user you have created has read authorization for the database. Follow menu path **Start · Settings · Control Panel · Administrative Tools · Data Sources (ODBC)** to create a new system DSN, also named **Books**. Refer to the suggested database table, Books. Access the database with user **EPUser** and with the user you assigned during installation. As noted, the user must have authorization to access the database; otherwise, the database is unavailable for selection.

Listing 9.7 shows the source text for the project described above. You don't have to use it immediately—it is provided here only as an example. You'll be able to use it by the end of this chapter.

```
package UniLibrary;
import java.io.*;
import java.sql.*;
import java.util.*;
import com.sapportals.portal.prt.component.*;
public class request extends AbstractPortalComponent {
   String url, sqlQuery, searchString;
   ResultSetMetaData metadata;
   Statement stmt;
   ResultSet rSet;
   int numcols, numrows, flag;
   Connection conn;
   String output;
   public void doContent(
      IPortalComponentRequest request,
      IPortalComponentResponse response) {
      searchString = request.getParameter("Title");
      flag = 0;
      if (searchString != null) {
         sqlQuery =
           "SELECT * FROM BOOKS WHERE
                upper(TITLE) LIKE upper('%"
                + searchString
                +"%')";
         try {
            Class.forName("sun.jdbc.odbc.JdbcOdbcDriver");
         }
```

```
catch (Exception exp) {
   response.write(
     "Error at bridge: " + exp);
}
try {
   url ="jdbc:odbc:Books";
   conn = DriverManager
     .getConnection(url,
     "epuser","<password>");
   stmt = conn.createStatement(
      ResultSet.TYPE_SCROLL_INSENSITIVE,
      ResultSet.CONCUR_READ_ONLY);
   rSet = stmt.executeQuery(sqlQuery);
   metadata = rSet.getMetaData();
   numcols = metadata.getColumnCount();
   getForm();
   while (rSet.next()) {
      if (flag == 0) {
         output += "<table border = 1
            class = \"gSAPTable\">";
         output += "<tr class=\"gSAPTr\">";
         output += "<th class=\"gSAPTh\">
            Book ID</th>";
         output += "<th class=\"gSAPTh\">
            Title </th>";
         output += "<th class=\"gSAPTh\">
            Author</th>";
         output += "<th class=\"gSAPTh\">
            Available</th>";
         output += "<th class=\"gSAPTh\">
            DateBack</th>";
         flag = 1;
      }
      output += "<tr class=\"gSAPTr\">";
      output += "<td class=\"gSAPTd\">"
         + leerCheck(rSet.getString(1))
         + "</td>";
      output += "<td class=\"gSAPTd\">"
         + leerCheck(rSet.getString(2))
         + "</td>";
```

```
            output += "<td class=\"gSAPTd\">"
               + leerCheck(rSet.getString(3))
               + "</td>";
            output += "<td class=\"gSAPTd\">"
               + leerCheck(rSet.getString(4))
               + "</td>";
            output += "<td class=\"gSAPTd\">"
               + leerCheck(rSet.getString(5))
               + "</td>";
            output += "</tr>";
         }
         if (flag == 0) {
            output += "</table><B class=\"gSAPB\">
               No data record found for this title.</B>";
            output += "</body></html>";
         }
         else
            output += "</table></body></html>";
         stmt.close();
         response.write(output);
         conn.close();
         flag = 0;
      } catch (Exception exp) {
         getForm();
         response.write(output);
         response.write("</body>");
         response.write("</html>");
         response.write("<B class=\"gSAPB\">
            No data record found for this
            title. </B>" + exp);
      }
   } else {
      getForm();
      response.write(output);
      response.write("</body>");
      response.write("</html>");
   }
}
```

```
    public String leerCheck(String text) {
        if (text == null)
            text = "";
        return text;
    }
    public String getForm() {
        output = "<html><head></head><body
            class=\"gSAPBody\">";
        output += "<form action=\
          "/irj/servlet/prt/portal/prtroot/
            UniLibrary.default\"method=POST>";
        output += "<br><B class =\"gSAPB\">
            BookTitle: </B>";
        output += "<input type=text value =\""
            + ((searchString == null) ? "": searchString)
            + "\"name=Title class=\"gSAPInputText\">";
        output += "<input type=submit value=\
          "Send\"class=\"gSAPInputButton\">";
        output += "</form>";
        return output;
    }
}
```

Listing 9.7 Source Text for the UL Search Portal

Comments on the source text

As you can see, Listing 9.7 consists of some enhanced Java language elements and uses a database access. Although the example is relatively simple, it does involve several lines of source text. It also uses portal-specific style statements to adjust the portal components to the design of the portal.

The example uses only a single program for input, evaluation, and display. The following sections describe the flow of the program. When the portal component is activated, it first checks its state: `if (searchString != null)`. If the content of the search field is initial, which can be assumed when the program starts, the search screen is displayed (`else` branch). If an entry is made, the database is queried for the title, even if only a fragment of the title has been entered. If matches are found, they are displayed. If no matches exist, an appropriate message is displayed. If no entry is made, all records in the database are displayed. If you wish to avoid this response, replace `if (searchString != null)` with `if (searchString != null && !searchString.equals(""))`. The user is also notified if an error occurs while searching the database. Figure 9.6 illustrates the flow step by step.

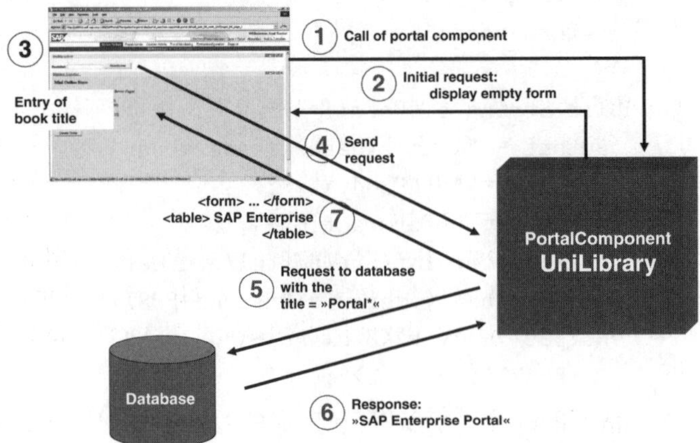

Figure 9.6 Flow When Calling the Portal Component

Technical requirements

After this introductory, but admittedly somewhat complex example, you can now learn, on your own, how to develop a portal component from the ground up. The basic tools you'll need are a ZIP tool (such as WinZip), an editor (if possible one that has syntax highlighting for Java—such as Text Pad), and a working portal. If you don't yet have a portal, you can download *SAP Portal Development Kit (SAP PDK)* from SAP for testing and development. Go to *http://www.iviewstudio.com*, where you can also find installation instructions. If you have not yet installed SAP PDK, the next section will show you how to install it on your computer. If you already have access to a portal or are fortunate enough to have SAP PDK installed on your computer, you can skip the next section.

9.2.1 SAP Portal Development Kit

When this book was published, Release 6.0 of SAP Portal Development Kit was available for SAP EP 5.0 SP 6 and as a business package for SAP EP 6.0 in the content catalog of the iViewStudio. It contains documentation, examples, and tools for the development of Java iViews. SAP PDK supports you with all the information and tools you'll need to develop portal components. It is available free of charge to registered users, and registration is also free. You will receive a user name and password via email after successful registration. No SAP license is required for SAP PDK for SAP EP 5.0. However, SAP PDK for SAP EP 6.0 is available only to those customers with a license for SAP EP 6.0.

This section describes the installation of SAP PDK and iView development for both SAP EP 5.0 and SAP EP 6.0 with the use of Eclipse. This approach ensures that users with a license for SAP EP 6.0 can also develop. It's entirely up to you if you want to use SAP NetWeaver Developer Studio (NWDS) (including Eclipse and SAP plug-ins) or only Eclipse (with SAP plug-ins) to develop portal components. SAP NWDS has an advantage: not only can you develop portal-specific components, but Web Dynpro applications as well. In any event, a complete SAP development environment assumes that sufficient computer resources exist. Sole use of Eclipse with SAP plug-ins makes available an alternative, "thin" development environment, but only for Java-based portal applications. Section 12.4.3 examines Web Dynpro development with SAP NetWeaver Developer Studio.

After installing SAP PDK, you have the complete documentation, all required libraries (*.jar* files), containers for testing and error detection, a workset for portal developers (business package for developers in SAP EP 6.0), plug-ins and wizards for IBM's Eclipse and Borland's JBuilder (only with SAP PDK for SAP EP 5.0). The only prerequisite that you must have is knowledge of Java programming, particularly experience with servlets and Java beans. In the first part of this chapter, we already touched on the importance of this knowledge. Whether you're a beginner or an experienced Java developer, it would probably serve you well to have one or more Java manuals on hand as a reference.

9.2.2 Installation of SAP PDK 5.0

Register at the iViewStudio and download SAP PDK. Download the Tomcat 3.3 application server (*jakarta-tomcat-3.3.1.zip*) from the Apache Web site. Extract the ZIP file and change the name of the *jakarta-tomcat-3.3.1* directory to *tomcat*. Follow menu path **Start · Settings · Control Panel · System · Environment Variables** to set the TOMCAT_HOME environment variable on your Tomcat directory (*c:\tomcat*) and extract the *pdk_tomcat.zip* file to this directory. You must then change the proxy settings in the *tomcat.bat* file in the *tomcat\bin* directory. In lines 48 and 49 of the file, enter the proxy settings in your Internet browser under `_PROXY_HOST`, `_PROXY_PORT`, and `_NONPROXY_HOSTS`. Start Tomcat with `\tomcat\binartup.bat`. The portal components and services are extracted and installed. You can follow the progress in the DOS console, where you will see the following error message:

```
Jul 31, 2004 7:54:21 PM # IRJ Init thread       Fatal
LOCK_CLIENT - OK: Lock client connected.
Server: xxx client: xxx port: 3299 pid: 1 #
```

But that's not really an error message, it's a sign of success. When the message appears, the installation worked. Now start your Internet browser with the following URL: *http://localhost:8080/irj/servlet/prt/portal*. You'll receive a warning informing you that you don't have a valid license. Confirm the message by clicking **OK** and continue. You can operate SAP PDK with two users—even without a license. If you have more than two users, you need a license key. You don't need an LDAP server or database to operate SAP PDK. The file system simulates both.

The decision on using SAP PDK for development is completely up to you. You can also develop portal components with Borland's JBuilder, IBM's Eclipse, or an editor and ZIP tool of your choice. Using an IDE is the easiest way to proceed.

Plug-In for JBuilder (only with SAP PDK for SAP EP 5.0)

JBuilder from Borland is an IDE for the development of Java programs. It contains syntax highlighting for Java keywords, supports you during the creation of development projects, enables user-friendly debugging of applications, and provides a test environment for all sorts of programs. The biggest plus with JBuilder is its ability to be expanded with *OpenTools* from third-party vendors.

To enable you to get to an operable portal quickly and without wasting time entering commands, SAP has developed a plug-in for JBuilder for SAP PDK (only for SAP PDK for SAP EP 5.0). The plug-in integrates a PDK wizard into JBuilder. You can use the wizard without having to be concerned with details. You can start directly with development and create portal components. The ready-made body of the program source text is already inserted, the directory structure for the portal components is created automatically, and the *property files* are previously created for you. You only have to enhance the corresponding source text as required. With a simple click, the portal component is compiled, automatically copied to SAP PDK, and activated in SAP PDK. If you want, the portal component is started in your standard browser immediately.

Installation

To install the plug-in, close JBuilder if you've already started it. In SAP PDK, change to **Downloads · IDE Plug-In** and load the *SAPPortalParWizards.jar* file into the *lib/ext* directory of JBuilder. This file contains the PDK wizard. Then, copy the *ParWizardDoc.jar* file into the *doc* directory of JBuilder. It contains a documentation file for the PDK wizard. Start JBuilder and follow the directions in SAP PDK to create portal components.

Plug-In for Eclipse

Eclipse is an open source IDE for Java programming; it was developed by IBM and is available free of charge. You can download Eclipse at *http://www.eclipse.org*. SAP PDK and the plug-in currently support versions 2.0 and 2.1. Like JBuilder, Eclipse offers syntax highlighting for Java keywords, help with project management, and debugging. Third-parties can also enhance Eclipse. To enable rapid and easy development of portal components, SAP has also developed a plug-in for Eclipse; it supports you throughout development—right up to activating your components in SAP PDK.

To install the plug-in, download the *SAPPDKEclipsePlugins.zip* file from SAP PDK and extract it into the Eclipse *plugins* directory. The file contains the SAP PDK plug-in. Start Eclipse and follow the directions in SAP PDK to create portal components. **Installation**

9.2.3 Installation of SAP PDK 6.0

Register in iViewStudio and download SAP PDK. Note that you need a complete installation of SAP EP 6.0 and an SAP license to use SAP PDK 6.0. A plug-in for Eclipse is delivered with SAP PDK 6.0. Copy the *com.sap.portal.pdk.PortalDevelopmentKit.epa* file into the *usr/sap/<Servername>/global/config/pcd/Import* directory. Follow menu path **System Administration · Transport · Import**, select the PDK business package, and import it (see Figure 9.7).

Follow menu path **User Administration · Role Assignment** to add the Java developer role to a user (com.sap.portal.pdk.JavaDeveloper; see Figure 9.8).

You can now find a new tab, **Java Developer**, in the uppermost navigation bar. Install Eclipse. Eclipse may not be running during installation of the plug-in. Extract the PDK plug-in for Eclipse into the *<Eclipse_directory>/plugins* directory and start Eclipse. SAP PDK for SAP EP 6.0 is now installed.

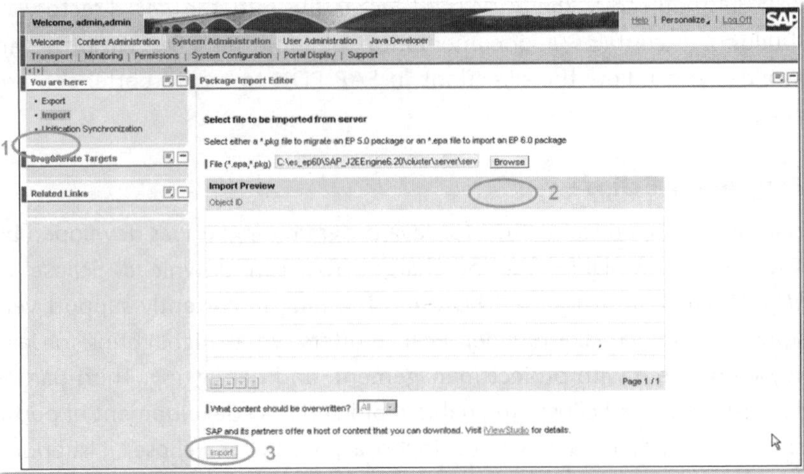

Figure 9.7 Importing SAP PDK Business Packages

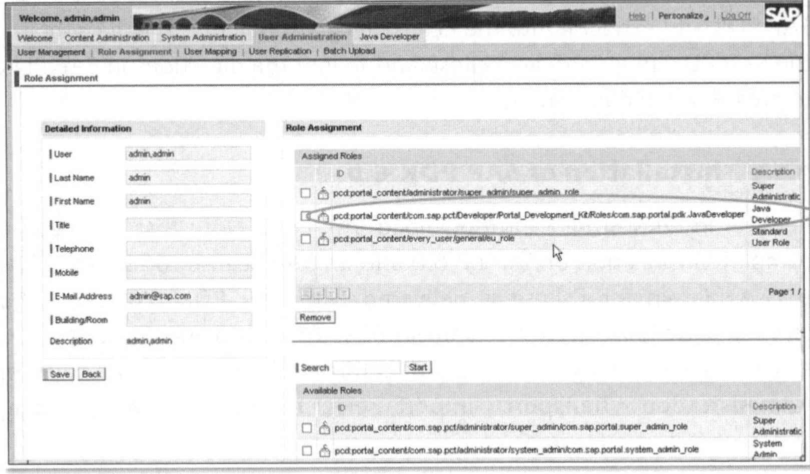

Figure 9.8 Role Assignment: Development Authorization

9.2.4 Editor and File System

If you prefer not to use either of the IDEs, you can use an editor, ZIP program, and the DOS console.

File structure

To develop a project, please set up the file structure shown in Table 9.5 in your project directory. This manual procedure is more involved than the PDK plug-ins, but it does show you the purpose of each directory, even if you use the plug-ins.

File Structure	Explanation	Release
private	Private resources: stored in the *WEB-INF* directory	
|___META-INF		6.0 only
|___MANIFEST.MF	Manifest file that contains versioning and origin	6.0 only
|___PORTAL-INF		6.0 only
|___portalapp.xml	Deployment descriptor (DD)	6.0 only
|___classes	Java classes (only API in 6.0): contains classes that can be shared with other portal applications	5.0 and 6.0
|___lib	**.jar* files (only API in 6.0): contains libraries that can be shared with other portal applications	5.0 and 6.0
|___pagelet	*.jsp files	5.0 and 6.0
|___profiles	Profile files (**.properties*).	5.0 only
|___src	Can be used for source texts (**.java*).	5.0 and 6.0
|___private/lib	Only CORE *jar* files: Only this application can use these libraries.	6.0 only
|___private/classes	Only CORE *class* files: Only this application can use these classes.	6.0 only
public	Public resources: accessible from the client	5.0 and 6.0
|___css	Styles	5.0 and 6.0
|___images	Image files	5.0 and 6.0
|___js (or scripts)	JavaScript	5.0 and 6.0
|___pages	Pages (HTML)	5.0 and 6.0

Table 9.5 File Structure of the Project Directory

You now have two directories, *private* and *public*, under your project directory. The *private* directory contains libraries (*.jar* files), classes, profile files, and, if you want, the source text. The directory and the files should be protected, so they are stored in a separate section. The *public* directory contains the mime formats that must be accessible in order for the component functions to work properly. You can now write your Java source text in an editor and compile your program in the DOS console with the following command:

```
javac -d classes FirstPortalComponent.java.
```

Adjusting the environment variables

You must also insert the required portal libraries into the environment variables with **Start · Settings · Control Panel · System** or store them in the in the *<JAVA_HOME>\jre\lib\ext* directory. If you fail to do so, you'll receive an error message stating that components have not been found. If the files compiled successfully, you must create a *default.properties* file in the *profiles* directory. The file must contain the following two lines (in order):

```
ClassName.value=MyTest.FirstPortalComponent

Title.value=FirstPortalComponent
```

The portal uses the file to localize your component in the correct package (`MyTest`): it looks for the `FirstPortalComponent` class in the `MyTest` package. As preconditions, your Java class must be named `FirstPortalComponent` and your package must be stored as `MyTest`. Figure 9.9 shows the directory structure for a *.par* file of SAP EP 5.0.

Figure 9.9 The File Structure in the File System

Deployment

Pack (with WinZip, for example) all the contents of *MyTest* into a file named *MyTest.zip*. Rename the file to *MyTest.par*. The file won't be changed, but the portal accepts only those files with the portal archive ending of *.par*. To deploy the file in the portal, log on to the portal with a user who has administrator rights. In SAP EP 5.0, select **Portal-Admin · Upload from PAR Files**; in SAP Enterprise Portal 6.0, enter URL *http://<servername>:<PortalPort>/irj/servlet/prt[/portal/prtroot/PortalAnywhere.Default]*. Select the file and then **upload**. Follow the status messages. If the result is positive, the component will be deployed and can be

tested with URL *http://<servername>:<port>/irj/servlet/prt/prtroot/MyTest.default*. In PDK 5.0, log on to the portal as a user who has administrator rights. Select **DevTools · ComponentManager** and upload the *.par* file into SAP PDK. With the **ComponentInspector**, select **MyTest · Details · Start**. The selections represent manual deployment. If you use the plug-ins of SAP PDK, you have simple options for deployment. However, you must configure Eclipse so that
SAP PDK 5.0 or SAP EP 6.0 can be addressed for automatic deployment. To do so, open an Eclipse window and select **Preferences · PAR Upload Settings**; enter the server name, the port, and the user for the upload.

9.2.5 Deployment Descriptor in SAP EP 6.0

The following sections briefly examine the deployment descriptor used in SAP EP 6.0 instead of the profiles file. Listing 9.8 provides an example.

```
<?xml version="1.0" encoding="iso-8859-1"?>
<application alias="com.sap.training.test">
  <application-config>
     <property name="myProperty1"
         value="myPropertyValue1"/>
     <property name="myProperty2"
         value="myPropertyValue2"/>
     ...
  </application-config>
  <services>
         ...
  </services>
  <components>
         ...
  </components>
</application>
```

Listing 9.8 Example of a Deployment Descriptor—portalapp.xml

After the *.par* file has been uploaded into the portal, the `components` listed here are visible in the portal. The name of the application is the name of the *.par* file. The deployment descriptor can contain a series of property elements, such as SharingReference, PrivateSharingReference, ClassLoadingPolicy, Startup, Release, ServicesReference, and DeploymentPolicy. The properties listed affect the portal application as a whole. Table 9.6 shows predefined properties along with the values used and the default values.

Name	Description	Possible Values	Default
SharingReference	Refers to other portal applications whose API definitions are used in the API definition of this application.	Comma-separated list of other portal applications or aliases.	None
PrivateSharingReference	Refers to other portal applications whose API definitions are used in the implementation of this application (non-public).	Comma-separated list of other portal applications or aliases.	None
Startup	Specifies if the application is called (initialized) when the server is started.	"true" or "false"	"false"
Releasable	Specifies if the application is releasable.	"true" or "false"	"true"

Table 9.6 Predefined Properties of the Deployment Descriptor

When an application is loaded, the portal runtime checks the dependencies given in the deployment descriptor (SharingReference and PrivateSharingReference). All other applications dependent on the application are also deployed and are loaded first. This approach guarantees the readiness of the ClassLoader of the dependent applications. Every application has its own ClassLoader. The SharingReference means that resources of other applications can be used. SharingReferences use API extensions, which you can specify as "transitive" with the SAP EP 6.0 policy.

PrivateSharingReferences specify APIs that are later used by the application's "private coding." Consequently, another application cannot use an API implementation when it is declared as a PrivateSharingReference. Therefore, this situation implies non-transitivity.

Deployment of a portal application considers the deployment policy given in the deployment descriptor. If its value is "5.0" (SAP EP 5.0 DeploymentPolicy), the deployment is compatible with SAP EP 5.0. Directories are not deleted: the deployment process simply overwrites the directories with the new content. The PreservedConfigPaths property from SAP EP 5.0 is also considered. It contains a comma-separated list of paths and files that are to be protected. A new version does not replace these files and paths. The ClassLoadingPolicy indicates how the definitions of this application are exported and how the definitions of other applications are imported. If the value of the ClassLoaderPolicy is "5.0"

(SAP EP 5.0 ClassLoading), the API definitions of referenced portal applications are not automatically visible for other referencing applications with the SharingReference property. Table 9.7 shows the configuration properties for downward compatibility.

Name	Description	Possible Values	Default
PreservedConfigPaths	With the SAP EP 5.0 deployment policy, you can specify a series of PAR directories to be protected during deployment.	Comma-separated list of application paths.	None
DeploymentPolicy	Specifies how the resources of a portal application are to be handled during deployment.	"5.0" <empty>	None
ServicesReference	Equivalent to the SharingReference property.	See SharingReference	See SharingReference
ClassLoadingPolicy	Specifies how the resources of the ClassLoader of other applications are available.	"5.0" "transitive"	"transitive"

Table 9.7 Configuration Properties for Downward Compatibility

Component area

As you can see above, the deployment descriptor includes a component area. The following example shows how this area is further subdivided into a config and a profiles area:

```
<components>
      <component name="myComponent">
            <component-config>
                  ...
            </component-config>
            <component-profile>
                  ...
            </component-profile>
      </component>
</components>
```

In the config area, you enter properties that configure the portal component (ClassName, ComponentType, JSP, and so on.). AuthRequirement is an important property. It determines the minimum authentication required to execute the component: **user**, **admin**, **none**, or role(s).

The profile area contains properties that represent the dynamic part of the portal component: options to adjust and personalize the component.

You can use another area, similar to the component area, to set the configuration for services.

9.3 The Development Cycle

Regardless of which IDE you use, the development cycle always remains the same (see Figure 9.10):

1. You create a new project, iView classes, and a *.par* file.
2. You create or modify the profile file.
3. You enter the Java source text.
4. You finalize the *.par* file, upload it into the SAP PDK, and activate it.
5. You test the iView in SAP PDK. When it functions without problems and quality assurance ends, you can upload it into the productive portal.

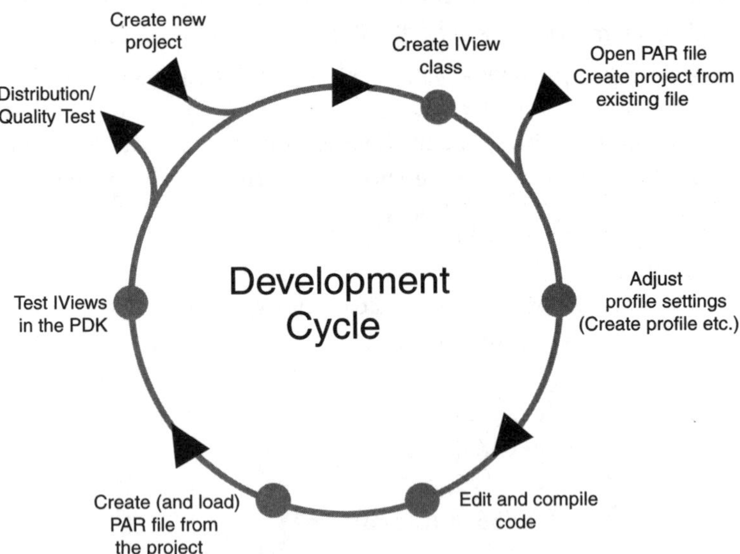

Figure 9.10 Development Cycle of a Portal Component

9.4 Java PortalComponents

In this chapter, you have already learned how PortalComponents function: they accept a request, process it, and transmit a reply. PortalComponents are related to Java servlets. Servlets and PortalComponents are well suited for simple applications. Because of their simplicity, they can be developed quickly and integrated easily into the portal.

Creating a project

You can now begin to use Eclipse to create your first portal component. Start Eclipse and select **File · New · Project · SAP Portal Development-Tools · PortalComponentProject.** In SAP PDK for SAP EP 6.0, select **File · New · Project · PortalApplication · Create a PortalApplicationProject**. Enter a name for the project, create the basic directory for the project (*c:\pdk_dev*, for example), and assign classes and package names.

Classes and package names are not yet entered in SAP PDK for SAP EP 6.0. Instead, the deployment descriptor, the *portalapp.xml* file is displayed first. Then select **File · New · Other · Create a new Portal Application Object**. Select the portal application project here and PortalComponent in the next screen. Next, assign the name, the location (CORE), the class names, and the package names.

Select `AbstractPortalComponent` and assign a class name and a package name like `MyFirstPortalComponent` and `FirstComponent` respectively. Then, select the `default` profile. The procedure is almost identical in JBuilder. The directory structure is also created automatically and the body of the Java component appears in the editor.

After you've created the project successfully, you should see the following fragment of source text in the editor:

```
package FirstComponent;
import com.sapportals.portal.prt.component.*;
public class MyFirstPortalComponent extends AbstractPor-
talComponent{
   public void doContent(IPortalComponentRequest
      request, IPortalComponentResponse response){
      /* Enter coding here */
   }
}
```

As you can see, the package and class names you assigned were transferred. A package named `FirstComponent` and a class named `MyFirstPortalComponent` were created. You can now enter coding in the area marked `/* Enter coding here */`. The first goal is to generate a simple "Hello World!" Replace the area marked with `/* ... */` with the following line:

```
response.write("Hello World!");
```

Compilation and deployment

Save your project and follow the menu path **File · Export · Create a portal archive (File · Export · PAR File** in SAP PDK for SAP EP 6.0:). Select your project here. In the next screen, select **Deploy Portal Component to Local Portal (to the referenced) Portal.** With SAP PDK for SAP EP 5.0, select the **default** setting at **Launch Browser**. The portal component is now compiled; when your PDK runs without errors, you can upload it into SAP PDK and deploy it.

With SAP PDK for SAP EP 5.0, the Internet browser is loaded; it displays your component. If the browser does not start automatically, you can start it with URL *http://localhost:8080/irj/servlet/prt/prtroot/FirstComponent*. The display should contain "Hello World!" You've now developed your first portal component.

In SAP EP 6.0, select your component with URL *http://localhost:8100/irj/servlet/prt/portal/prtroot/PortalAnywhere.Go* and select **Go**. From SAP PDK, you can also test your component with **JavaDeveloper · Development · ComponentInspector**, the selection of your component, and **Start**. In Eclipse, you can use the *portalapp.xml* file, the **Overview** tab, and the **External Preview** window beneath it to test your component.

Because a simple "Hello World!" is somewhat humdrum and you certainly want to see an interactive program, let's develop a portal component now that accepts your name as a parameter in a form and then returns it when you click a button.

Interactive example

As described above, create a new project named `NameTest`. Name the class `MyNameTest` and the package `NameTest`. Supplement the body of the program with the source text in Listing 9.9.

```
package NameTest;
import com.sapportals.portal.prt.component.*;
public class MyNameTest extends AbstractPortalComponent {
   String name;
   public void doContent(
      IPortalComponentRequest request,
      IPortalComponentResponse response) {
```

```
        name = request.getParameter("Name");
        response.write("<html><head></head><body
           class=\"gSAPBody\">");
        response.write("<form
           action=\"/irj/servlet/prt/portal/
           prtroot/NameTest.default\"method=POST>");
        response.write(
          "<br><B class =\"gSAPB\">Your name:
           </B><input type=text size=20 name=Name
           class=\"gSAPInputText\"> <input type=submit
           value ="\Submit"
           class=\"gSAPInputButton\">");
        response.write("</form>");
        if (name != null){
           if (!name.equals(""))
              response.write("<B class =\"gSAPB\">Your
                 Name is:<\B>" + name);
           else
              response.write("<B class =\"gSAPB\">
                 No name was entered</B>");
        }
    }
}
```

Listing 9.9 MyNameTest—Entry and Output of the Name

Comments on the source text

The required amount of source text is rather small. The example borrows from the somewhat more complex library example given in Section 9.2. You implement the `MyNameTest` class derived from `AbstractPortal-Component`. The `doContent()` method queries the `Name` parameter. The parameter can also be empty, which is usually the case at the first call. That's why the next step displays the "empty" form. The problem here is that the when the submit button is clicked, the iView must return the text that has been entered to itself. Therefore, we specify the URL for the servlet itself, */irj/servlet/prt/portal/prtroot/NameTest.default*, as a `form action` parameter. Alternatively, you could call the `request.createComponentURL()` method to generate an event and transfer the following as a parameter: `request.createComponentURL(request.createRequestEvent("submit"))`. The advantage of the latter is that you can react to various events. Because the example evaluates only the `submit` action, the first variant will suffice. It also clarifies how the PortalComponents borrow from servlet technology.

You have now become familiar with the simple variant of iViews and can use this knowledge to create your own small applications.

Disadvantages of PortalComponents

The disadvantage of PortalComponents and servlets is that they don't clearly separate content (data) from formatting (presentation of data). They don't separate the program text from the presentation of data in the portal. Imagine that you've created a large application that uses several pages for input and output. As you've seen, we'd have to insert the output of our application as HTML text or as text with an explicit stylesheet statement into the response object of the portal component. The application might not change, but it may have to be modified frequently. You can't expect a Web designer to work through the Java source text to find all the places where HTML is to be inserted or changed. In addition, *event handling* should occur separately from data storage. The next section introduces the techniques that meet these requirements.

9.5 Java Server Pages and DynPages

UML

UML stands for *Unified Modeling Language*, a descriptive language and notation to support structured software development. A good developer does not simply write something and develop something, but analyzes the problem, develops the design for a solution, and then implements the design. That's when testing starts.

DynPages

Java server pages and *DynPages* (from SAP) were created precisely to support this model; to avoid opening the door to chaotic programming; and to avoid destroying the good designs of XML, stylesheets, and the separation of content, data, and formatting. As seen in the previous section, you could not sensibly separate data, output, and event handling with simple PortalComponents. All actions occur in a single method or at least in the same class. Data output had to be hard-coded into the Java program and any change required recompilation of the program.

Observer pattern

UML supports design pattern, particularly the *observer pattern*. An example can clarify the pattern. Imagine a company that operates a warehouse. Many employees can use their computers to access warehouse files: purchasing agents, the production manager, and employees in materials management. Constant withdrawals and replenishments update the data. That's why the company has central data storage: several employees read the database and modify it. It would be unpleasant for "Production I" to withdraw parts without letting "Production II" know about it, so that Production II would not have the parts that it needs. And purchasing agents must always have up-to-date information so that they can reorder the right amount of materials. The goal here must be to ensure that every company employee with access to the database must log on to the system and then have a *view* of the database. The database represents the data *model*. The only thing missing is a *control* that handles communication between the multiple views and the database.

If the database changes, the views must be updated. If the view changes because of a withdrawal or a delivery, the database and the other views must be updated. You can easily understand the observer pattern from this example. The views or the controller observe the data source (model), and the controller observes the views to determine whether they change (see Figure 9.11). Views are often for display only.

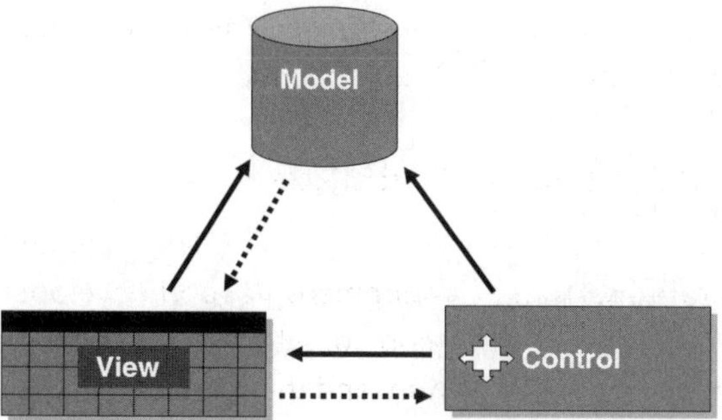

Figure 9.11 Model View Controller (MVC)

Therefore, a data model exists that is based on Java and that provides methods to read or change the data. One or more views exist that display the data from the data model and are updated as soon as the model changes.

Controller

The third part of the system is the controller. If a view changes or if a user performs an action in the view, the model changes the view and rereads the updated data. A double coupling can also update the views when the data of the model changes for any reason.

What does all this have to do with DynPages? DynPages, Java beans, and Java server pages are the counterpart of the design pattern of the observer or of the model view controller (MVC) for the portal in realization.

DynPages and JSP

DynPages are responsible for the data model and the controller. The Java server pages, which will come into play later on, stand for the various views. You don't have to use Java server pages; you can also generate the view from the DynPage. However, SAP recommends that you use

DynPages with JSPs and the HTMLB taglib. HTMLB stands for *HTML Business*; it provides a library for the graphical depiction of iViews in SAP EP.

The following example (see Listing 9.10) shows how DynPages function—first without JSPs.

```
package FirstDynPage;
import com.sapportals.htmlb.page.DynPage;
import com.sapportals.htmlb.page.PageException;
import com.sapportals.portal.htmlb.page
   .PageProcessorComponent;
import com.sapportals.htmlb.*;
import com.sapportals.htmlb.enum.*;

public class MyFirstDynPage extends
   PageProcessorComponent {
   public DynPage getPage() {
      return new MyDynPage();
   }
   public static class MyDynPage extends DynPage {
      /* Initialization: executed one for each user. */
      public void doInitialization() {
      }
      /* Handling the entry: called after user input. */
      public void doProcessAfterInput() throws
         PageException {
      }
      /* Create output. Called once for each request. */
      public void doProcessBeforeOutput() throws
         PageException {
         Form myForm = this.getForm();
         TextView myText = new TextView();
         myText.setText("Hello World!");
         myText.setDesign(TextViewDesign.LABEL);
         myForm.addComponent(myText);
      }
   }
}
```

Listing 9.10 Sample DynPage: "Hello World!"

Comments on the source text

Class PageProcessorComponent is derived from class AbstractPortalComponent. Therefore, all the methods of AbstractPortalComponent are also available for PageProcessorComponent through inheritance. PageProcessorComponent must also overwrite a getPage() method; getPage() returns a DynPage. Listing 9.10 implements a class derived from DynPage as an inner class from a class derived from PageProcessorComponent. This approach makes possible something akin to a multiple inheritance, which is normally impossible in Java, where classes can come from only a super class. The inner class (MyDynPage) can access PageProcessorComponent. It can have the same affect as a PortalComponent, even though it's derived from DynPage and inherits completely different methods there. You could say that the DynPage takes over processing for all the processes of the PageProcessorComponent.

Because the AbstractPortalComponent class supports the IPortalComponent interface, you can use its service()method to access the request and response objects. PageProcessorComponent inherits the accesses, and the DynPage also has access as an inner class. If JSPs are used, the getPage() method returns a JSPDynPage instead of a DynPage. JSPDynPage is a class derived from DynPage that also implements a setJSPName() method. This feature allows you to use JSPs and set them dynamically. The DynPage makes the required data available to the JSP with a Java bean and communicates with the JSP about the Java bean. The JSP takes data from the Java bean and creates the GUI for the user. Figure 9.12 clarifies the process.

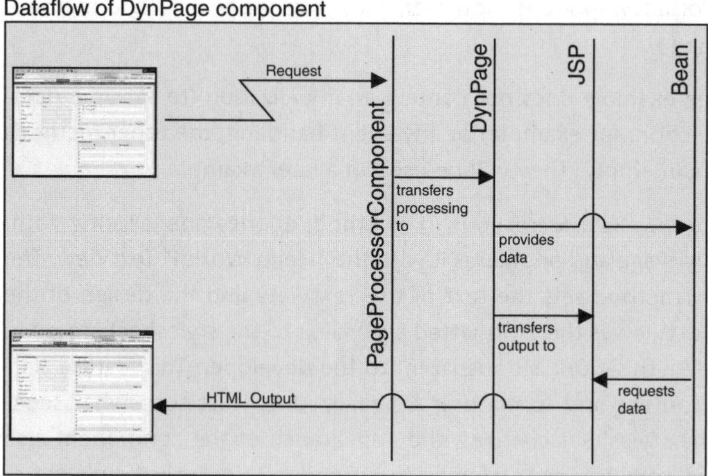

Figure 9.12 Data Flow of a PageProcessorComponent with a JSPDynPage

As explained, the `MyDynPage` class is an inner class of the `MyFirst-DynPage` program. The property file receives the name of the external class because the portal runtime (PRT) does not call the DynPage but the `PageProcessorComponent` derived from `AbstractPortalCompo-nent`. After the PRT starts the iView, the DynPage and its methods are also called. Because `DynPage` is an abstract class and contains abstract methods, the methods must be overwritten; otherwise, the class could not be instanced and it would be an abstract class itself. The methods to be overwritten are:

- **`doInitialization()`**
  Called only once during initialization of the instance
- **`doProcessAfterInput()`**
  Called when data is sent to the server (event handling)
- **`doProcessBeforeOutput()`**
  Always called: it handles graphic elements

PAI and PBO

The terminology shows the relationship to the backend of SAP R/3. SAP Dynpros in the ABAP/4 language from SAP also use the *Process After Input (PAI)* and *Process Before Output (PBO)* keywords. These methods are called in ABAP before a screen is displayed or after user interaction in a screen.

In the example, it's important to understand that all methods must be overwritten, regardless of whether they contain something or should process something. The example contains only one programmed method, and although the others are not programmed, they must still be overwritten. The PortalComponent, however, must overwrite only one method: `doContent()`.

Because the example does not contain an initialization (to set up a database connection, for example) or any event handling, the other methods simply remain empty. They will be used in a later example.

The `doProcessBeforeOutput()` method queries the existing form from the DynPage and populates it with the "Hello World!" TextView. The `setText()`method sets the text of the TextView and the design of the text. The TextView is then formatted according to the stylesheet stored in the portal. All this work is transparent to the developer. This feature clarifies how content and formatting are realized at least somewhat separately. If the stylesheet changes, the appearance of the component also changes, without having to change the program. No explicit style statements are required: the formatting is oriented to the current portal design. But it's still unfortunate that the design of the form—the alignment of the components—must be done in the Java source text. If that design changes, the Java source text must—as was the case previously—be modified.

Your IDE already changed the property file: it inserted the `ServicesReference=htmlb` entry. The entry is required because you are now using a service reference. To display the graphic components, HTMLB uses the same program as it does for the GUI. If the entry is missing, you receive a linkage error in the portal runtime for Java. HTMLB later replaces the form components with HTML components by using the portal's style defaults.

Separation of content and form

Finally, to create the actual separation of content and formatting, we turn to the JSPDynPages. As noted, the GUI is not assembled in the Java source text, but in a separate JSP that is created dynamically at runtime.

Create a new project for a JSPDynPage instead of for a DynPage. The only special feature here is that you must also assign a name for the Java bean and the JSP. For example, name the Java bean `MyBean` and the JSP `MyView.jsp`.

You should recall that we used the `doProcessBeforeOutput()` method in the DynPage to assemble the GUI. We do the same here with the JSPDynPage, except that in this case the JSP page is integrated with the `setJSPName()` method and the interface is not assembled with Java objects. First, you should generate a Java bean in the JSPDynPage. The Java bean establishes the connection between the JSP page and the application and, therefore, enables data exchange. You can use the `doInitialization()` method:

```
MyBean myBean;
public void doInitialization() {
   myBean = new MyBean();
}
```

Java bean registration

Now you must register the Java bean so that the JSP can find it and access its data:

```
public void doProcessBeforeOutput()
   throws PageException {
   ((IPortalComponentRequest) getRequest())
      .getServletRequest()
      .setAttribute("myBean",myBean);
```

```
  myBean.setValue("Hello World!");
  this.setJspName("MyView.jsp");
}
```

Java bean implementation

Next, you must implement the Java bean. Traditionally, a Java bean contains only set() and get() methods. These methods must exist for every GUI component. Because our example outputs only a simple "Hello World!" we need just one TextView. Insert the following entries into the source text fragment of the Java bean:

```
// Properties TextView
public String text;
// set()/get() TextView
public String getText() {
  return text;
}
public void setText(String text) {
  this.text = text;
}
```

You must then make some entries in the JSP:

```
<hbj:textView id="line1"encode="false">
   <% line1.setText(myBean.getText()); %>
</hbj:textView>
```

You have created a GUI with these lines. The complete JSP appears in Listing 9.2:

```
<%@ taglib uri="tagLib" prefix="hbj"%>
<jsp:useBean id="myBean"
   scope="request" class="View.MyBean"/>
<hbj:content id="myContext">
   <hbj:page title="PageTitle">
      <hbj:form id="myFormId">
         <hbj:textView id="line1" encode="false">
            <% line1.setText(myBean.getText()); %>
         </hbj:textView>
      </hbj:form>
   </hbj:page>
</hbj:content>
```

Listing 9.11 Source Text of the Complete Java Server Page

The Taglib in use is specified in the first line. The connection to the Java bean registered earlier is established on the `myBean` instance rather than on the `MyBean` class. A new context, a new page, and a new form are created. The form contains exactly one TextView with one line; the line is populated with the content of the data model from the application. You can't really speak of a true data model here because we've populated only one value for the TextView in the application, but it's enough to clarify the theory.

Comments on the source text

In another step, you transfer the earlier application of the portal component to the JSPDynPage. The user should enter a name in the input field; a TextView outputs the name.

For this application, you need an input field, a button to trigger an action, and the TextView that you already used. Create a new project. Check your results against the source text for the JSPDynPage given in Listing 9.12.

```
package FirstJSPDynPage;
import View.MyBean;
import com.sapportals.htmlb.*;
import com.sapportals.htmlb.page.*;
import com.sapportals.htmlb.event.*;
import com.sapportals.portal.htmlb.page.*;
import com.sapportals.portal.prt.component.*;

public class MyFirstJSPDynPage extends
   PageProcessorComponent {
   public DynPage getPage() {
      return new MyDynPage();
   }
   public static class MyDynPage extends JSPDynPage {
      MyBean myBean;
      public void doInitialization() {
         IPortalComponentRequest request =
            (IPortalComponentRequest)
         this.getRequest();
         myBean = new MyBean();
         myBean.setText("Submit");
         request.getComponentContext()
            .getProfile().putValue("myBean",
               myBean);
      }
```

```
      public void doProcessAfterInput() throws
         PageException {
         IPortalComponentRequest request =
           (IPortalComponentRequest)
         this.getRequest();
         myBean = (MyBean)
            request.getComponentContext()
            .getProfile().getValue("myBean");
            InputField input = (InputField)
               getComponentByName("InputName");
            if (input != null)
               myBean.setText_view(
                 "Your name is: "
                  + input.getValueAsDataType()
                  .toString());
      }
      public void doProcessBeforeOutput() throws
         PageException {
         this.setJspName("MyView.jsp");
      }
      public void onClick(Event event)
         throws PageException {
      }
   }
}
```

Listing 9.12 First JSPDynPage—Entry and Output of the Name as a JSPDynPage

Creating a Java bean for data exchange

Now you must create the Java bean that will be used to exchange data between the JSP and the JSPDynPage (see Listing 9.13).

```
package View;
import java.io.Serializable;
public class MyBean implements Serializable {
   // Properties Button
   public String text;
   // Properties TextView
   public String text_view;
   // TextView
   public void setText_view(String text) {
      text_view = text;
   }
```

```
  public String getText_view() {
     return text_view;
  }
  //Button
  public String getText() {
     return text;
  }
  public void setText(String text) {
     this.text = text;
  }
}
```

Listing 9.13 Java Bean for Data Exchange (MyBean)

Creating the JSP

Finally, you must create the JSP (see Listing 9.14).

```
<%@ taglib uri="tagLib" prefix="hbj"%>
<jsp:useBean id="myBean"
  scope="application" class="View.MyBean"/>
<hbj:content id="myContext">
  <hbj:page title="PageTitle">
     <hbj:form id="myFormId">
        <hbj:tray id="example" design="BORDER"
          width ="500" title="NameCheck"
          isCollapsed="false">
           <hbj:trayBody >
              <hbj:inputField id="InputName"
                type="STRING" design="STANDARD"
                width="100" maxlength="100"
                tooltip="Please enter your name">
              </hbj:inputField>
              <hbj:button id="MyButton"
                text="<%=myBean getText() %>"
                onClick="click" tooltip="submit">
              </hbj:button>
              <br><br>
              <hbj:textView id="line1" encode="false"
                tooltip="Ihr Name">
                 <% line1.setText(myBean
                    getText_view()); %>
              </hbj:textView>
           </hbj:trayBody>
```

```
            </hbj:tray>
        </hbj:form>
    </hbj:page>
</hbj:content>
```

Listing 9.14 Display for the User (MyView.jsp)

Flow of the JSPDynPage The following sections describe the flow of the JSPDynPage. First, the components are called in the portal. The `doInitialize()` method is executed. It writes (sets) data to the Java bean. Because the Java bean does not yet exist, it is created and the text for the button that will be clicked when a name is entered is set. The Java bean must be registered because the JSP cannot access it otherwise.

Scope The design of Java beans offers several options for storing data and determining which components can access the Java bean. The *scope* sets the standard. The example uses the `application` scope, which allows access to the Java bean only within the portal component. Both the JSP and the JSPDynPage can access the Java bean, but no other components can do so. Other variants are also available, such as those that store the Java bean outside the context of the application or component. This approach is especially vital for more complex applications that must access the data jointly. However, typically, you can use a database for an extreme case and therefore should not be concerned with this issue. The only important consideration here is that you understand why Java beans are used.

Figure 9.13 shows the schematic flow of the execution of a JSPDynPage.

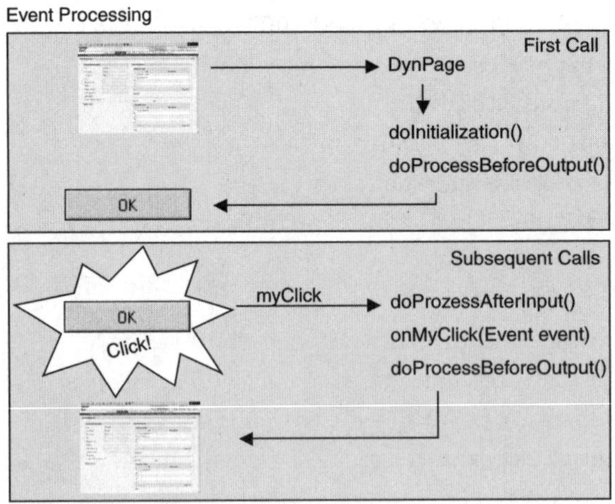

Figure 9.13 Event Handling During the Execution of a JSPDynPage

If initialization has been performed, the doProcessBeforeOutput() method is executed. The JSP is called (set) and displayed in the portal. The JSP is compiled, dynamic elements are read from the Java bean and inserted dynamically, and the HTML output is generated.

Event

The generated HTML page now waits for user action. When the **Submit** button is clicked, an event is triggered. The JSPDynPage then receives the event. The event is transferred and the doProcessAfterInput() method is called. This method is now responsible for calling the values of the request from the HTML page and evaluating them. In this case, the input field that is to display the name is to be evaluated. You can use the getComponentByName() method to read and evaluate components. In this case, the input field is InputName. Once the component has evaluated the entry in the field, the value must be transferred to the JSP because the JSP should then display the name.

You could call a second JSP page now or populate a TextView that you included in the JSP for future use but that has not contained any text thus far. Because the JSPDynPage does not and should not have direct access to the JSP because we're using the MVC concept, we must first supply the Java bean with the new values. To have renewed access to the Java bean, you must use the context to access the profile and the stored value to access the Java bean. You can then set the text of the TextViews.

The onClick method is called next. But, because no other actions are required, it remains empty. In conclusion, the doProcessBeforeOutput() method is called to redisplay the JSP in the portal. If you use several JSPs, you must use a status flag to monitor whether the component was called for the first time or an additional time. The initial call displays the first JSP with the form; later calls display the resulting JSP if you don't want to enable another entry as the example does.

Property file

You must also make two entries to the property file as follows:

```
tagLib.value=/SERVICE/htmlb/taglib/htmlb.tld
tagLib.inheritance=final
```

The entries are required to grant the JSPDynPage access to the HTMLB Taglib.

You have now learned all the requirements to develop your own PortalComponents, DynPages, and JSPDynPages. In the simplest cases, you'll develop PortalComponents; for more complex applications, you'll develop JSPDynPages. In general, JSPDynPages are preferable to DynPages for the reasons noted above.

Migration from SAP EP 5.0 to SAP EP 6.0

Because SAP EP 5.0 uses *.par* and *.zar* files in a different format than SAP EP 6.0 files and because it doesn't use the XML-based deployment descriptor, you must consider the following aspects when migrating to SAP EP 6.0 iViews:

- *.zar* files must be renamed to *.par* files.
- The SAP EP 6.0 deployment descriptor is generated dynamically during the upload and stored in the repository (the file system in SP2 and the database in SP3).
- The generated deployment descriptor permits deployment and sets the ClassLoadingPolicy.

10 Connectivity

Connections to the outside world are the sine qua non for the portal. Content is available only outside the portal and integrating content into the portal requires connectors. This chapter provides you with a look into the world of connectivity.

Data is available everywhere, however, it is often in a format that you can't use, or that doesn't meet the requirements necessary for your applications to process it.

10.1 SAP Java Connector

There's a solution for almost every one of these cases. Do you want to access an SAP system but not use the powerful SAP GUI to do so? Do you need access to specific data but don't have power-user access over the GUI? Don't worry. You can use the *Java Connector (JCo)*. It's lightweight—in terms of its components—and it's easy to use. And with some additional help in development, you can easily call a function module from an SAP system.

Download

The JCo is already partially integrated into SAP Enterprise Portal. It is usually employed to call specific modules in the background. If you want to use the JCo and use SAP PDK 5.0, you'll find many interesting sources, tutorials, and sample programs in the *<tomcat_home>\webapps\irj\docs\sapjco* directory. You can download the SAP JCo from SAP Service Marketplace with the alias */connectors*. Simply integrate the *sapjco.jar* file into the libraries of your Integrated Development Environment (IDE).

Example

Let's use a sample program delivered with the JCo to illustrate the simple use of the JCo in the portal. It tests an RFC connection to an SAP system (see Listing 10.1). The function module returns the system data of the system that was addressed.

```
package JCoTest;
import com.sapportals.portal.prt.component.*;
import com.sap.mw.jco.*;

public class SimpleJCoTest extends
   AbstractPortalComponent {
   public void doContent(
```

```
IPortalComponentRequest request,
IPortalComponentResponse response) {
JCO.Client client = null;
try {
  response.write("<br><br>Version of the JCO-
    library:<br>"
    + "----------------------------<br>"
    + JCO.getMiddlewareVersion());
    client = JCO.createClient("000",
    "UserID",
    "Password",
    "EN",
    "hostname",
    "00"); // system number
  client.connect();
  JCO.ParameterList input =
    JCO.createParameterList();
  input.appendValue("REQUTEXT",
    JCO.TYPE_CHAR, 255, "This is my first Jayco
    example.");
  JCO.ParameterList output =
    JCO.createParameterList();
  output.addInfo("ECHOTEXT",
    JCO.TYPE_CHAR, 255);
  output.addInfo("RESPTEXT",
    JCO.TYPE_CHAR, 255);
  client.execute("STFC_CONNECTION",
    input, output);
  response.write("<br>The function
    'STFC_CONNECTION'
    returned the following parameters:<br>"
    "---------------------------------------
    ---------------------------");
  for (int i = 0; i < output.getFieldCount();
    i++) {
    response.write(<br>Name: " +
    output.getName(i)
    + " Value: " + output.getString(i));
  }
  client.disconnect();
```

```
            response.write("<br><br>Congratulations!
               It worked.");
         } catch (Exception ex) {
            response.write("Caught an exception: <br>"
               + ex);
            if (client != null)
               client.disconnect();
         }
      }
}
```

Listing 10.1 Calling Function Module STFC_CONNECTION to Test an RFC Connection

You need to enter only a user ID, password, application server, client, and system number and you can execute the program yourself (see Figure 10.1).

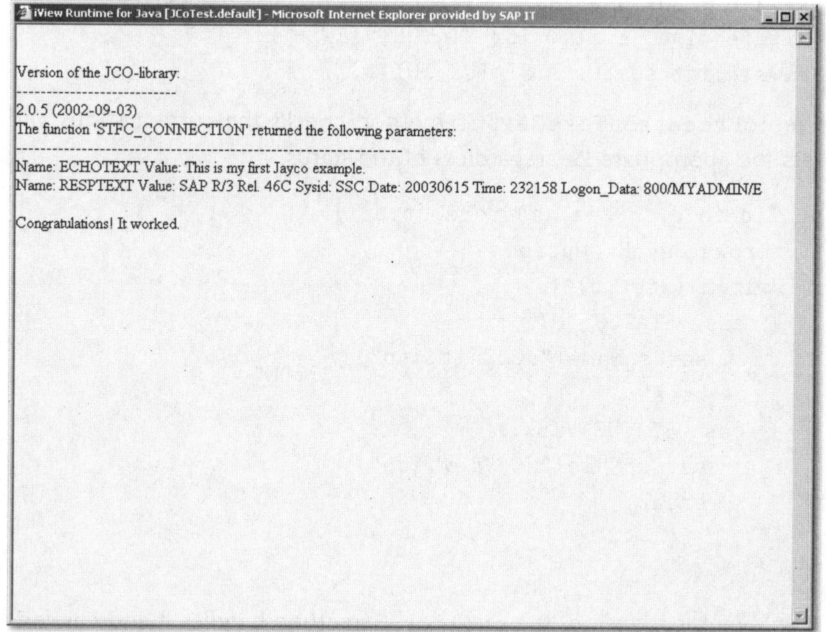

Figure 10.1 Testing the Connection to SAP R/3 with the Java Connector

Reading a table with RFC

Another example clarifies how you can read from a table with remote function call (RFC). To strengthen your understanding of JSPDynPages from Chapter 9, the example is realized with a JSPDynPage rather than a PortalComponent. The goal here is to create a PortalComponent with a **Display Company Codes** button that connects with the specified SAP system and calls function module BAPI_COMPANYCODE_GETLIST when activated. It then displays all company codes in a TableView in which you can scroll by line or page.

You can find the complete program at the following Web site for this book: *http://www.sap-press.com*

The following sections examine only special considerations. With these interactive components, it's important that two different statuses exist. The `Init` status occurs when the program starts—a selection button, not the table, should be displayed at this point. If you were to insert a TableView element into the JSP, without having a TableView with an appropriate data model, you'd receive an error message. For that reason, you need two JSPs—one with a selection button and one that incorporates the table after selection. You must insert a variable that indicates the current status:

```
private final static int STATUS_INIT = 0;
private final static int STATUS_VIEW = 1;
private int status = STATUS_INIT;
```

Checking the status

The `doProcessBeforeOutput` method checks the current status and sets the appropriate JSP, regardless of the status:

```
public void doProcessBeforeOutput()
   throws PageException {
   switch (status) {
      case STATUS_INIT :
         setJspName("JCoInit.jsp");
         break;
      case STATUS_VIEW :
         setJspName("JCoView.jsp");
         break;
   }
}
```

Event handling

If an event is triggered, the `onClick()` method handles it and converts the status:

```
public void onClick(Event event) {
   myBean.doSelect();
   status = STATUS_VIEW;
}
```

It's also important to handle navigation events appropriately:

Handling navigation events

```
public void onNavigation(Event event) {
   if (event instanceof TableNavigationEvent) {
      TableNavigationEvent tne =
         (TableNavigationEvent) event;
      visibleRow = tne.getFirstVisibleRowAfter();
      if (myBean != null) {
         myBean.setVisibleRow(new Integer(visibleRow).
            toString());
      }
   }
}
```

Accessing SAP systems

Now you'll learn how to use the SAP JCo to access an SAP system from the portal. The Java bean handles all data storage and data capture for the JSP and the JSPDynPage.

As you can see in the `onClick()` method, clicking on the selection button triggers data selection in Java with the `doSelect()` method. The `doSelect()` method establishes the connection over a JCo client. The client logs on to the SAP system, captures the data, and returns it. The data returned by the JCo can simply be displayed in a list. However, it's much more interesting to output the data in a table. But you should consider that the list can become rather long and that it should not populate the entire portal page with entries. That's why it's best to spread the table across several pages and provide a navigation bar. The component would then appear in the portal as shown in Figure 10.2.

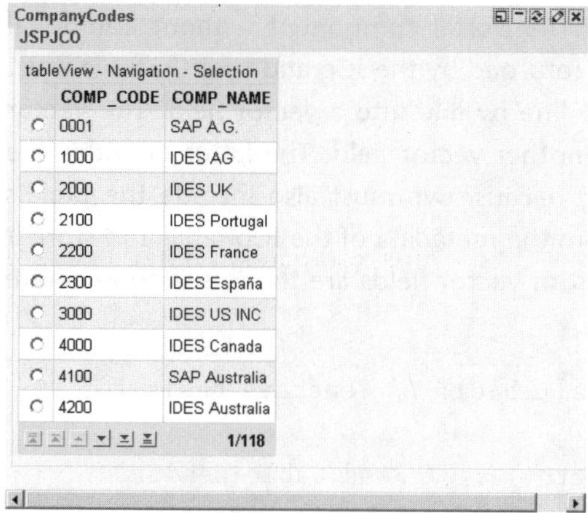

Figure 10.2 JCo Table in a TableView with Navigation Elements

Generating a JCo client object

To connect to an SAP system, you must first generate a JCo client object. The connection data used in the preceding example is not enough to log on to an SAP system:

```
JCO.Client client = JCO.createClient("000", "UserID",
   "Password", "EN", "hostname", "00");
client.connect();
IRepository rep = new JCO.Repository("DDIC", client);
IFunctionTemplate ftemplate =
   rep.getFunctionTemplate("BAPI_COMPANYCODE_GETLIST");
JCO.Function function = new JCO.Function(ftemplate);
client.execute(function);
JCO.Table compTab =function.getTableParameterList()
   .getTable("COMPANYCODE_LIST");
model = createNewTable(model, compTab);
```

Creating a connection to the repository

You create a connection to the repository and use the template to call the function module—this next step is not new to you. The last line of the above code fragment is interesting—it generates a data model. The background for this procedure is that the data returned by the JCo cannot be used as is in a table. As discussed in Chapter 9, a table in the context of Java means a separation of data between the display and the controller: the model view controller pattern is used here.

The table to be displayed in the portal must be based on a data model and react to modifications or events in the view. We can't really speak of changes in the data here, so we don't need to pursue this design any further. The goal here is to define an appropriate data model based on the table to be displayed. The data model of the JCo cannot simply be transferred to the data model of the portal component without additional steps, which is why the data returned by the JCo and the JCo table must be evaluated and transferred line by line into a vector field. The vector field is then transferred to another vector field. The latter provides the basis for our data. However, because we must also include the table's header data, we extract it from the metadata of the JCo table and store it in yet another vector field. Both vector fields are then used to generate the final data model:

```
Vector data = createData(table); // Generate basis for
data
Vector columns = new Vector(); // Read table header
for (int i = 0; i < table.getNumColumns(); i++) {
   String columnName = table.getName(i);
```

```
   columns.addElement(columnName);
}
// Generate data model
model = new DefaultTableViewModel(data, columns);
```

The data is generated with the vector fields:

```
Vector dataVector = new Vector();
Vector retVector = new Vector();
String field;
for (int j = 0; j < table.getNumRows(); j++) {
   table.setRow(j);
   for (int i = 0; i < table.getNumColumns(); i++) {
      field = table.getString(i);
      if (field == null)
         field = "";
      dataVector.addElement(field);
   }
   retVector.addElement(dataVector);
   dataVector = new Vector();
}
```

Now the data model is present and the JSP can use the `getTableModel()` method to access the data and generate the table. The JSP determines how the view will be displayed in the portal component and which actions the user can take. When users navigate (scroll) in the view, an event is triggered and redirected to the JSPDynPage.

You can see that it's not very complicated to read data from an SAP system with the JCo and then display it in a JSP. You can also insert input fields into the JSP, evaluate them on the server side, and use the JCo to select data. In this manner, you can create interactive reports in the portal and have easy access to the data in an SAP system.

10.2 SAP Business Connector

Automating business processes

You should use SAP Business Connector when you want to automate or enhance business processes. Using SAP Business Connector is particularly helpful when you want to employ open, non-proprietary standards. You can access most common formats with it. And if a format is not available in the standard package or in an enhancement package, you can always develop mappings yourself to access external formats.

Access to external data SAP Business Connector enables SAP systems to access external formats and converts the proprietary SAP IDoc format into standard or external formats. It therefore supports bidirectional access in real time or asynchronous communication to and from an SAP system.

If you use SAP Business Connector, you can use its services to call BAPIs or RFCs in a straightforward manner. You can also define mappings in SAP Business Connector proactively.

Note OSS note 571530 indicates that SAP is removing SAP Business Connector from its portfolio. The last release will be Version 4.7, after which SAP Business Connector will no longer be developed. There is no direct successor for SAP Business Connector. SAP Web Application Server (SAP Web AS) and SAP Exchange Infrastructure (SAP XI) support some of the functionality of SAP Business Connector, such as HTTP maintenance, parsing XML documents, or routing messages to the appropriate recipient.

10.3 SAP Exchange Infrastructure

Chapter 12 presents the new SAP strategy for interoperability and data exchange between SAP and non-SAP systems and examines components of SAP NetWeaver. For more information on SAP Exchange Infrastructure, see Chapter 12.

10.4 Additional Connectors

The SAP environment includes several additional connectors, including *SAP DCOM Connector*, *SAP MarketSetConnector*, and *SAP .NET Connector*. It also contains additional tools, such as the RFC Library and a SOAP processor (delivered with SAP Web AS 6.20). You can use most of these connectors from the portal, depending on the available and targeted area of use.

However, typically, communication for Java iViews occurs over the SAP JCo. If you're not a power user, and you don't want to use SAP Internet Transaction Server (ITS) to call SAP Dynpros, and would prefer to develop in Java instead of ABAP or BSPs, you'll find the JCo an indispensable tool.

11 Portals and Security

Security plays an integral role in networks and therefore in portal environments. Data must be transferred securely. It must be realizable. The operability of an application should never suffer because of security mechanisms. This chapter shows you how to secure a portal and integrate security components into the portal.

11.1 Overview

Via the Internet, SAP Enterprise Portal is linked to or can be linked to the entire world. All possible types of components can be integrated into the portal: simpler Internet sites, Web services, and complex applications. Most components are located outside of a company's own network or simply on a server other than the portal server. Communication is always occurring—between various servers, between hardware and software, and among hardware and software components (several server instances can run on one computer). It occurs within and beyond your own network.

As a hardware unit, servers are generally secure because firewalls and upstream (reverse) proxy servers offer protection from direct attack. But something can still go wrong in the connections between servers and data can be manipulated. *Secure Network Communications (SNC)* protected connections ensure secure communications between two SAP systems. HTTP can use an encryption technique—*secure sockets layer (SSL)*.

Digital signature

A digital signature is another security technology. It is used to uniquely identify the sender of a message and to provide a means to validate the integrity of a message.

General security requirements

The security measure noted so far deals with secure and confidential communications among individual portal components, applications, and the outside world. But the portal must also use authentication mechanisms to ensure that only authorized personnel can access the portal and its resources. That's why a user must log on to the portal at least once so that the portal can confirm the user's identity. Users authenticate themselves with a combination of user ID and password, a digital certificate, or by using an SAP system or a third-party product, such as *NT LAN Manager (NTLM)* or *Java Authentication and Authorization Services (JAAS)* interface.

You can use the SSL protocol to protect the data while it is being transferred from the Web browser to the server. You can assign authorizations and roles to grant users or groups of users access to the applications, information, and iViews that they require. User management administers these users, groups, and role. *Access control lists (ACL)* define authorizations for various objects of the portal content directory, which administers and stores portal applications.

Single Sign-On

Users should find it easy to use applications in the portal. The diverse sources of applications integrated into the portal and the various technologies used should be transparent to users. But ease of use also means that the portal cannot demand that users log on separately to each application. Doing so would destroy transparency. After users have been authenticated, their portal ID (if it differs) is mapped to the user ID of the integrated systems with user mapping. This approach enables comprehensive *single sign-on (SSO)*. Users retain all their assigned roles and authorizations to access the applications, data, and services integrated into the portal or referenced by the portal. SSO offers an option to log on to SAP and non-SAP system. With SSO, users are required to sign on to the portal only once. They are automatically logged on to all the systems and applications they use in the portal.

Once users are logged on to the systems and applications, they need authorizations. The SAP and non-SAP systems handle the authorizations: the portal does not assign authorizations. In addition to authentication, SSO, authorization, user management, and the configuration of secure communication within and outside of the portal, you must also ensure that the portal is part of a secure network environment. Figure 11.1 provides an overview of the security architecture of SAP EP.

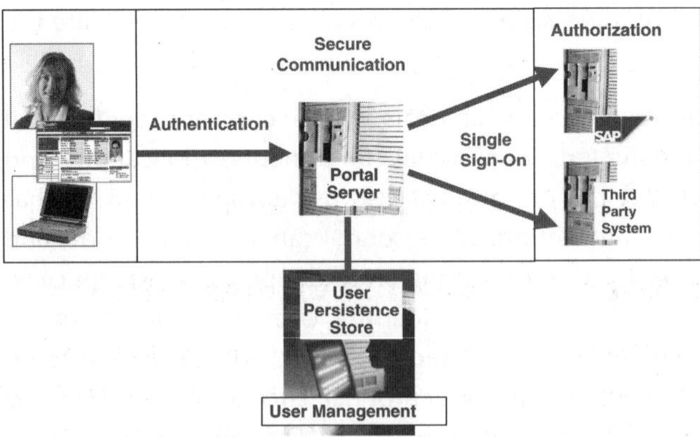

Figure 11.1 Security Architecture of SAP Enterprise Portal

The following sections provide an overview of the security architecture of SAP EP. This overview is by no means complete, especially because of the multitude of possible options. Topics are described on the basis of practical experience with SAP customers. The first topic addresses the security improvements in SAP EP 6.0.

11.2 New Security Features in SAP Enterprise Portal 6.0

Before we look at individual security topics in SAP EP, we'll provide you with an overview of the new security features in SAP EP 6.0 and then introduce the conventional security features. When appropriate, we have noted how the new features enhance or replace previous features.

SAP EP 6.0 includes the following new security features:

- Parallel use of various authentication methods
- Parallel use of various user persistence layers
- Use of an anonymous user (to request a new user over self-service, for example)
- Authorization depending on the authentication method: iViews require a specific logon method (a digital X.509 certificate, for example)
- Interface for third-party authentication (*pluggable*) and support of *Java Authentication and Authorization Services (JAAS)*
- Support for partner products
  - Support of Web access management products
  - Support of other external authentication services, such as hardware tokens
- The last status in the portal is reestablished after the SAP logon ticket expires and a user is authenticated again
- Ticket verification library for Windows and UNIX platforms (Java)
- Web server filter for additional Web server platforms

11.3 Secure Network Communications (SNC)

Secure Network Communications (SNC) offers end-to-end security between SAP systems at the application layer. SNC can secure communications between two components, such as two SAP application servers. Along with SNC, SAP supports other external security products.

SAPCryptoLib SNC offers protection (channel encryption) to the connection between one server and others with *SAP Cryptographic Library (SAPCryptoLib)* or with a certified partner product. SAP customers can download SAPCryptoLib from SAP Service Marketplace at *http://service.sap.com/swdc* (**Download • SAP Cryptographic Software**) free of charge (see Note OSS 397175 on export controls). The license disclaimer for SAPCryptoLib states that it may be used only as an integral element of SAP products, not as part of non-SAP products. Legal use of SAPCryptoLib for SNC is limited to the protection of back-end server components made available for SAP or SAP partners.

SNC supports three security grades:

- Authentication
- Protection of integrity
- Protection of confidentiality

Authentication guarantees the identity of a communications partner; it is not primarily concerned with protecting the data. Protection of the data checks its integrity to determine whether the transmitted data was changed on the way from the sender to the recipient. The highest level of security protects confidentiality—all data to be transmitted is encrypted.

SNC in the portal You can configure the portal server of SAP EP and SAP back-end systems for the use of SNC-protected connections as a matter of course. If an SAP system is used for user management (*user persistence store*), the connection can also be protected with SNC. You can find documentation on configuring the connection between the portal server and an SAP system in the *SAP Enterprise Portal Security Guide*, available from SAP Service Marketplace at *http://service.sap.com/securityguide*.

When using SAP Internet Transaction Server (ITS), you must distinguish between configuration of the *WGate* and the *AGate*. The AGate of SAP ITS communicates with the SAP back-end system over a proprietary SAP protocol. You can configure this connection for protected communications with SNC. The same applies to the connection between the AGate and the WGate. You can find documentation on the required configuration in the SNC user manual, available from SAP Service Marketplace. The WGate communicates with the Web browser over HTTP; you can use the SSL protocol to secure the connection. Secure HTTP is HTTPS (*HTTP Secure*). See the following section for more information on SSL. Figure 11.2 illustrates the protocols and components used in the portal, except for SAP ITS, which plays a special role.

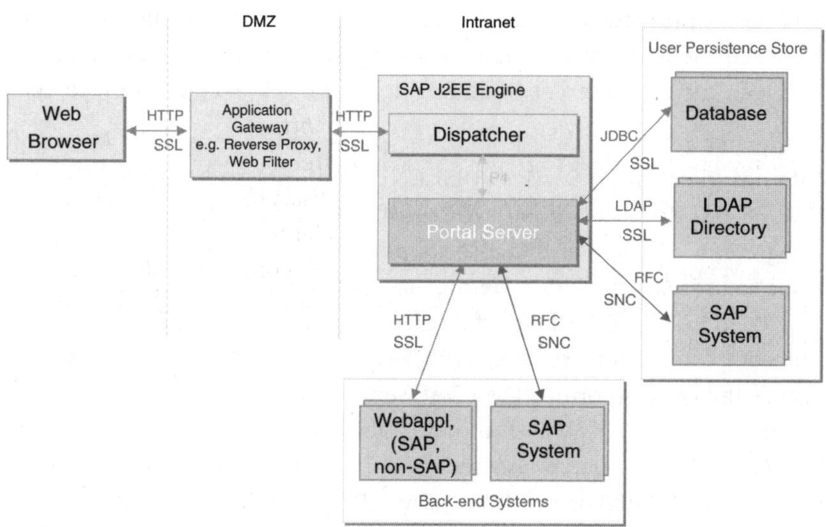

Figure 11.2 Use of SNC and SSL in the Portal

11.4 SSL

Secure sockets layer (SSL) was developed by Netscape to encrypt confidential data between clients and servers. SSL uses a hybrid encryption procedure consisting of a symmetrical algorithm (DES or RC4, for example) to encrypt data and an asymmetrical algorithm (RSA, for example) to manage the session key. Use of the SSL protocol is available for portal operators with a high level of security requirements. In general, use of SSL is highly recommended, as will become clear in this section.

How SSL works

An SSL connection is set up when a client asks a server to communicate with it over a connection protected by SSL. The server then sends the client its certificate with a public key. The client verifies the certificate and generates a session key. The session key is encrypted with the server's public key and returned to the server. The server decrypts the session key with its private key. Both the client and the server now have the session key used to encrypt the channel between the client and the server. To use SSL, it's essential to user server certificates. You can also use SSL to authenticate clients. In this case, the client has an X.509 certificate, which it sends to the server for inspection along with the initial request. See Section 11.5.2 for more detailed information.

The portal supports both SSL and SNC. Together, the technologies ensure a seamless, encrypted data transmission between the Web browser (portal client) and the portal Web server (required for SAP EP 5.0, optional for

SAP EP 6.0—optional because it's integrated into the portal server); between the portal Web server and the portal server (J2EE Engine); and between the portal server (J2EE Engine) and the SAP application server.

Portal server architecture: SAP EP 5.0 and SAP EP 6.0

In the architecture of SAP EP 5.0, the portal server consists of Microsoft Internet Information Services (IIS) (.NET runtime) and the J2EE Engine. SAP EP 6.0 does not require Microsoft IIS because the portal platform integrates a Web server that also supports SSL. If you want, you can continue to use Microsoft IIS as before: it's required to authenticate a user via NTLM. In SAP EP 6.0, the portal server consists only of the J2EE Engine. For complete system security with SAP EP 5.0 and 6.0, you must also secure the connections to the LDAP server (although use of this server is optional in SAP EP 6.0) and to the database with SSL. Depending on the database driver, you can also secure the connection between the portal server and the database with SSL (SAP EP 5.0 and SAP EP 6.0).

11.4.1 Configuration of Microsoft IIS

If you use Microsoft IIS, you can configure support for SSL with the Internet services manager, which you can start with **Start • Settings • Control Panel • Administrative Tools • Internet Services Manager**. Select **Properties** from the context menu of the default Web site and then select the **Directory Security** tab. Next, select **Server Certificate** and follow the instructions of the wizard. You can also generate a key pair here and create a certificate. For SLL-protected communication between the J2EE Engine and Microsoft IIS, you must install an additional ISAPI filter on the IIS. You can find directions in the file system at *<SAP_J2EEngine6.20>\tools\lib\IIS_module\ssl*.

11.4.2 Configuration of the J2EE Engine for SSL

You can also configure the J2EE engine for the use of SSL. The required steps are described in a special publication, *SAP J2EE Engine SSL Installation Guide*, also located at *<SAP_J2EEngine6.20>tools\lib\IIS_module\ssl*. A service of the J2EE Engine generates a key pair and creates a certificate for you. For more information on SSL configuration of the J2EE Engine, visit SAP Service Marketplace with the alias */securityguide*. You'll find the *SAP Enterprise Portal Security Guide* (for SAP EP 5.0 and SAP EP 6.0) and *SAP J2EE Engine Security Guides* for various releases (6.20 and 6.30).

11.5 Authentication

Before users can log on with SSO to the systems integrated into the portal, they must be authenticated for the portal. Authentication can occur in any of the following ways:

Authentication techniques

- User ID and password
- Digital X.509 certificate
- SAP authentication (SAP Web AS or SAP R/3)
- Third-party authentication
  - Windows authentication: (NTLM or HTTP basic authentication) with the domain controller
  - Others: Java Authentication and Authorization Service (JAAS) interface (pluggable JAAS login module)

11.5.1 User ID and Password

During authentication with a user ID and password, the portal server compares the data supplied by users with the values stored in persistent user management (SAP EP 5.0: LDAP directory; SAP EP 6.0: database and LDAP directory, SAP Web AS, or SAP R/3). Basic and form-based authentication are supported. After the logon data passes inspection, the user ID might also be mapped to the SAP user ID (see authentication schema for SAP systems in Section 11.6.1). A user is then issued an SAP logon ticket. If the user data or password does not pass inspection, access to the portal and its resources is denied. Figure 11.3 illustrates the logon process with user ID and password.

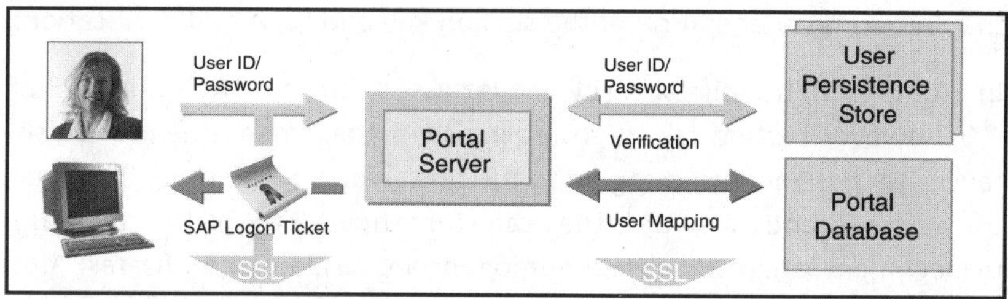

Figure 11.3 Authentication with User ID and Password

11.5.2 X.509—Digital Certificates

X.509 certificates permit implementation of higher standards of security. SAP EP allows certificate-based authentication with the use of the SSL protocol, which uses X.509 certificates. With certificates, passwords are no longer necessary. For client authentication with SSL however, the client needs an X.509 certificate.

Certificate-based authentication requires implementation of a *public key infrastructure (PKI)*. A PKI establishes a trusted connection between two partners. Both partners trust a *certificate authority (CA)* operated by a trust center. The CA issues digital certificates (X.509) that represent the digital identities of the partners. See Section 11.6.5 for information on how you can request a certificate with a certification agency, such as SAP Trust Center Service.

PSE

If you use SECUDE software to secure the client/server environment, you will use a *personal secure environment (PSE)*. Once users log on to the PSE and are authenticated, a digital X.509 certificate is stored in the Web browser. You can use the digital certificate to set up an SSL-encrypted connection with client authentication to the portal server via X.509. In this case, the portal server knows and trusts the client. Use of SSL without X.509 certificates means that the client remains anonymous. SAP Trust Center Service also issues certificates; you can use a server to store them in the portal, even when you're not using a PSE.

Flow of authentication

Authentication flows as following when using X.509 certificates. Along with a request to communicate via SSL, the Web browser sends the Web server its X.509 certificate and a document with random data that it is signed digitally. The Web server verifies whether the issuer of the certificate is trustworthy. If it is, the Web server verifies the digital signature with the public key contained in the user certificate. Checking the digital certificate ensures that the client has the private key that first public key contained in the user certificate. The remaining flow is similar to the way that SSL works (generation of the session key and server authentication).

In SAP EP 5.0, the digital certificate is passed, but not stored. In SAP EP 6.0, however, certificates are stored in user management (the user persistence store). When users log on to the portal for the first time, they must use a user ID and password. They can store their X.509 certificate in user management later on. Subsequent logons are based on certificates. After a successful check of the certificate, the client (and thus the user) is authenticated. The user certificate and *credentials* (cn = Goebela, ou = consulting, and so on) must be mapped to the portal user (arnd.goebel, for example) in a second step. This data is also stored in user management. If a matching portal user is found, the user is granted access to the portal and its resources. Figure 11.4 illustrates the flow of authentication with digital X.509 certificates.

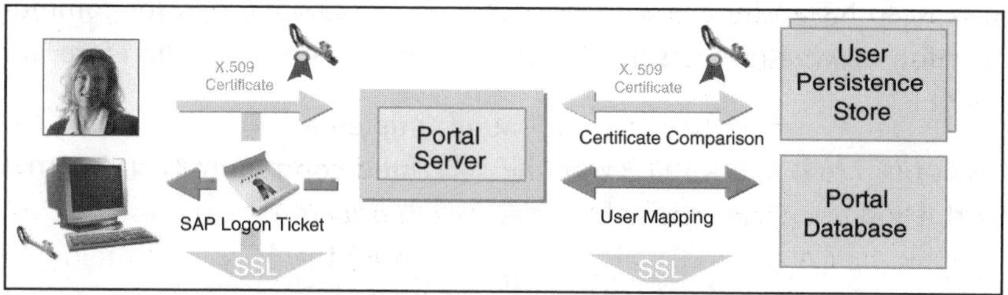

Figure 11.4 Authentication with Digital X.509 Certificates

11.5.3 SAP Authentication

Synchronization of SAP user IDs with a company's corporate LDAP directory means that users can authenticate themselves based on the data in an SAP Web AS or SAP R/3 system. Portal users enter their SAP user IDs and passwords when they first log on to the portal so they can have access to it. The passwords remain in the SAP system and are not written to the LDAP directory. This procedure is required only with SAP Web AS 6.10 and SAP R/3 4.5B/4.6x. If you use a SAP Web AS release that is higher than 6.20, you can configure the portal so that SAP Web AS is used directly as user management. In this case, having access to an LDAP server would not be imperative.

11.5.4 External Authentication

SAP Enterprise Portal supports mechanisms for external authentication of users.

Windows Authentication—NTLM

SAP EP supports the use of Windows Domain Controller and *NT LAN Manager (NTLM)* for authentication. With NTLM, users have already authenticated themselves to a
Windows 2000 or Windows NT Domain Controller. To use this authentication for the portal, configure the portal so that a direct logon to the portal is no longer required. The portal then trusts the users' authentication on the operating system—in this case, the Windows Domain Controller.

NTLM is an authentication process used by Windows NT or Windows 2000 to authenticate connections, such as those between the Web browser and the Web server. With NTLM, two systems handle access to a resource with a challenge–response process. The procedure uses a hashing process that does not require passwords. Because Microsoft has enhanced NTLM for use with HTTP, NTLM can also be used for communication between Microsoft IIS and Internet Explorer, and therefore, for SAP EP.

Use of NTLM is appropriate when SAP EP functions purely as an Internet portal and uses Internet Explorer exclusively.

Figure 11.5 illustrates the logon process when NTLM is used.

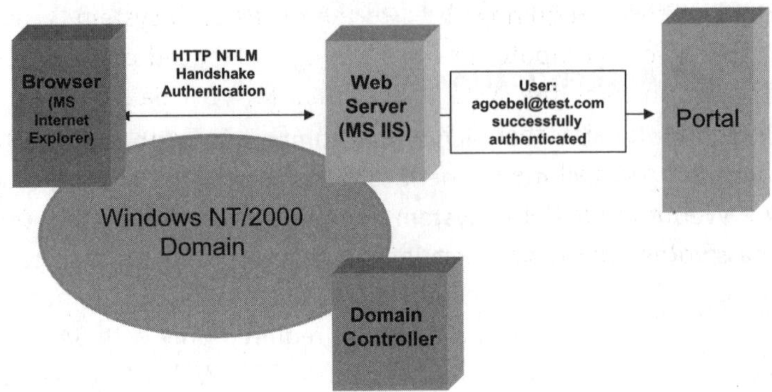

Figure 11.5 Logging on to the Portal with NTLM

Windows Authentication—HTTP Basic Authentication

In addition to NTLM, you can also authenticate users with HTTP basic authentication. You can select this approach when SAP EP is used as an extranet as well as an Internet portal.

Web Access Management Products

Web Access Management (WAM) Products can be used to grant users access to e-business Web sites. Users must authenticate themselves to the WAM product. The HTTP header data then sends the user ID to the portal server with an indication that the user has already been authenticated. The portal server compares the user ID it receives with the stored profile: if they agree, it grants access to the portal. Certified SAP partners offer WAM products. SAP EP 6.0 SP1 includes delivery of a generic module you can use to integrate a WAM product with HTTP header variables. No certification is required to use this solution.

JAAS Interface

The *Java Authentication and Authorization Service (JAAS)* is a standard defined by Sun Microsystems. SAP EP supports the external authentication methods with an *application program interface (API)* based on the

JAAS standard. The procedure is similar to that with WAM products. After a successful check by an external server, the user is logged on to the portal. For more information on the JAAS standard, visit *http://java.sun.com/products/jaas*.

11.6 Single Sign-On

Single Sign-On (SSO) allows portal users to work on several systems simultaneously, without requiring them to log on to each system. Once you have started your computer in the morning and logged on to the portal, you can log on to all the systems you need for your daily work without requiring additional authentication. You need only your user name and password to access all the required systems, assuming that you're authorized to use them or the portal administrator has granted you access to them. Security in the systems is still guaranteed.

Less administrative effort

The advantages of SSO are readily apparent. When complex system landscapes involve a countless users, administrators often have to reset passwords several times a day. Highly secured production systems also require users to change passwords at regular intervals. But users often forget their passwords and have to approach user administrators in the company to reset their passwords, which results in increased administrative and support costs. Users are often overwhelmed with the number of passwords they must remember, so they simply write them down in insecure locations or select the same password for all systems. Both cases lead to security risks. The use of SSO not only reduces administrative and support costs, but also significantly increases security in the system infrastructure.

SSO represents a key function for SAP EP. With SAP EP, SSO not only allows automatic logon to SAP component systems, but also to external systems and Internet applications, such as Web mail, Yahoo! stock portfolios, and many other applications and Web services.

Three variants of SSO in the portal

You can use any one of three variants of SSO with the portal. The variants differ in their security requirements and in the back-end support required for SSO. The following variants are available:

- SSO with SAP logon ticket
- SSO with user ID and password
- SSO with X.509 certificate

None of the three variants require a special logon to the connected systems after successful authentication in the portal. The difference between

SSO with SAP logon tickets and SSO with user ID and password is that the former uses secure SAP logon tickets and the latter transfers the logon data directly in the URL or in the body. We strongly recommend SSL encryption for both procedures. Otherwise, the user data and passwords are transmitted in clear text and can be viewed by third parties. SAP logon tickets also need the security of SSL encryption to avoid any kind of misuse. SSO with user ID and password stores the passwords in the database in encrypted form (triple DES algorithm).

When you use SSO with X.509 certificates, you must distinguish between a direct connection of the user with the SAP system and a connection that involves the portal server. If an SAP system is addressed directly from the Web browser over ITS, it can log on the user based on a certificate. In this case, no additional configuration in the portal is needed. But if users access an SAP system from an iView or a portal component, the certificate and the digital signature must be redirected from the Web browser to the portal server and from the portal server to the SAP system. SAP EP 5.0 SP5 (with patch level 1) supports this procedure as long as the J2EE Engine 6.20 (with patch level 10) or higher is used. For configuration, you also need the *Enabling SSL for the SAP J2EE Engine* and the previously mentioned *SAP Enterprise Portal Security Guide* documents. You can find both in SAP Service Marketplace under alias */epinstall* (**EP 5.0 SP5 Roadmap · Installation, Upgrades & Patches SP5**). Generally, however, the portal uses SAP logon tickets for SSO.

Figure 11.6 provides an overview of the authentication methods for SAP EP and both SSO variants for access to applications.

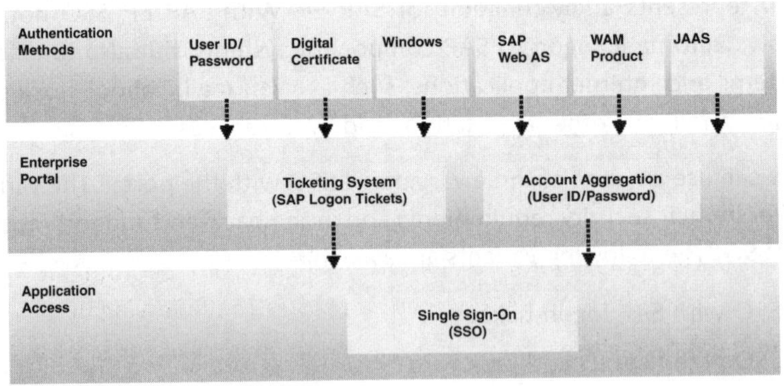

Figure 11.6 Authentication and Single Sign-On with SAP Enterprise Portal

11.6.1 Single Sign-On and SAP Systems

Authentication schema

SAP logon tickets

SAP logon tickets represent users' logon data (credentials). After a successful initial logon, the portal server issues logon tickets to users. The logon ticket is stored as a non-persistent cookie in the client browser; it is transmitted to the server that offers the required application each time the client issues a request to the server.

Figure 11.7 illustrates the process of issuing logon tickets.

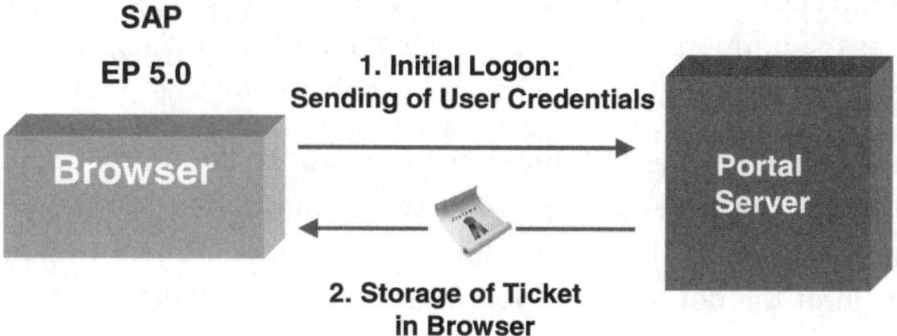

Figure 11.7 Issuing Logon Tickets by the Portal Server

SAP systems then use the logon ticket to log portal users on to the system without additional authentication, as shown in Figure 11.8.

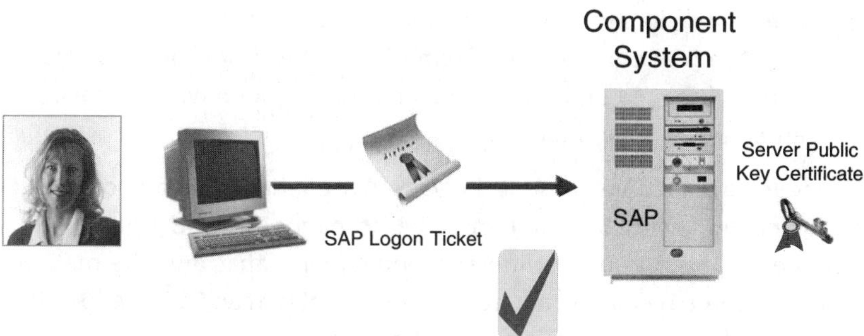

Figure 11.8 Logging on to an SAP Component System with an SAP Logon Ticket

Contents of logon tickets

SSO tickets contain information on the logged-on user, but they don't contain passwords. An SAP logon ticket stores the following information:

- User ID of the portal user and, optionally, the mapped SAP user ID (if it differs from the portal user ID). For example: *arnd.goebel* as the portal user and *Goebela* as the SAP user
- Validity period

- Information that identifies the issuing system (PL3, for example)
- Digital signature of the portal server
- Authentication schema (from SAP EP 6.0)

Flow

Technically, the use of SSO flows as follows in the standard case:

1. If the portal server is started for the first time or has no certificate, the portal engine generates a cryptographic key pair. The private key is used to generate the logon ticket. If the certificate keystore manager is not changed, the certificate always remains the same.
2. If a portal user logs on to the portal successfully, the portal server issues the user a logon ticket. The ticket is stored in the client browser as a non-persistent cookie.
3. At each access from the Web browser to an SAP system in the same domain, the logon ticket and the request are transmitted to the SAP component system. If the SAP component system is located outside the domain of the portal server, you must note some domain restrictions, which are treated below.
4. The SAP component system checks the validity of the logon ticket by verifying the digital signature of the portal server and the expiration date of the logon ticket. To do so, it uses the portal server's public key, which is part of the digital certificate.
5. If the digital signature is verified and the logon ticket is valid, the user ID for the SAP component system is extracted from the logon ticket. The user is logged on to the SAP component system without having to reenter a user ID and password.

SSO scenarios

The following sections present the various scenarios available to use SSO in connection with SAP systems. The scenarios depend upon various parameters. Each also has different requirements that must be met. For example, some scenarios require that the user IDs of an SSO user be identical in all the SAP systems accessed with SSO.

Figure 11.9 provides an overview of all the scenarios. The following sections explore individual scenarios in detail.

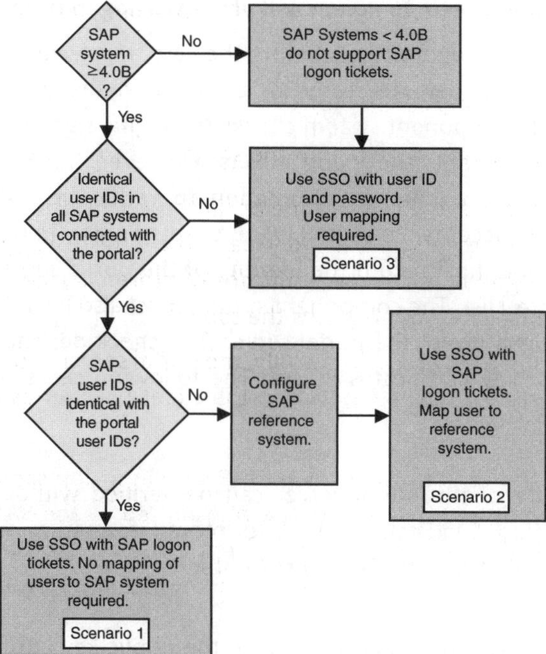

Figure 11.9 Use of Various Scenarios with SSO

Scenario 1: SSO with Logon Tickets and Without User Mapping

Standard scenario

In the scenario, the portal users must have the same user ID in all the SAP systems they address with SAP logon tickets. If the SAP user IDs are identical to the portal user IDs, user mapping is unnecessary. This situation is standard.

Normally, the portal server generates and signs SAP logon tickets for users. In principle therefore, no additional setting are required. Small adjustments are needed only in special cases.

- **Configuration of the portal server for SSO with SAP logon tickets**

  Various settings are required regardless of who signed the SAP logon tickets.

  If the portal server has a public certificate signed by the *SAP Trust Center Service (TCS)*, add the following line to *<SAP_J2EEngine6.20>\alone\services\servlet_jsp\work\jspTemp\irj\root\WEB-INF\plugins\portal\services\usermanagement\data\usermanagement.properties*:

```
login.ticket_include_cert=1
```

- **Configuration of the SAP system to accept and verify SAP logon tickets**

  The portal server signs SAP logon tickets before they are transferred to the portal user or before they are stored as a cookie in the user's browser. After the SAP component system checks the digital signature of the logon tickets, it accepts the logon tickets. However, the SAP component system needs additional information to verify the SAP logon tickets. To ensure acceptance of SAP logon tickets only from the issuing portal server, you must record the identity of the portal server in the SSO access control list. The component system must also be able to check the digital signature of the portal server. The check depends on the type of public key certificates in use. The following can sign public key certificates:

  - SAP Trust Center:
    The digital signature of the portal server can be verified without additional information. See Section 11.6.5 for more information on requesting a certificate from the SAP Trust Center.
  - The portal itself:
    The SAP component system requires access to the public key information of the portal server. The information must be recorded in the certificate list of the component system.
  - Another trust center (TrustTC or VeriSign) or the company:
    A public key infrastructure is required here.

- **Requirements for SSO with an SAP component system**

  - The portal plug-in that corresponds to the release of SAP EP must be installed on the component system.
  - The required kernel patches have been downloaded to the component system (up to SAP R/3 4.6C. Note 177895 provides additional information. You might have to download additional patches because of SAP patches.
  - The *SAP Security Library* (SAP SecuLib) must be installed on all application servers of the SAP component system. You can download the latest version from SAP Service Marketplace at *http://service.sap.com/swdc* (**Download · SAP Cryptographic Software**).

For SAP component systems higher that SAP R/3 4.6C, you can use transaction STRUSTSSO2 for the step given above. This chapter provides additional details below.

If you want to use more that one portal server in the same access control list, you must configure the portal server separately. This chapter provides more details below.

Note

Scenario 2: SSO with Logon Tickets and User Mapping

Different user IDs

Scenario 1 represents the standard situation, in which the portal user IDs and the user IDs for the SAP systems are identical for every user. However, some limited exceptions exist in which the portal user ID differs from the SAP user ID and that require user mapping. For this scenario, however, all the user IDs in all SAP systems must be identical. You can then define an SAP reference system and map the user ID of each portal user to the user ID of the reference system. In this scenario, the following steps are required:

1. Define an SAP R/3 reference system (ZBV, for example).
2. Configure the portal server for SSO with SAP logon tickets in the *usermanagement.properties* file, as described above.
3. Configure the SAP system to accept and verify SAP logon tickets. Use Transaction STRUSTSSO2 as described below.
4. Have users map their own portal user ID to the user ID of the SAP reference system.

Scenario 3: SSO with User ID, Password, and User Mapping

SAP R/3 4.0B and below

You must select this scenario if you use an SAP component system below SAP R/3 4.0B or if the users' IDs in the SAP component systems differ from each other. The portal configuration option requires that you map the portal user ID to the user ID of each SAP component system. To do so, you must select the appropriate system in the user settings of each portal user and enter the user ID and password for each system. The same procedure is required for non-SAP systems that don't support SAP logon tickets for SSO.

11.6.2 Configuration of the Systems

To call transactions in SAP component systems from SAP EP while using SSO and SAP logon tickets, you must configure the SAP components systems (SAP R/3 4.0B and higher) accordingly. The component system must accept SSO logon tickets and verify the digital signature of the portal server. Only when the portal can rely on the system that issued the requests can users log on to the system and process their requests. The following describes the steps that you must take, listed by keyword.

Profile Parameter

Both of the following profile parameters must be set for each instance profile:

```
login/accept_sso2_ticket = 1
login/create_sso2_ticket = 0
```

ITS Service Parameters

For access with SAP ITS, you must set the following parameters in service file *global.srvc* on each ITS server of the component system:

Parameter	Value	Description
~login	(space)	No user because of the logon ticket.
~password	(space)	No password because of the logon ticket.
~mysapcomusesso2cookie	1	Allows users to log on to an SAP system with an existing SAP logon ticket.

Configuration of the SAP System

SAP R/3 systems at or above SAP R/3 4.6C must be configured with Transaction STRUSTSSO2:

1. Copy the *verify.der* portal certificate from *<SAP_J2EEngine6.20>\alone\services\servlet_jsp\work\jspTemp\irj\root\WEB-INF\plugins\portal\services\usermanagement\data* into your *\temp* directory.
2. Start Transaction STRUSTSSO2 and upload the certificate from the *\temp* directory to your SAP R/3 system.
3. Select **Add to List of Certificates.**
4. Then, select **Add to ACL.**
5. Enter WP3 and 000 for **WPS client,** but only when a single portal accesses this SAP R/3 system. The alternate procedure is described below.
6. Save your entries.

The entries are displayed in the system PSE and in the SSO access control list.

Reference system

If the user IDs in your portal differ from those in the SAP systems, but if all user IDs for a user are identical in the SAP systems, you must specify a reference system for log on. Figure 11.10 illustrates this condition.

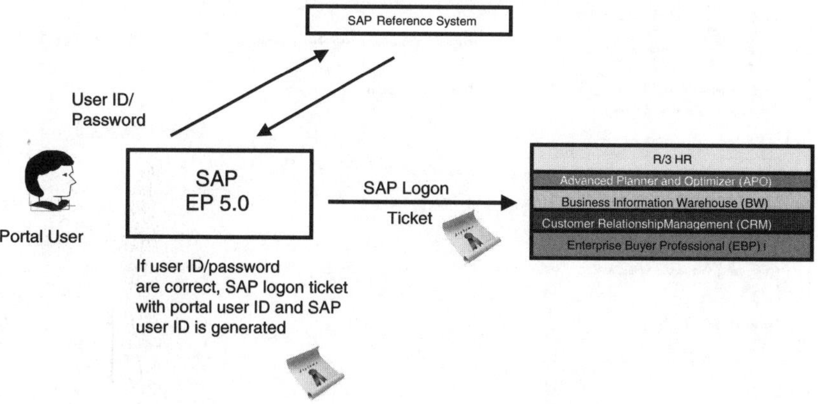

Figure 11.10 Use of an SAP Reference System

Maintenance of the system file

The procedure to maintain the system landscape file differs in SAP EP 5.0 and SAP EP 6.0. In SAP EP 6.0, maintenance occurs with a graphical interface. The following explains the instructions for SAP EP 5.0:

1. First copy file *<SAP_J2EEngine6.20>\alone\services\servlet_jsp\work\jspTemp\irj\root\WEB-INF\plugins\portal\services\landscape\xml\Systems.xml* into your *\temp* directory. Open the file and insert the following two attributes into your SAP system to configure it as a reference system:

```
<System name="EBP">
...
<Attributes>
   <pcd:Attribute name="UserMappingType" value="user"/>
   <pcd:Attribute name="r3usernamereference" value="1"/>
</Attributes>
```

2. Follow menu path **System Configuration • System Landscape** to upload the file into your portal (see Figure 11.11).
3. All users must then use the personalization function (**Personalize • Portal**) to enter their user ID for the SAP R/3 reference system. Select the reference system in personalization and enter your user ID. Users, not administrators, should perform this task because the end users' passwords are required in the reference system.

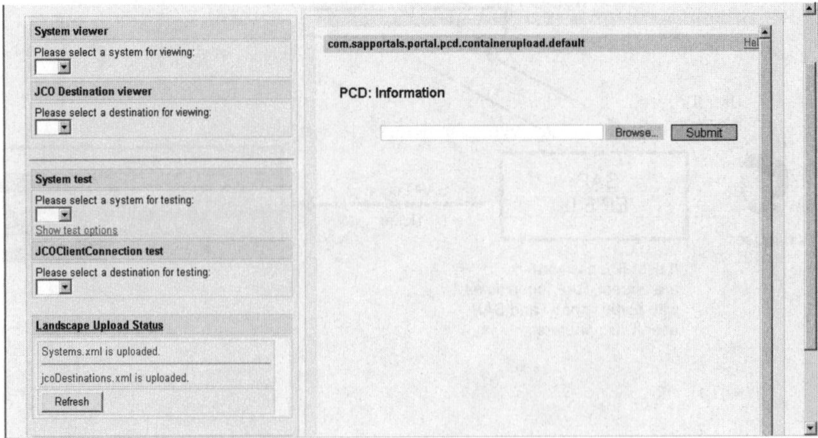

Figure 11.11 Modifying and Uploading the System Landscape Files

Configuration of SSO with the Use of NTLM

Proceed as follows to configure SSO with the use of NTLM:

1. Select **System Configuration · User Management Configuration** in the portal. Under **General Settings** create a user configuration that differs from the **default** configuration or you face the prospect of losing all access to the portal. You can always recreate the **default** configuration if something goes wrong.
2. Select **Authentication Server** and **User Authentication Type** "NT.". Check **Disregard domain in user name**.
3. Select **Apply** and start the J2EE Engine.
4. To configure the default Web page of the IIS, select **Start · Program · Administrative Tools · Internet Services Manager** and then **Default Web page**. Use the context menu to select **HTTP Keep-Alives Enabled**.
5. From the **Directory Security** tab, select **Anonymous Access and Authentication control · Edit** and then **Integrated Windows Authentication**.
6. Repeat this step for each SAP EP Web server instance.
7. Start the IIS.
8. In Internet Explorer, select **Internet Options · Security · Internet Sites · Custom Level** and then **Automatic Logon with current username and password**.

SSO Access to an SAP R/3 System from Several Portals

When you add a portal to the access control list of SAP R/3, a system ID, client, and the certificate normally identify the portal. If two portals are connected to an SAP R/3 system, the data for each portal must be identical.

To configure the portal correctly, you must make the following settings in at least one portal:

1. Stop the J2EE Engine.
2. Open the *<SAP_J2EEngine6.20>\alone\services\servlet_jsp\work\jspTemp\irj\root\WEB-INF\plugins\portal\services\usermanagement\data\usermanagement.properties* file.
3. Enter any combination of three letters (except "WP3") for the `login.ticket_issuer` parameter.
4. Enter a three-character string (except "000") for `login.ticket_client`.
5. Enter the **distinguished name**, such as "CN=NP5," "OU=Americas," "O=myorg.com," or "C=US." This value must correspond to the issuer of the certificate in X.509.
6. Delete the files that begin with *ticketKeyStore* and *verify* in the *<SAP_J2EEngine6.20>\alone\services\servlet_jsp\work\jspTemp\irj\root\WEB-INF\plugins\portal\services\usermanagement\data* directory.
7. Start the J2EE Engine.

You have now learned how SSO functions with the portal and how to configure the portal so that you can use SSO.

11.6.3 Single Sign-On and Non-SAP Systems

You can also connect to external systems (non-SAP systems) with SSO. You must decide whether the non-SAP systems can use SAP logon tickets. Typically, the applications will be unable to understand logon tickets. That's why you can use the "SSO with user ID and password" scenario. The procedure is similar to Scenario 3, *SSO with user ID, password, and user mapping*. You must specify a data source for non-SAP systems. The data source contains the information (particularly the URL) on how to address the target system and what authentication method is being used. You can map portal user data to user IDs in the target system with the **User Mapping** button. SSL is absolutely necessary here because without it, the user data would be transmitted without protection.

11.6.4 Domain Restrictions

Some domain restrictions can occur when setting up SSO with SAP logon tickets. The following describes the restrictions and how they can be overcome.

Various domains

In one possible scenario, SAP EP might be located in one domain, but some SAP component systems might be located within the same domain (*mycompany.com*) and others might be located in another domain (*mycompany.biz*). SAP logon tickets are cookies and are transmitted only within the domains or subdomains in which the logon ticket was issued. For example, the logon tickets would be sent to *mycompany.com* and all **.mycompany.com* subdomains, but not to other domains (see Figure 11.12).

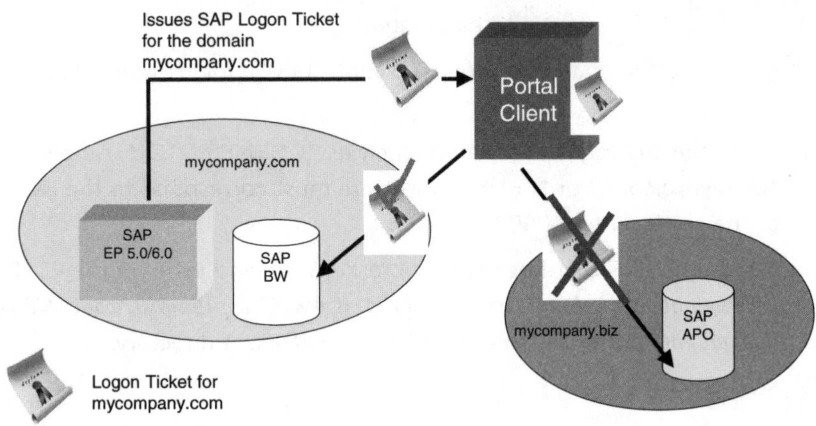

Figure 11.12 Domain Restrictions with SSO When Using SAP Logon Tickets

Working around the restrictions

Because SAP logon tickets are valid only for the domain in which the portal operates, the Web browser that holds the ticket at any given moment will not transmit it to other domains. This restriction arises from general Internet technologies. Because the SAP component system is located in another domain, the portal user cannot log on to it; the logon ticket would never get to it. You can solve the problem by changing a property file on the portal server. The file must record entries for the domains in which the SAP component systems are located. You must then install either an IIS with a Web server filter or an *iView runtime for Java (IRJ)* on the receiving server that resides outside the domain of the portal. With this setup, the client or portal server can transmit a request and an SAP logon ticket issued for its domain to Web servers (or an IRJ) in other domains. The request informs the Web server (or IRJ) that an SAP logon ticket is to be issued for the external domain. The Web server filter (or IRJ) issues an SAP logon ticket for its domain and copies the portal user name into the new SAP logon ticket. The ticket, which is now valid for external domains, is then stored in the user's Web browser along with the logon ticket that is valid for the portal server's domain. The portal user can now address SAP component systems in other domains, as illustrated in Figure 11.13.

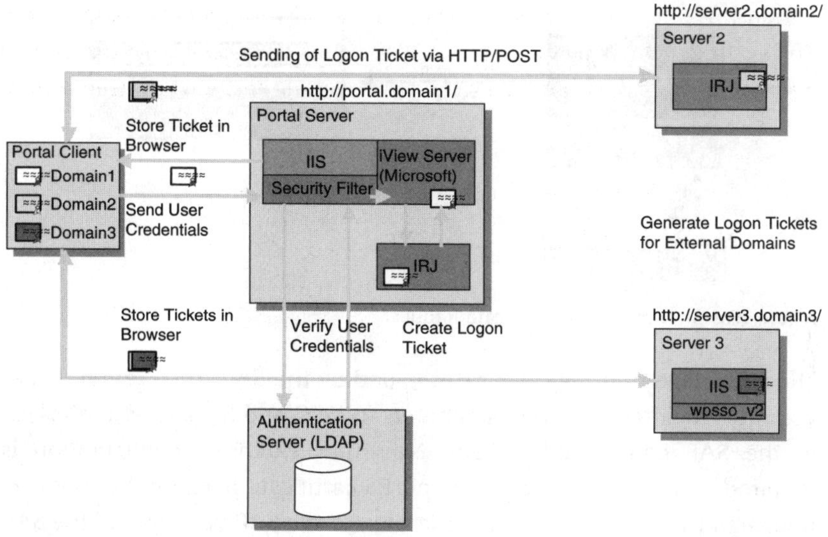

Figure 11.13 Using SAP Logon Tickets Beyond the Limits of a Domain

11.6.5 Requesting Portal Certificates

In the standard case, the portal server generates and signs its own certificate and uses it to sign SAP logon tickets. If you want to request a certificate signed by the SAP Trust Center Service that you can use to sign SAP logon tickets or to request client certificates, you must generate a certificate request and transmit it to the SAP Trust Center.

You then import the response from the SAP Trust Center, which is in binary code, into the keystore of the portal server.

Flow of requesting a certificate

The following workflow explains the procedure (see Figure 11.14):

1. The keystore manager (delivered with the portal) creates a data block. You create an OSS message in the BC-SEC component in an SAP OSS system and append the data block as an attachment.

2. The SAP Trust Center Service responds by sending you a message that contains the server certificate and the root certificate of the SAP Trust Center.
3. Upload this data block (in binary form) into the portal with the keystore manager.
4. The portal now has a public key certificate signed by the SAP Trust Center. It can now use the corresponding private key to digitally sign SAP logon tickets for use with SSO in SAP EP.

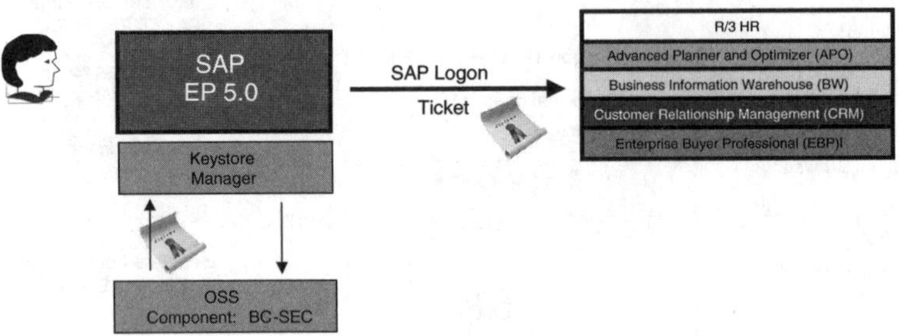

Figure 11.14 Transmitting a Certificate Request

No additional configuration

The advantage of using certificates issued by the SAP Trust Center is that you must maintain only the parameters for SSO and the access control list in the SAP component system. No other extensive configuration is required and you don't have to import a certificate because the root certificate of the SAP Trust Centers is known to the SAP systems and the SAP component systems trust the center.

You can also request a certificate from an external supplier—the same advantages apply.

If you use your own PKI, you can also use certificates that you have issued yourself.

11.6.6 Risks with SAP Logon Tickets and User IDs and Passwords Without SSL

A number of risks are involved with the use of SAP logon tickets:

- The use of SSL should protect SAP Logon tickets from unauthorized parties who can intercept the logon tickets and create unauthorized access to SAP systems. When logon tickets are intercepted, a danger exists that the person who intercepted them can use the roles and authorization of the tickets' owners to access SAP systems. This problem can occur because the logon ticket stores the user ID of the owner.

▶ In addition, an increased risk exists when using SSO with user ID and password but without SSL. To protect against external access to the logon data, we strongly recommend using SSL. It is indispensable for a secure environment.

11.7 User Management, Roles, and Authorizations

Companies have many databases and directories that store user information. Consistent user management must combine these locations. SAP EP allows you to use the user management of your existing infrastructure for the portal without having to change it because the portal receives access to the required user data, such as an existing corporate LDAP directory, a database, or an SAP system. The portal handles central user management and saves you administrative work: you can administer user management from one location. Figure 11.15 illustrates the architecture of user management.

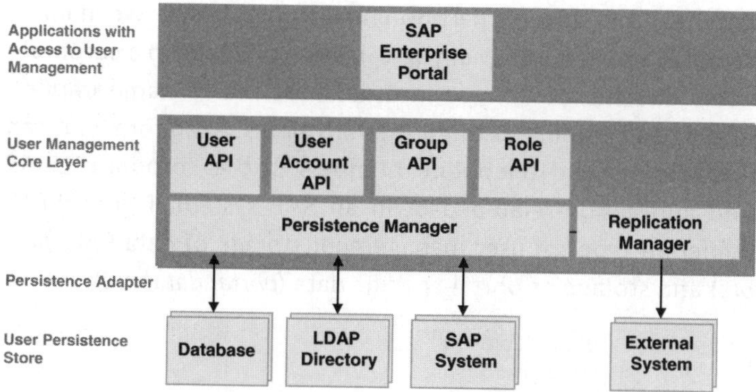

Figure 11.15 User Management Architecture

11.7.1 Persistence of User Data

Persistence adapters

SAP EP allows the transfer of existing user databases into the system infrastructure with the assistance of *persistence adapters*. You can use persistence adapters to read and write data to and from various data sources. For example, you can read user data from a corporate LDAP directory and then store it in a database. Persistence adapters are available for databases, LDAP directories, and SAP Web AS. You can find details on the LDAP servers and databases supported by the adapters in the product availability matrix in SAP Service Marketplace at *http://service.sap.com/pam*. Figure 11.16 shows an overview of the persistence of user data.

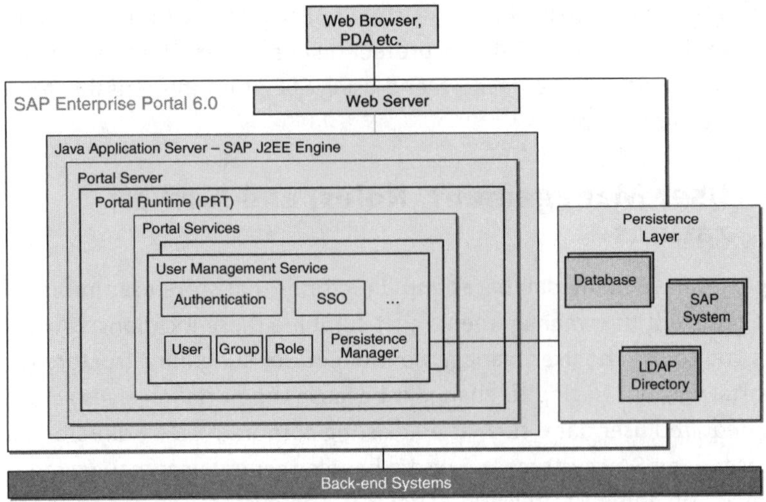

Figure 11.16 Persistence of User Data

Partitioning user data

The portal also allows partitioning of user data. You can store user data by users or attributes. User-specific partitioning distinguishes between internal and external users. For example, you can store one type in a corporate LDAP directory and the other type in a database. As its name implies, attribute-specific partitioning distinguishes attributes. Therefore, you can store email addresses and telephone numbers in the corporate LDAP directory and application-related data in an SAP system. Figure 11.17 shows the different types of user management storage of data (*user persistence store*) and storage of portal-specific data (*portal database*).

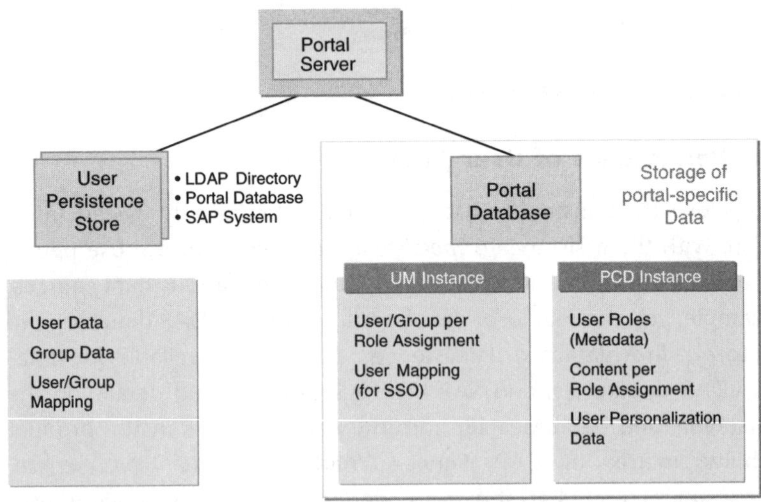

Figure 11.17 User Management in Various Databases and Directories

User data can also be replicated. To do so, the replication manager creates an XML document with the user data and transmits it to external applications that then process it further to use the user database for SAP CRM, for example. Replication occurs automatically. Replication is currently supported for user data for SAP Basis 4.6D and SAP Web AS 6.10.

Replicating user data

If you use SAP Central User Administration (CUA), you can synchronize the CUA and the corporate LDAP directory.

SAP Central User Administration

11.7.2 Roles and Authorizations

Chapter 9 introduced the role concept in the portal with iViews. Because roles are a central element of security, we will revisit that subject here. Figure 11.18 can help you to better understand the topic. The graphic shows portal navigation and role hierarchy in SAP EP 5.0 (see Chapter 8 for information on SAP EP 6.0). As you have already seen, SAP EP can utilize user data from existing LDAP directories, SAP systems, and databases. If you don't yet employ user management, you must set it up and can use the portal LDAP directory in SAP EP 5.0 to help. SAP EP 6.0 has a user management engine that enables more complex structures for managing and partitioning user data. You can also assign users to groups in a flat or multilevel hierarchy.

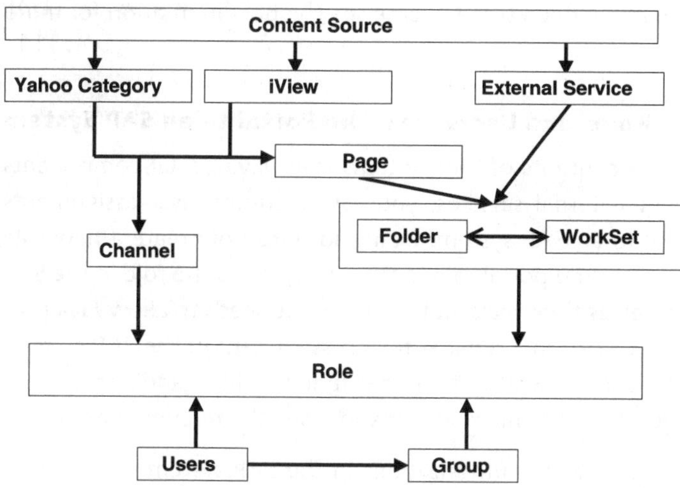

Figure 11.18 Portal Navigation and Role Hierarchy

You can assign users and groups to portal roles in the portal. With roles, portal users and members of groups receive access to the portal's resources, which can include folders, worksets, pages, roles, iViews, and channels. See Chapter 8 on the specifics and characteristics of SAP EP 5.0

Assignment to portal roles

and SAP EP 6.0. SAP EP 5.0 uses indirect assignment; SAP EP 6.0 uses direct assignment. For example, a role can be assigned directly in SAP EP 6.0 but not in SAP EP 5.0. Except for iViews, these objects can contain other objects. Therefore, roles are really a collection of information and services, which determine the information that a portal user can access and the actions that a portal user can trigger. A role defines navigation in the portal—what can be called and what cannot be called. Roles are stored in the portal content directory (PCD).

Master iViews are portal components that you learned about in Chapter 8 and Chapter 9. If you assign master iViews to a role, the users assigned to the role have authorization to use this component.

You maintain roles with the role administrator. For information on the maintenance of roles, see the portal documentation at *http://help.sap.com* (*Administration, Developer and End User Documentation*).

Role Migration from SAP Systems into the Portal

You don't have to create new roles for portal users who access an SAP system. You can use a tool in the portal to import roles from an SAP system into the portal. The content of individual and collective roles remains the same. As noted, the authorizations remain in the SAP system and continue to be maintained there. Please see the documentation for more information.

Distributing Roles and Users from the Portal to an SAP System

If you access the contents of SAP systems from Java portal components (Java iViews) or external services, you can distribute user assignments from the portal to an SAP system. Doing so does not create a new role that corresponds to the portal role in the SAP system. The role in the SAP system then receives the special authorizations it needs to allow Java portal components or external services to access content in the SAP system. Both the portal and the SAP system offer functionalities and transactions for this configuration. For more information, see the documentation.

Authorizations

You should note that the authorizations in the SAP system remain constant and are checked there. The portal merely enables access. Therefore, it's entirely possible for a user to have access authorization to an SAP system from the portal, but not have the required authorization in the target system. That's why you must always look at both sides: the role in the portal and the authorization in the target system.

11.7.3 Authorization Model for PortalComponent/Services

SAP EP allows you to do more than assign authorizations at the role and user level. Because Java iViews can be called directly with the entry of the portal runtime URL (PortalComponents)—or with Web services with SOAP (PortalServices)—you must also monitor this access. As of SAP EP 6.0, you can use two concepts to do so:

- Security zones
- Safety level

Security Zones

Security levels

Security zones (see Figure 11.19) enable abstracting the various security levels for PortalComponents and PortalServices at runtime. You can use the portal application descriptor (see Chapter 9 for information on the deployment descriptor) and a character string to set the security zone in the configuration area. Ensure that you adhere to the naming convention. This is how you define a logical catalog of specific portal objects. The portal administrator assigns the users, groups, and roles to the zones with ACLs. The ACLs set the authorization required to access specific zones. The following naming convention applies:

{Namespace of the business application}/{Safety level}/{Portal application}

Specification of a portal application is optional. It allows the portal administrator to assign authorizations separately at the portal application level.

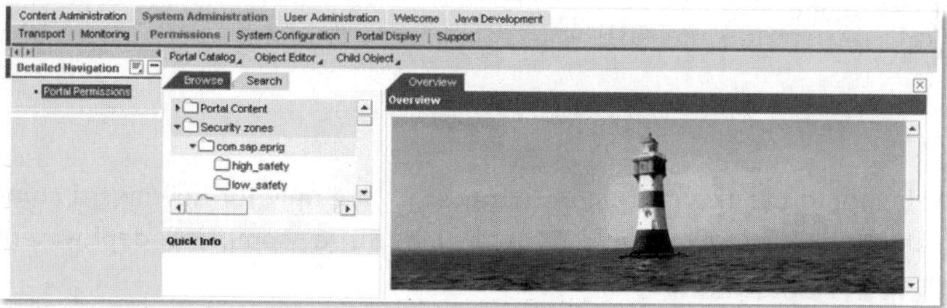

Figure 11.19 Security Zones

Safety Level

You can define various safety levels within a security zone and assign different authorizations to each level. You use a character string to set the safety level and the security zone: be sure to adhere to the naming convention or naming recommendation.

Recommendation The SAP recommendation for names is as follows:

Safety Level	Description
HIGH_SAFETY	Administrator rights required
MEDIUM_SAFETY	Specific role required (content_admin, for example)
LOW_SAFETY	User must be authenticated
NO_SAFETY	Allow anonymous access

You set the security level in the deployment descriptor of the portal component as follows:

```
<component-config>
   <property name="SecurityZone"
      value="com.sap.portal/high_safety"/>
   </property>
</component-config>
```

The entry is similar for portal services in the `<service-config>` area:

```
<services>
...
<service-config> ...
   <property name="SecurityZone"
      value="com.sap.portal/high_safety"/>
   </property>
</service-config>
...
</services>
```

You should use the `<AuthRequirement>` tag only for downward compatibility. The following sample listing for a complete deployment descriptor does not do so.

```
<?xml version="1.0" encoding="iso-8859-1"?>
<application alias="myportalapp">
  <application-config>
    <property name="ClassLoadingPolicy" value="5.0"/>
    <property name="DeploymentPolicy" value="5.0" />
    <property name="AuthenticationPolicy" value="5.0" />
```

```
  </application-config>
  <services/>
  <components>
    <component name="MyTest">
      <component-config>
        <property name="ClassName"
          value="com.sap.test.MyTestComponent" />
        <property name="SecurityZone"
          value="com.sap.portal.ep50/ep50_safety" />
      </component-config>
    <component-profile/>
    </component>
  </components>
</application>
```

11.8 Digital Signatures

The international economy requires legal security for electronic transactions. For example, in 1997 the United States Food and Drug Administration (FDA) issued a regulation 21 CFR Part 11 (Code of Federal Regulations Electronic Records) entitled "Electronic Records and Electronic Signatures." The regulations provide guidance for the use of electronic records and electronic signatures in the biotechnology, pharmaceutical, medical devices, radiological health, food, cosmetics, and veterinary medicine fields.

11.8.1 What Are Digital Signatures?

Electronic signature

An electronic signature is a computer data compilation of any symbol or series of symbols executed, adopted, or authorized by an individual to be the legally binding equivalent to the individual's handwritten signature.

Digital signature

A digital signature is an electronic signature based on cryptographic methods of originator authentication, computed by a set of rules and a set of parameters such that the identity of the signer and the integrity of the data can be verified.

11.8.2 Procedure for Using Digital Signatures

Use of a digital signature requires at least two persons or institutions (*A* and *B* in the following example) and a certification authority (CA).

A and *B* want to exchange an important document electronically. *A* and *B* don't know each other and therefore don't (yet) trust each other. To sign a document electronically, *A* needs a certificate. A certification authority—a trustworthy institution—checks the identity of *A* and issues a certificate to *A*. The certificate can be stored on a SmartCard or on a SmartToken. The certificate contains *A's* certified *public key*). Both *A* and *B* trust the CA.

Signing process

A now signs the document to be sent with the private key issued by the CA. Doing so maps a checksum (hash value) to the document. The hash value is transferred with a card reader to *A's* SmartCard, where it is signed digitally with the *private key*. The signing process uses the public key algorithm and the private key to represent the hash value on the document. The operation results in a signature value along with the document and the certificate that contains *A's* public key that is then sent to *B*. It's important that the private key never leave the SmartCard. The private key is written to the SmartCard or the SmartToken by the CA when it issues the private key, the internal trust center, or the user. This process is called *personalization*. The private key cannot be downloaded from the card, but it can be deleted or overwritten.

Verification process

Upon receipt of the document, *B* also uses the cryptographic checksum of the document and calculates a hash value. Now *B* has *A's* public key, which can be extracted from the certificate. *B* then applies a (different) public key algorithm to the signature value while using the public key, and receives the hash value generated by *A*.

All that remains is a comparison of the checksums or hash values. If they agree, the document has been received without any modifications. If they don't agree, the document is a forgery that has been changed on the way from *A* to *B*.

Checking the CA

In an additional step, the certificate from the CA is inspected and checked to determine whether it has been recalled in the meantime. You can also check on the accreditation of the CA. This procedure can occur with varied methods that depend on the security requirements in effect in the company. For more information, see the subsection on mass signatures in Section 11.8.6.

11.8.3 Types of Signatures

Various types of signatures are common, including the following:

- PKCS#7
- S/MIME
- XML signature

PKCS#7

Public key cryptography standards (PKCS) are specifications developed by RSA Security (*http://www.rsa.com*) against the background of secure information exchange over the Internet. PKCS#7 stands for the *cryptographic message syntax standard*, which sets the general syntax or a format for encrypted and signed messages. PKCS#7 is a precondition for S/MIME.

S/MIME

Secure multipurpose Internet mail extension (S/MIME) uses PKCS#7 to secure email. The message and any attachments are transmitted in their entirety in a PKCS#7 packet.

XML signature

With an XML signature, one XML document stores the document to be signed and the signed hash value. The document can contain the XML signature, the XML signature can include the document, or the XML signature can be stored separately with the XML document.

The advantage of an XML signature over S/MIME and PKCS#7 is that XML can sign only individual parts of a document. PKCS#7 always signs the entire document; S/MIME signs the entire email. An additional problem with S/MIME and PKCS#7 is that they don't enable you to view the signed documents. PKCS#7 is not legible: it consists of binary code. XML offers legible characters and can be enhanced with *Extensible Style Language (XSL)*. If the style sheet is also signed, the document and its formatting can be viewed in any browser. In this way, the signature doesn't encapsulate the document: the document and the stylesheet are stored in separate branches of the XML document—separately from the signature.

SAP support

SAP uses Java components to support PKCS#7, S/MIME, and XML signature. ABAP stack supports only PKCS#7.

11.8.4 Legal Foundations

Most of the laws began with the Utah Digital Signature Act of 1995, which focused on a narrow set of Digital Signature technologies based on public key infrastructure (PKI). California realized that focusing on specific technologies in law was pointless because technology advances so quickly. Therefore, a technology-neutral approach was adopted, which became the foundation of the US E-Sign Act.

In order to avoid each American state from having conflicting laws, the National Conference of Commissioners on Uniform State Laws (NCCUSL) developed the Uniform Electronic Transactions Act (UETA), while the European Union proposed its Directive on a Common Framework for Electronic Signatures for the European Union.

In the United States, all of these incompatible state laws were superseded by the Electronic Signatures in Global and National Commerce Act (US E-Sign Act), which was signed into law in 2000. It is technology-neutral, provided certain disclosures are made available and the basic requirements of Electronic Signatures are adhered to.

By *electronic signature*, we mean an electronic sound, symbol, or process that is attached to or logically associated with a contract or other record, and executed or adopted by a person with the intent to sign the record.

However, for such an electronic *symbol* to be legally binding, it is important that this symbol can provide authentication of the party who created it, ensure that what was signed cannot be altered, confirm that the party understands that by creating the symbol, the said party has willingly signed and can keep an original of the data and his or her electronic signature for his or her own records.

Can anything be signed electronically?

Not everything can be signed electronically. The E-Sign Act specifically forbids the electronic signing of certain documents such as wills, testamentary trusts, papers pertaining to adoption or divorce, court orders, termination of utilities, repossession, foreclosure, eviction, cancellation of life insurance, product recalls, and documents associated with the transportation of hazardous materials.

11.8.5 Potential Cost Savings

According to a study on the potential cost savings by the EU commission, a traditional invoice costs an average of € 1.40[1]. The cost of an invoice sent electronically averages about € 0.40 and reduces processing time. The difference represents a savings of 72% of today's costs for customers. Because the German government has accepted tax payments for invoices with a digital signature since January 1, 2002, there's no need to send a traditional invoice and the costs can be saved.

1 At the time of writing, € 1.00 equals $ 1.35.

Documents used	Costs	Comment
Traditional invoice	€ 1.40[2]	No SRM/EBP, EBPP or similar system in use
Traditional and electronic invoice	< € 1.40[3]	e-solution (SAP) in use
Electronic invoice only (and digital signature as of 01/01/2002)	€ 0.40[2]	SAP EBPP/EBP (additionally the processing time is reduced)

Table 11.1 Average Costs for an Invoice with and without a Digital Signature

Sample invoice

According to the numbers given above, a midsize or large company that works with 1,000 invoices per day can save the following costs:

1,000 invoices × 220 working days × € 1.40	€ 308,000
./. 1,000 invoices × 220 working days × € 0.40	€ 88,000
Potential cost savings, not including implementation costs	**€ 220,000**
./. Implementation of the solution	€ 27,000
Cost savings	**€ 193,000**

Table 11.2 Cumulative Cost Savings

It has been said that "The invoicing department of social services could save—conservatively—about a billion marks (about 10% of the administrative costs) just with invoicing if employees worked with digital signatures."

11.8.6 Digital Signatures at SAP

SSF interface

Because SAP EP represents a new interface to the user, the question arises regarding the implementation of a digital signature on the frontend SAP EP. SAP currently offers several options for working with digital signatures. A *secure store and forward (SSF)* interface is implemented in every SAP Basis system (as of 4.0). The SSF interface enables the use of the following four functions:

- Sign
- Verify

---

2 Source: a study by the EU Commission

3 An electronic solution saves the costs of manual creation.

▶ Encrypt

▶ Decrypt

The first two functions are essential for a digital signature. The application calls the sign/verify transaction and triggers the signing and verification process with the software and hardware of an SAP-certified security provider. Because SAP itself is not a security provider, it requires a certified security provider.

If the software and hardware of the provider are available, users can use the SSF interface to sign and verify with the following:

▶ SAP application server (with SAP SecuLib 4.5 and higher)

▶ SAP GUI for Windows (Complimentary Software Program) 4.0 and higher (see Figure 11.20)

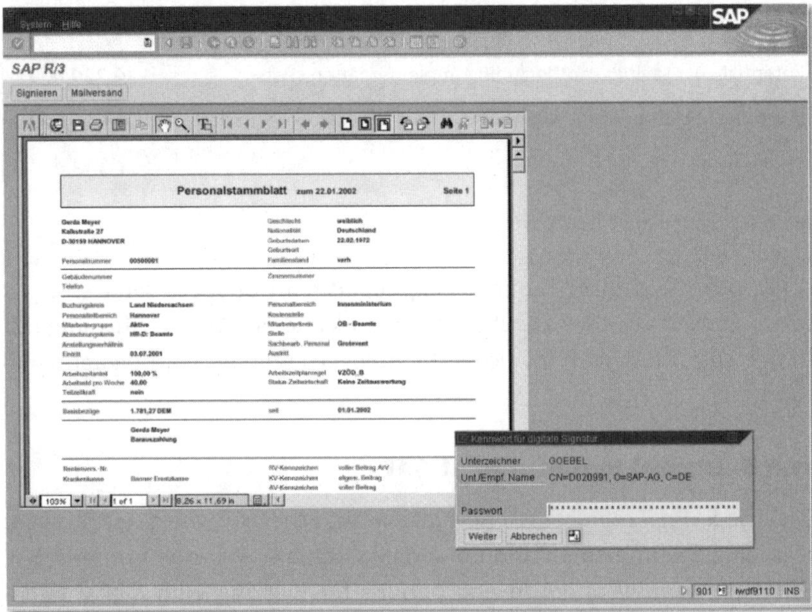

Figure 11.20 Digital Signature with SAP GUI for Windows

▶ Web browser (signed SAP Signature Control in Internet Explorer 6.10 and higher (see Figure 11.21)

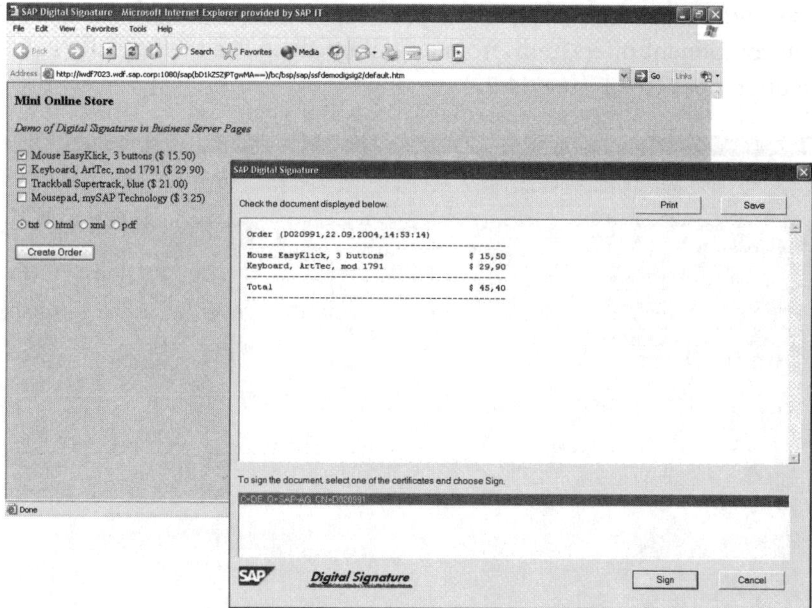

Figure 11.21 Digital Signature in the Web Browser with SAP Signature Control (Signed by VeriSign)

Differences in the signature process

The three options differ in the way that a digital signature is executed:

- If a digital signature is executed on an SAP application server, the request comes from the application: the application server signs the document and the user does not see the document. The signature is executed in the background. Therefore, the document can be displayed only after it has been signed.
- If the digital signature is executed in the SAP GUI for Windows or the Web browser, users are active. They trigger production of the signature by selecting the **Sign** button and view the document before they trigger the action. In the SAP GUI for Windows, the document is displayed in the GUI. Users enter the PIN in a popup window.
- If the signature is executed in a Web browser, the signature control appears in a separate window: the PIN is entered in a popup window.

Example

You can also integrate applications that execute a digital signature into SAP EP. The following sample application displays this ability. The example uses a small store in which users can select items. A digital signature closes the order process.

Users first call a portal component from which they can access the store. The component offers items from a catalog, much like the SAP SRM/EBP solution does (see Figure 11.22).

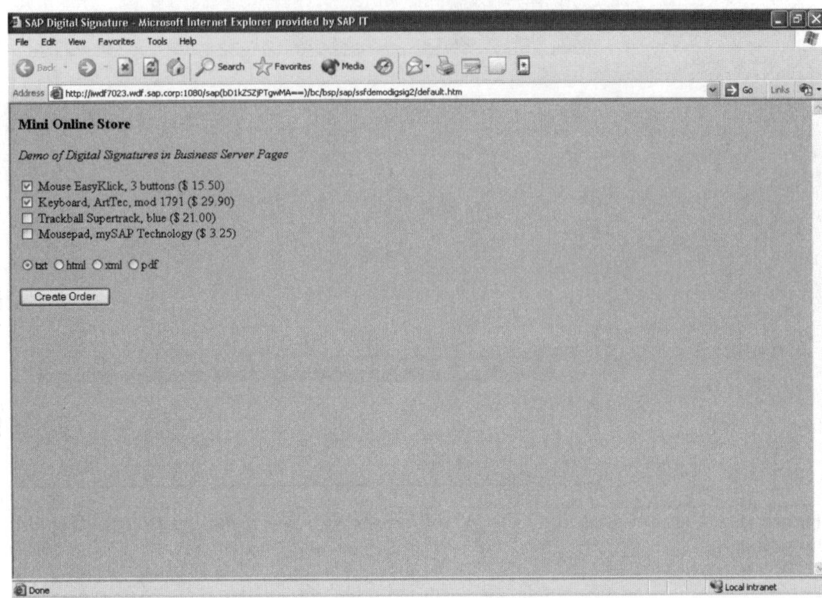

Figure 11.22 Signing in the Portal with Signed SAP Signature Control and SAP Web AS

The user then selects the desired item. The SAP system uses the signature control to ask the user to confirm the order with a digital signature. The lower area of the screen displays the certificates stored in the browser. A card reader could be addressed in the same manner so that the user would be prompted to insert a signature card and enter a PIN (see Figure 11.23).

After it has been signed, the document is transmitted and the order is triggered in the backend. To clarify the process, this sample application also checks the digital signature and displays the user data of the signer (see Figure 11.24).

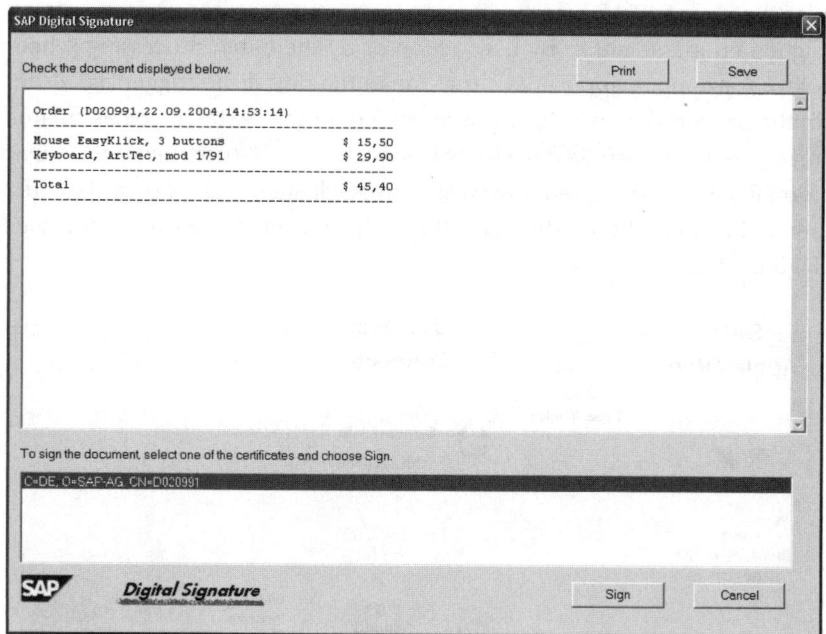

Figure 11.23 Display of the Document to Be Signed and Selection of the Certificate to Be Used to Sign the Document

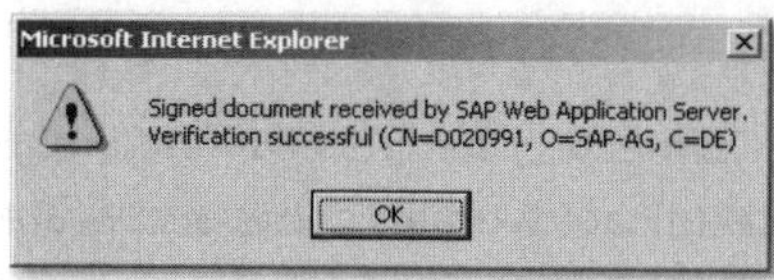

Figure 11.24 Receipt of the Document and Verification of the Digital Signature

Signature in the SAP GUI

As an additional option, you can produce a digital certificate in the SAP GUI for Windows. In this case, you can display an SAP R/3 transaction in the portal instead of using the Windows GUI to display the Web GUI. You can also execute the digital signature at the frontend. Because the portal might be called on a computer without a Windows GUI by the Web browser, we don't recommend this approach. Instead, it's better to execute the digital signature directly in the Web browser with the signature control.

You can also distinguish between digitally signing a single document or a group of documents. For SAP EP, the signature executed in the frontend is particularly important. But not all digital signatures can be executed in the frontend. Just imagine a large company that sends millions of invoices each month: manual digital signatures would be unthinkable.

Mass signature For these cases, SAP offers an option for mass signatures. Documents are signed en masse either by user action or by the batch processing schedule. For example, applications that run in the portal can trigger signatures in the backend or on a signature server. For example, the invoices created on a given day with SAP Business Connector in the proprietary SAP IDoc format can be converted into XML format, digitally signed by a signature server in an additional step, and then transmitted to their recipients (see Figure 11.25).

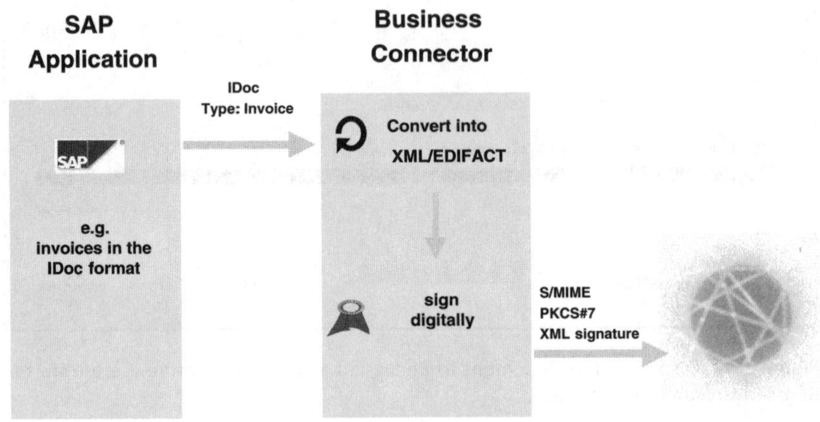

Figure 11.25 Signing During Mass Processing of Documents

In the same manner, SAP Business Connector can receive incoming invoices and check the validity of the certificate with an *online certificate service protocol (OCSP)* responder.

Checking validity You must check the validity of the certificate when you require the highest security level to check documents. You can check the validity of a certificate with a list of blocked certificates in offline mode. However, the list should be updated once or several times a day. If a company wants to delegate this task, it can also be performed by an OCSP responder.

The trust centers that issue certificates are arranged in a tree under the root node of the regulatory agency for telecommunications and mail. If the trust center does not trust the issuer of a certificate, the check is undertaken by the next highest authority—it might even go as far as the regulatory agency itself. The highest level verifies whether the issuing trust center is accredited and valid.

Processing in the SAP system If the check of the digital signature and certificate was successful, the signed document is archived for any future audit and the XML document is converted into the proprietary SAP format. The IDoc is transmitted to the SAP component system along with the archive ID. The component system generates a document header (BKPF) that contains the archive ID and a reference to the digitally signed document. You can always access the original document with the posting line in the SAP component system, check it, and display it (see Figure 11.26). In the ideal case, a PDF document would also be delivered for better display and archiving. As before, a check would use the signed XML document.

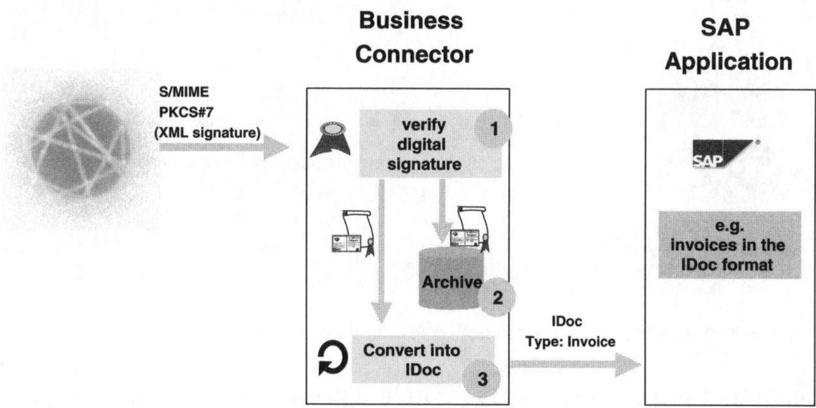

Figure 11.26 Receipt of Digitally Signed Documents During Mass Processing

Figure 11.27 illustrates the use of a digital signature to sign an event log for production instructions in a process industry. If an SAP application does not yet support the digital signature, you can easily execute it with customizing in Business Add-Ins (BADIs), customer exits, or enhancements to existing programs. The Secure Store and Forward (SSF) interface is called directly as a Basis component. Implementation of the digital certificate cannot be described globally because countless usage areas exist in SAP applications. The standard delivery covers the most important areas; project solutions implement the rest.

As we have seen, you can integrate a digital signature in SAP EP with little effort. As business processes continue to become increasingly more electronic—from purchasing requests to approval procedures—the digital signature will play a more critical role. SAP EP offers an interface for the application and the end users, be they department directors or clerks in an agency. With a card reader, a signature card, or a SmartToken, SAP EP simplifies and eases approval processes.

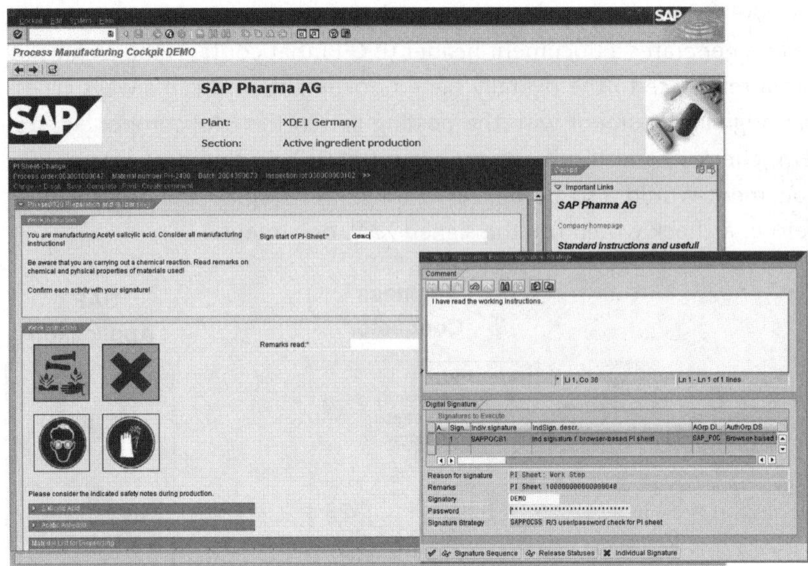

Figure 11.27 Event Log for Production Instructions in the Processing Industry

SSO with a signature card

Note that you can also use SSO with a signature card. The operating systems allow authentication with SmartCards and SmartTokens. If you have authenticated yourself to the domain controller with one of the two solutions, you can use NTLM to log on to the Web server, and thus SAP EP. Because the portal trusts the domain controller, you can also log on to the connected systems with SSO, as long as the configuration is appropriate. Once you have inserted the card into a card reader or the token into the USB port, you simply authenticate yourself to the operating system with your PIN and are then automatically logged on to all the applications integrated into the portal. If you think that you'll need an even greater number of user IDs and passwords than the hundreds you needed 10 years ago, you'll be relieved to know that you can now save your mental resources for more important matters.

11.9 Secure Networks

Network architecture must protect its electronic business data and processes. It's important that no one other than authorized personnel receive access to the data and processes. How the protection is performed depends on the level of confidentiality of the data, the software and hardware in use, and the overall infrastructure. The operating system plays a key role in the protection of systems and the authentication of users. Security providers build on that foundation and offer help with the integration of the public key infrastructure (PKI). Compatibility requires that SAP certified security providers who want to work with SAP solutions be certified. SAP also offers customers its own products, so that in many cases, such as SAP EP, you don't have to provide your own PKI. SAP Cryptolib is available to customers free of charge and ensures secure server-to-server connections. SAP Trust Center Service issues client and server certificates to SAP customers.

Protocols such as SNC and SSL secure network and Internet communications. You can also use X.509 client certificates for secure authorization with SSL. User management in SAP EP is responsible for the authorization concept, the assignment of authorizations, and role management. SSO allows user-friendly logon to connected systems—with additional authentication. When sending important documents with a digital signature, you can check the authenticity and integrity of a message.

The security mechanisms noted, SNC, SSL, authentication, SSO, user management, and digital signatures always represent portal security for a subarea only. You also need additional security mechanisms to ensure that the protection offered by any of these techniques is never compromised. To protect against any misuse and ensure maximum security, secure network architecture should surround the entire infrastructure. As a highly sensitive unit within the architecture, the portal servers should be installed in a separate area to protect it from external and internal attacks. Installation of a demilitarized zone (DMZ) and several firewalls among the individual components must shield sensitive components. Figure 11.28 illustrates a recommended approach to secure network architecture for SAP EP.

Firewalls

Firewalls protect your network and its resources from attacks and unauthorized access. Firewalls evaluate information in the header data of transmitted packets. Based on the sender and receiver data and the protocols in use, the packets are inspected and accepted or rejected. The use of multiple firewalls filters requests evermore finely and the restrictions become gradually greater. Therefore, only regulated and authorized requests reach the application server, database server, and user management.

Proxies

Proxy servers or reverse proxy servers prohibit direct external access to a company's servers and thus prevent attacks or paralysis. The servers can always be accessed by the proxy servers. For example, they permit transmission of outgoing requests but prohibit or strongly regulate incoming requests. Each Internet service (FTP, HTTP, TELNET, and so on) requires special proxy software. The use of a cache can buffer data and information frequently requested externally (a reverse proxy server can buffer the same for internal requests) and thus significantly reduce the load on the network. This approach looks at the resources of the connected systems very carefully.

Intelligent use and combinations of these technologies and services ensures maximum protection for your most sensitive data. See the professional literature on network security for more details on firewalls, reverse proxy servers, and demilitarized zones.

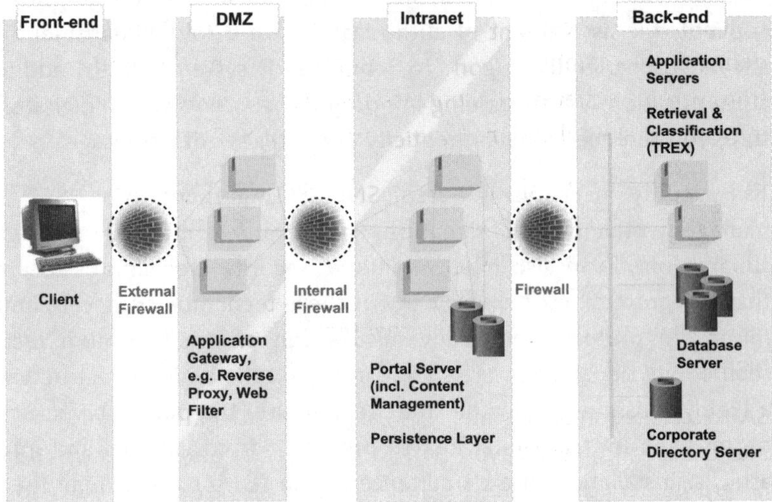

Figure 11.28 Secure Network Architecture for SAP Enterprise Portal

12 New Technologies and Development Platforms

In this age of modern information technology, it's especially important to open new areas (customers, business processes, and so on). SAP NetWeaver and SAP Exchange Infrastructure (SAP XI) create the technological foundation and a solid basis for implementing designs for integration.

Collaborative processes within a company and cross-company workflows demand the combination of structured and unstructured information from various systems. This process assumes openness to and compatibility with other applications located outside of SAP system landscapes.

Standards guarantee openness

In particular, openness applies to the products of strategic partners and those of competitors who have had a long-term, dominant position in the market. Companies can use the support of standard protocols (such as HTTP and SOAP), metalanguages (XML), and Web services[1] to create this essential compatibility with external technologies. In this context, we can highlight platforms such as IBM WebSphere, Microsoft .NET, and J2EE.

Enterprise Services Architecture

SAP NetWeaver comes into play as a new integration and application platform. SAP NetWeaver provides the technological foundation for *Enterprise Services Architecture*, a blueprint for flexible business applications that links SAP's knowledge of business processes and applications to the flexibility of Web services and open technologies.

SAP Exchange Infrastructure (SAP XI)

SAP Exchange Infrastructure (SAP XI) comes into play as a part of SAP NetWeaver to process message-based integration of internal and external systems. Integration occurs in the context of business processes, information, and people (users). In addition to SAP XI, SAP NetWeaver consists of SAP Web Application Server (SAP Web AS), SAP Enterprise Portal (SAP EP, including knowledge management and collaboration), SAP Business Intelligence (SAP BI), SAP Master Data Management, and SAP Mobile Infrastructure.

1 The Internet Communication Manager (*ICMan*), which is a subcomponent of SAP Web AS, enables both Webservices and Web Dynpros. The ICMan supports HTTP(S) and SMTP, thus building the technological framework for various Internet protocols. It can be used within a communications process as a server or a client.

12.1 SAP NetWeaver

Over the past several years, many companies extensively invested in their software landscapes to meet the wide-reaching demands of business users. The actual solutions disillusioned some companies: the results didn't meet their requirements. Consequently, they put immense pressure on their IT departments to lower costs, implement scalable solutions, and reflect the value of the company in the IT solutions (management information systems).

The sustained increase in the complexity of the value chain meant that traditional software solutions were no longer capable of meeting these requirements. Companies wanted a design that combined information seamlessly and created a modular and reliable application landscape.

Irreconcilable basic technologies

The situation has been complicated further because two basic technologies have found a place in the market: Java and Microsoft .NET. So far, these technologies have been irreconcilable due to their heterogeneity. Because of their diverseness, the IT departments in most companies had to compensate for this existing lack of uniformity.

To reduce the effort required for integration and the associated costs, the goal was to minimize the number of heterogeneous applications. Simultaneously, companies looked for ways to leverage their existing systems. Due to the new awareness of IT departments to avoid technological heterogeneity in the system landscapes in all circumstances, many companies decided to use SAP, IBM, and Microsoft products exclusively.

The promise to bridge the gap between these application worlds and technologies and to standardize interfaces supported this approach. The organizations that drive this standardization include the *World Wide Web Consortium (W3C)*, the *Web Services Interoperability Organization (WS-I)*, the *Organization for the Advancement of Structured Information Standards (OASIS)*, and so on.

Three layers of integration

The three cornerstones of SAP NetWeaver arise from business requirements to derive as much benefit as possible from existing applications and to enable modifiable structures:

- ▶ People integration (customers, employees, and business partners)
- ▶ Information integration (of the existing information)
- ▶ Process integration (business processes)

Figure 12.1 illustrates the various integration layers of SAP NetWeaver.

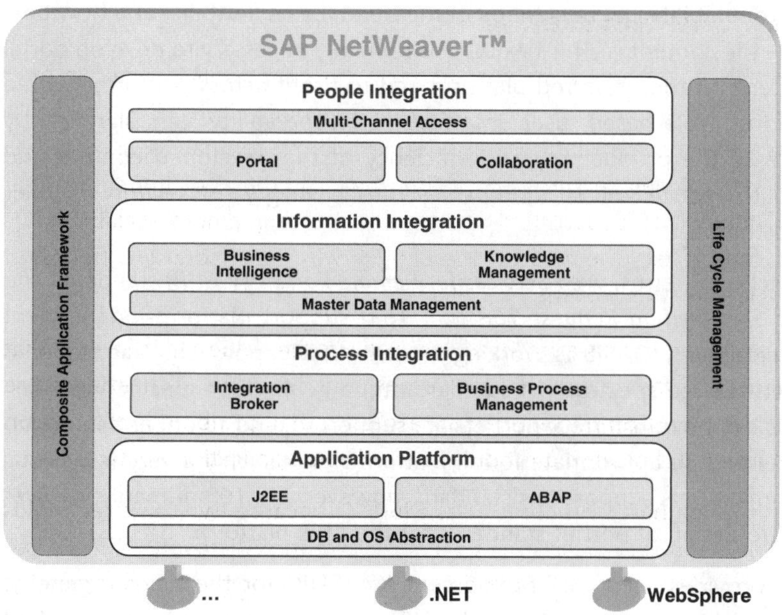

Figure 12.1 Integration Layers of SAP NetWeaver

Both core technologies, J2EE and ABAP are used for the application platform. J2EE delivers the framework architecture to develop, distribute, and control server-side, multilayer, and business-logic applications. The framework contains various key technologies: *Enterprise Java Beans (EJB)*, *Java Database Connection (JDBC)*, *Java Servlets*, *Java Server Pages (JSPs)*, *Java Transaction API (JTA)*, *Java Transaction Service (JTS)*, *Remote Method Invocation (RMI)*, and so on.

The strengths of ABAP are particularly apparent in its high-performance and easy-to-use access to databases. In addition, conventional SAP R/3 applications are based on the ABAP programming language.

In the following section, we examine the integration layers of SAP NetWeaver in more detail.

12.1.1 People Integration

Portal-Enabling, Interoperability, and Independence from End Devices

The key functionalities for application integration with SAP NetWeaver are made available by SAP EP and SAP Mobile Infrastructure: collaborative functions, the interoperability of different technologies, and alternate access with many types of end devices.

Interoperability Interoperability can be defined or measured by its flexibility and how portable the content is. This flexibility is primarily necessary to develop portal content on the preferred platform and to use it across platforms with a uniform, role-based user interface. Interoperability can significantly increase the productivity and efficiency of the developed content and lead to reduced costs. Companies thus have greater security in their investment.

Platform-independent development In technical terms, *Web Services for Remote Portals (WSRP)* standards and *Java Specification Request 168 [JSR 168]* support platform-independent development. OASIS is working on the WSRP approach. This standard meets a large spectrum of standardization goals (user-specific Web services can be transferred, portlets are supported, and so on) and in principle would be appropriate for all platforms. So far only a very few portal manufacturers support this standard, however. JSR 168 primarily involves the definition of portlet standards for the J2EE platform.

PDK: APIs as Web services SAP provides a Portal Development Kit (PDK) for the development of IBM WebSphere and Microsoft .NET portal components (see Section 9.2.1). This development environment far exceeds simple HTML integration and allows the use of SAP EP services (user management, personalization, support of roles, and so on) even within a non-SAP portal environment, much like direct access to Application Programming Interfaces (APIs) does. This feature is available because the underlying APIs are presented as Web services. Web services form the central interface technology for SAP components. SAP EP handles the actual presentation and formatting preferred by end uses. The following section looks at the SAP Exchange Infrastructure (SAP XI), which helps to integrate and link processes of heterogeneous applications from various manufacturers. SAP Web AS enables the execution of Web services in Java and ABAP. Complete documentation, including examples and ready-made enhancements, are part of the portal development environment.

Collaboration The integration of users occurs in *collaboration rooms* (see Figure 12.2), which enable realtime collaboration, regardless of geographical location. You can build temporary or permanent teams and provide them with discussion forums, e-distribution, document storage, and so on.

Although SAP NetWeaver can meet most requirements for virtual collaboration, you can also integrate other groupware products and collaboration solutions to leverage the use of existing investments and functionalities.

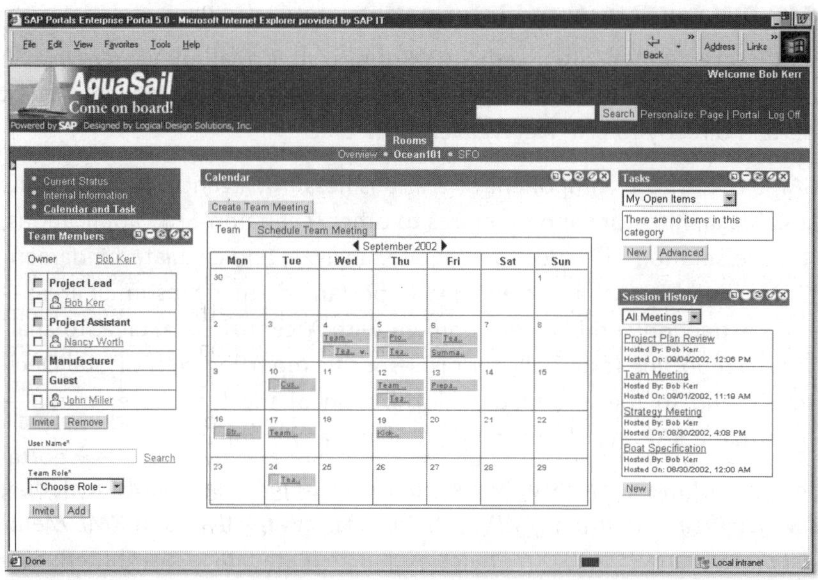

Figure 12.2 Collaboration Room in SAP EP 5.0

Mobile integration

SAP Mobile Infrastructure provides a high-grade, scalable, and flexible platform that enables companies to run applications on mobile devices, regardless of their connection status (on or offline). The original portal environment for which the end application was developed makes no difference whatsoever: a transfer (from IBM WebSphere to SAP EP, for example) can occur easily.

SAP Mobile Infrastructure currently supports end devices based on Pocket PC and Linux, so that it covers the majority of devices on the market.

12.1.2 Information Integration

The information layer of SAP NetWeaver consists of the following components:

- SAP Business Information Warehouse (SAP BW) for structured information
- Knowledge Management (KM) for unstructured information
- SAP Master Data Management (SAP MDM): central management of master data to ensure the consistency and integrity of data throughout the system

Now, let's look at these components in more detail.

SAP BW for Structured Information

In Chapter 4, we discussed SAP Business Information Warehouse in detail. Therefore, in this section, we will examine only the key points that pertain directly to SAP NetWeaver.

SAP BW is a core component of SAP Business Intelligence. Because of its scalable architecture and openness to other (even non-SAP) applications, it is the solution of choice to integrate, analyze, and circulate fundamental information within a company. Important partnerships in all areas—from extraction and ETL development with Ascential DataStage, to analysis, to reporting (especially for pixel-specific reporting with Crystal Decisions), and to the information distribution of the three-layer model—have made SAP BW *the* reporting tool in many companies.

Metadata

In terms of metadata, SAP BW supports a variety of standards, including *Java Metadata Interface (JMI)*, *XML for Analyses (XMLA)*, and *XML Metadata Interchange (XMI)*. XMI helps exchange metadata in distributed, heterogeneous system landscapes and can be used in .NET or J2EE development environments. The OLE DB for OLAP interface provides generic access (with the limitations noted in Chapter 4) to the data stored in SAP BW for a broad range of non-SAP applications.

XMLA also offers reliable access for platform-independent components, Web and Internet applications, and mobile end devices.

KM for Unstructured Information

Knowledge Management (KM) functions are an integral component of SAP EP and support the use, exchange, and distribution of unstructured information stored in a heterogeneous system landscape. In such a landscape, the connection to specific (document) storage is established with partially preconfigured connectors. You can also set up a connection with standard protocols such as *Web-based distributed authoring and versioning (WebDAV)*, HTTP, or connectors that you program yourself. Comprehensive search and classification mechanisms are also part of KM and allow the searching or setting up of taxonomies throughout the stored documents. Users always work in the familiar portal environment and are free to employ all KM services, such as discussion forums, evaluations, feedback, attributes, and so on.

SAP MDM for Cross-System Consistency and Integrity of Data

SAP Master Data Management (SAP MDM) collects and integrates data from various distributed IT systems and applications: it provides central management of master data. The consolidated master data creates an important precondition for continuous business processes within and among companies.

SAP MDM has three basic tasks:

- Consistent storage of data. You can filter master data by specific criteria and eliminate redundancies in the data.
- Significantly better integration of company processes. You can make data available to other systems by distributing it.
- Central maintenance of master data. You can modify and distribute logically related objects at a central location. You access the data based on roles integrated into SAP EP. The availability of Web services ensures flexible and efficient access to master data.

This section shows that the subcomponents for storing information with SAP NetWeaver consider, to a great extent, the type of information involved. This implies that they don't involve an apparent exactitude of information or—in the case of structured information—that you have to tolerate information deficits.

12.1.3 Process Integration

The core components of SAP NetWeaver in the area of process integration include the *integration broker* and *business process management (BPM)*. The functions are made available in the context of SAP Exchange Infrastructure (SAP XI), which is the topic of the following section.

12.2 SAP Exchange Infrastructure (SAP XI)

Process integration through open standards

SAP Exchange Infrastructure (SAP XI) is required to implement processes within an enterprise and among enterprises—across systems and independently of the platform. Support of open standards is the focus here. You can integrate not only non-SAP systems and platforms into an SAP system landscape, but also support metalanguages such as XML and platform-independent programming languages such as Java. What is important is that you consider such platform-independence as early as possible when defining the interfaces you use. The *Web Service Description Language (WSDL)* is used for the description.

Integration Repository

Before you an use an SAP XI solution, you must store the mapping information from the WSDL description in the integration repository. This "library" contains the potential structures created during the design phase. The next step, configuration, transfers the structures (assignment to a logical routing) and stores them in the integration directory. You can call the XI structures (components, interfaces, mappings, and so on) from the integration directory.

12.2.1 Uses of SAP XI

Synchronous and asynchronous exchange of messages

SAP XI supports the synchronous and asynchronous exchange of messages among any desired number of heterogeneous systems. Synchronous communication means that the sending system waits until the receiving system processes the last message. Asynchronous communication transmits additional messages regardless of the status of the receiving system. The interfaces used here can be created from scratch (which would make them platform-independent) or integrated into the existing (platform-dependent) system landscape with adapters. Mapping can be generated if needed to transform the contents of messages (adjusting values and structures) as they pass from sender to recipient.

Routing

The use of logical routing permits central maintenance of the flow of messages among logical systems. Ultimately, a logical sender is assigned to a logical recipient. You can also link the flow of a message to predefined conditions. The message is redirected to a specific recipient only when a freely defined number of conditions has been met. In addition to logical routing, you can also use technical routing, which links a recipient to a logical system (see Figure 12.3).

Logical and technical routing enable you to substitute the technical recipient address. Because both mapping and logical routing specify a dependence between only the logical sender and recipient, these types of changes don't affect the actual makeup of a business process.

The openness and independence of SAP XI can thus model cross-platform business processes that prove to be thoroughly flexible in the event of structural changes.

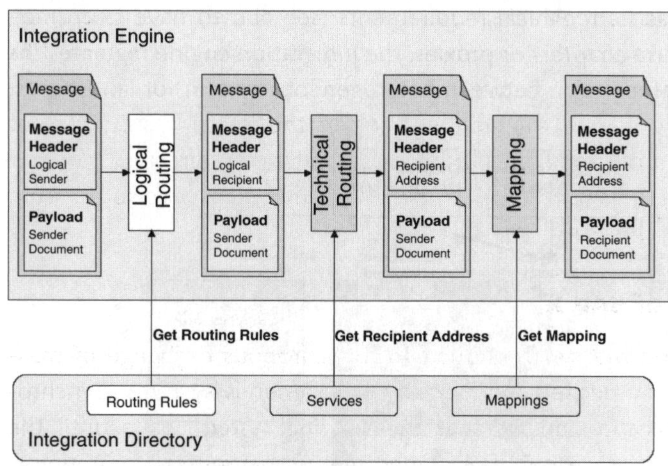

Figure 12.3 Logical and Technical Routing and Mapping

12.2.2 Runtime Components of SAP XI

The Architecture of SAP XI consists of the following:

Integration engine

The *integration engine* is the core element of SAP XI. Messages (in XML format) are generated directly within an SAP component or made available with external applications and an HTTP interface. Adapters offer an alternative to use intermediate documents (IDocs) and remote function calls (RFC).

Adapters

Adapters are required to communicate with SAP systems (later than the 6.20 release) and non-SAP systems. Current SAP systems support direct system connections without adapters. Adapters convert XML and HTTP documents into IDocs and RFCs (and vice versa). In the future, adapters will be made available with *Java connector architecture (JCA)*. The advantage of adapters is that they don't require a separate program runtime. You can use adapters for applications or messages (to convert protocols).

Integration repository

As described above, all the interfaces required for an integration scenario are stored in a central *integration repository*.

Proxy framework

The *proxy framework* offers a particularly promising scenario for the future: it enables platform-independent specification of interfaces even in the area of the integration repository. You can use the fixed definition of interfaces to generate proxies automatically in Java for SAP systems and for applications.

Figure 12.4 provides an overview of the components. In particular, it shows that the proxy framework is preferable to the adapters in every case, as long as its technical requirements (see above) have been met. Whether you use adapters or proxies, the integration engine regulates the exchange of information between heterogeneous systems or landscapes.

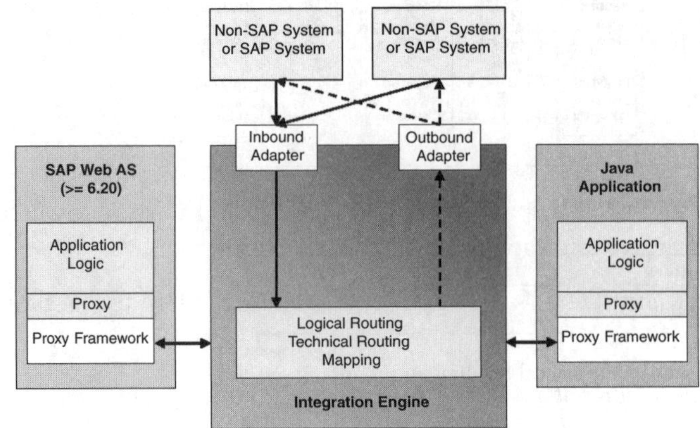

Figure 12.4 Communications with Adapters or the Proxy Framework

12.2.3 Creating Messages

The messages exchanged between the systems are created in XML format. XML is a method for depicting structured data in a text file and it is a metalanguage for the definition of document types. For more detailed information, see Appendix C.

12.3 SAP NetWeaver Developer Studio

12.3.1 SAP NetWeaver Developer Studio: Introduction

SAP NetWeaver Developer Studio (NWDS) is based on Eclipse, the open source product from IBM. Eclipse is a development environment to implement Java-based applications in a business context. Its open architecture makes it especially well suited to integrating additional functionalities.

SAP NWDS enables the realization of comprehensive Java development projects for standard technologies (J2EE, XML, and so on) or for SAP-specific technologies (Web Dynpro and so on).

Local storage of source code maintains a high degree of flexibility in the development process: you can even test the generated coding on a local server. The use of wizards can drastically reduce the development effort, especially when creating complex interfaces.

12.3.2 Plug-Ins for Eclipse

Extension points

Because of its open architecture, Eclipse allows you to develop your own tools that you can integrate into the basic application as plug-ins. *Extension points* enable these enhancements. Plug-ins add special, individual functionality to enrich the basic platform—the iView plug-in is a good example. Extension points can almost be created iteratively. As needed, plug-ins can make specific extension points available.

Eclipse itself is modular: even the required standard components are attached as plug-ins. Additional examples of plug-ins include the resource management system and the Eclipse workbench itself.

PDE and JDT

As Figure 12.5 illustrates, two components exist in addition to the basic platform:

- *JDT* (*Java development tooling*) adds basic functions to *edit*, *test*, and *debug* Java programs to the basic platform.
- *PDE* (*Plug-in developer environment*) creates the conditions for implementation and efficient use of your own plug-ins.

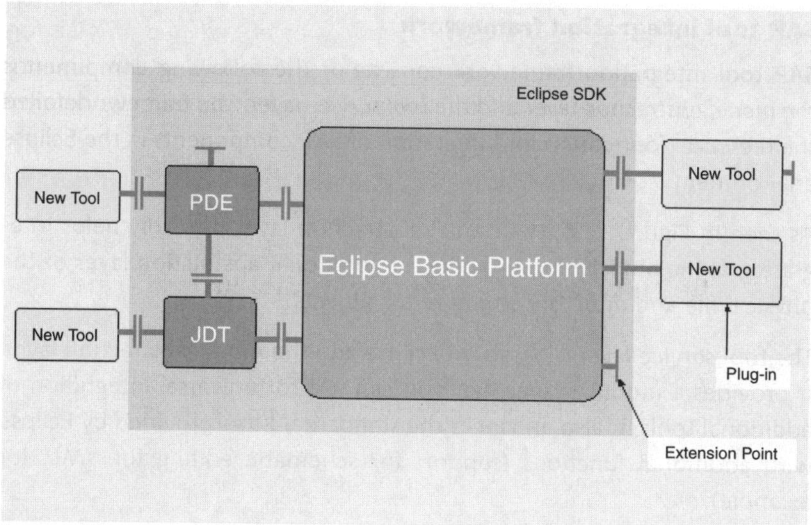

Figure 12.5 Structure of Eclipse

12.3.3 Plug-Ins for SAP NetWeaver Developer Studio

Because SAP NetWeaver Developer Studio is based on the infrastructure provided by Eclipse, you can insert SAP-specific supplemental components into the basic platform by using plug-in technology.

Three layers SAP NWDS consists of the following three layers:

- Eclipse as the basis for the adoption of plug-ins
- SAP tool integration framework
- Additional toolsets

Figure 12.6 shows the divisions between the individual layers. In the subsequent sections, we introduce the following topics: SAP tool integration framework and additional toolsets.

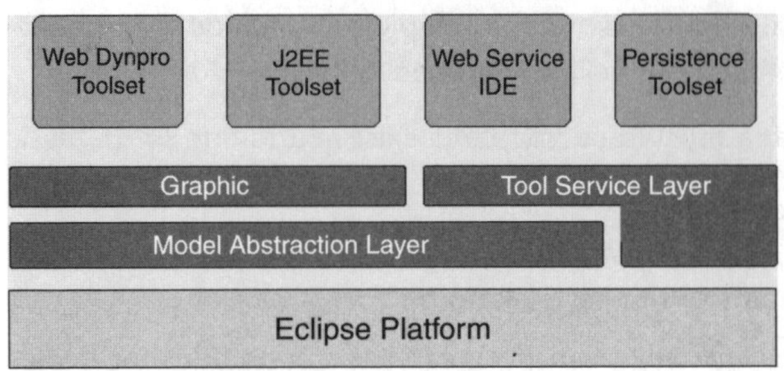

Figure 12.6 Three Layers of SAP NetWeaver Developer Studio

SAP tool integration framework

SAP tool integration framework consists of the following components: the *model abstraction layer* and the *tool service layer*. The framework forms the technical foundation for integration of SAP components in the Eclipse environment.

Model abstraction layer As seen in Figure 12.6, the model abstraction layer primarily helps integrate graphic objects and provides an additional abstraction layer of the physical file and directory structure for objects.

Tool service layer The tool service layer is based on Eclipse and the model abstraction layer. It provides a modular layer that you can use for universal integration of additional tools. It also enhances the standard editors provided by Eclipse with additional functions (support for schematic editing for XML, for example).

The *action and menu framework* exclusively offers a clear separation between action functionality and its visual representation. Its structure is quite similar to the Model-View Controller (MVC) design that we discussed in Chapter 9.

Toolsets

Toolsets are realized via the SAP tool integration framework. The toolsets contain individual tools that can be combined into a perspective, based on the requirements of specific tasks.

The Developer Studio offers a range of tools covering all aspects of application development. As is usual in Eclipse, the associated tools are generally bundled together in Perspectives according to the task at hand. For a short overview of the uses and features of each toolset, refer to the following documents as appropriate: *http://help.sap.com/saphelp_webas630/helpdata/en/48/fb411e8ebd5b4bbeff225dcd2f07fd/content.htm*

The following lists the most important toolsets:

- Web Dynpro toolset
- J2EE toolset
- Web service IDE
- Persistence toolset
- SAP enterprise connector
- SAP Java test tool

Web Dynpro toolset

Web Dynpros enable the user-friendly creation of business applications because wizards handle most of the development effort. Only event and error-handling require manual programming work.

The application modeler is also a component of SAP NWDS. It contains the view designer, which provides a large quantity of predefined view elements. Web Dynpro tools then populate these interface elements seamlessly with back-end logic. For example, the context editor combines the data fields of the view with the model data created later (see Figure 12.7).

J2EE toolset

In addition to the development of Web Dynpros, SAP NetWeaver Developer Studio also provides all the components required to develop J2EE applications (as of J2EE Engine 6.30).

Various types of projects are often formed as part of a J2EE development project—a project frame is generated for each type of project. Project types are categorized as *source*, *archive*, and *application*.

A source project is created first (see Figure 12.8): either as an Enterprise Java Bean (EJB) or a Web project. As shown in Figure 12.8, an EJB project involves the integration of several different Java beans. A Java bean is a software component whose methods are named according to a naming scheme. Wizards can automatically generate code templates for the integrated EJB classes.

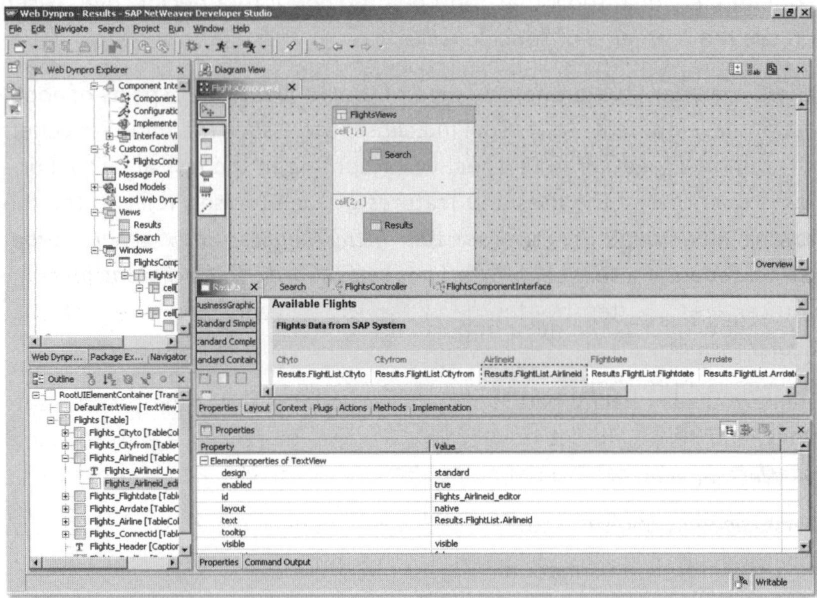

Figure 12.7 Application Modeler and Web Dynpro Explorer in SAP NetWeaver Developer Studio

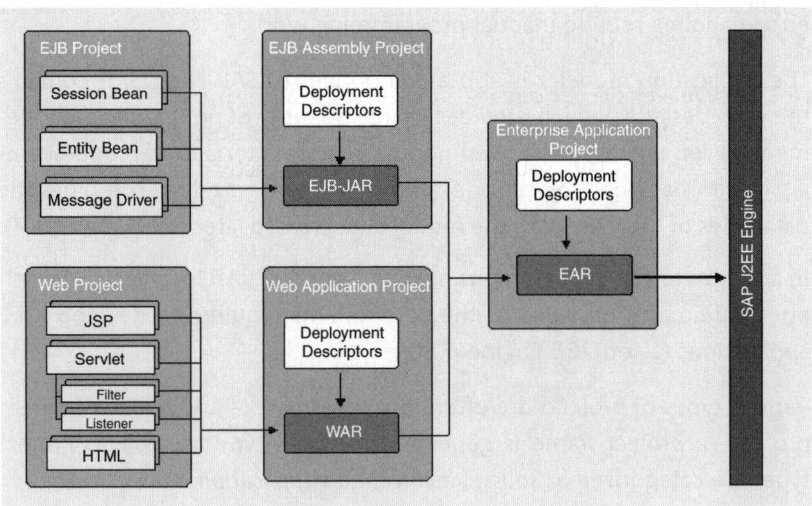

Figure 12.8 J2EE Toolset

Web projects, however, are appropriate to record diverse Web sources (JSPs, HTML pages, servlets, and so on). Archive projects are created from source projects. Standardized deployment descriptors are inserted into archive projects. You can then bundle several archive projects into a resource for the type of application project (EAR file) before starting the deployment process.

Web services IDE

SAP NetWeaver Developer Studio also supports Web service providers and Web service clients.

You have two ways of actually defining Web services. You can use a wizard to generate a service in only a few steps (with predefined values) or, you can create a step-by-step definition to build a Web service with particular properties.

Then, you can specify parameters, the interfaces used, the security settings, and so on. To set the parameters, you must also specify a virtual interface, a Web service definition, and a Web service configuration.

Persistence Toolset

Persistence tools are another important element of the development environment. Data is considered persistent when it is stored for a longer period, which is normally the case when using a database.

You can use Open SQL (for Java) to create portable and high-performance database applications. A central Java dictionary holds all tables. Applications can then access the data with SQLJ, JDBC, and so on, without having to consider the properties of a database.

SAP NetWeaver Developer Studio also uses SQLJ to support static SQL access. This feature is particularly interesting because SQL statements embedded within Java sources can be edited directly. If a SQLJ source is then stored, the resulting Java calls are generated automatically.

The *SQLJ translator*, including the *SQLJ checker* components, are implicitly called to check the SQL sequences. The *SQLJ translator* then leads to a direct realization of the SQL statements in the corresponding Java calls. Figure 12.9 illustrates this flow.

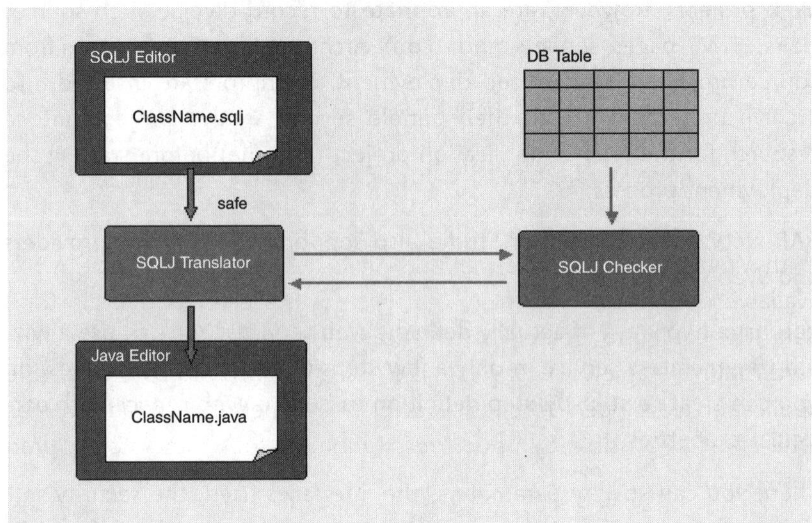

Figure 12.9 SAP NetWeaver Persistence Framework

SAP Enterprise Connector

SAP Enterprise Connector is yet another element: it redirects the corresponding Java proxy classes from the RFC function modules. Compared to a direct call of the RFC function modules, proxies have the advantage of enabling user-friendly and familiar access to SAP data.

SAP Java test tool

JLin is a tool that you can use to check the properties of Java source texts. In addition to a pure syntax check, it can also check the syntax for metrics, compatibilities, language restrictions, authorizations, and so on. You can also enhance these checks with check routines, which combine individual checks to cover one or more source texts if necessary. The results of these checks include warnings, errors, and a list of test results.

As you can see, SAP NetWeaver Developer Studio covers a broad range of technologies, including those from third parties. The modular structure of SAP NetWeaver Development Studio allows integration of any enhancements and updates without a great deal of effort. In the future, it will occupy a central position in the development of Web applications in the SAP NetWeaver environment.

12.4 Web Dynpro Development

SAP Web Dynpro for Java is a revolutionary step in the development of Web-based user interfaces. It is a completely new design created by SAP and represents a quantum leap in the development of Web-based ERP applications.

12.4.1 The Design Pattern

MVC

The design pattern of the Model-View Controller (MVC, discussed in Chapter 9) is the design philosophy behind Web Dynpros. It is based on a clear separation of data presentation and storage and on event handling. The views or the controller observe the data source (the model) and the controller observes the views.

With Web Dynpros, you determine which elements should be made available on the user interface and where these elements obtain their data. The coding to create the user interface is generated from the standard runtime framework. The primary goal of Web Dynpros is to enable application developers to create powerful Internet applications with as little effort as possible by using "descriptions of tools" and a structured design process.

Description of applications

We should now describe applications; development and programming plays a lesser role in the description. Imagine that you want to develop a new Internet application. As a rule, you would first design the user interface in HTML with or without the support of a development tool. You must then enliven the static HTML pages and program the actions behind them in Java, PHP, or JavaScript. Maintenance of these applications usually involves a good deal of effort and time. Web Dynpros make it easy for customers and partners alike to tailor or enhance applications. The applications should also be able to work on a variety of devices, especially regarding the collaboration of applications.

The main idea is that as little self-written code as possible should be required for the user interface. Web Dynpros pursue this goal in two ways. First, a descriptive language is used to define the user interface, without requiring any programming. The code for a functioning program for the user interface is generated completely, and metadata that can execute a generic engine at runtime is derived. Adjustments are required only for user-specific modifications. Secondly, Web Dynpros offer functionalities for internationalization, interactions, and a clear separation of business logic from the user interface. The separation occurs with the use of the MVC design pattern. Code for the runtime environment of the J2EE Engine and the ABAP stack of SAP Web AS can be generated from the metadata. The .NET runtime environment should also be supported.

12.4.2 Requirements

Software

To develop Web Dynpros, you need SAP NWDS and the J2EE Engine. You also need the SAP GUI and a user ID with sufficient authorizations in the SAP system for BAPI and RFC calls.

Hardware

SAP NetWeaver Developer Studio and the J2EE Engine can be installed on separate servers. SAP recommends that each server have 512 MB of RAM. If you install the studio and engine on the same server, SAP recommends 1 GB of memory on the server.

12.4.3 Developing a Sample Application

This example develops a Web Dynpro application that starts a Web Dynpro component that displays a graphic in the Web browser. To develop the application, start SAP NetWeaver Developer Studio (see Section 11.3 for a general overview of SAP NWDS). Select **File · New · Project · Web Dynpro · Web Dynpro Project**. Enter the name of the project in the project wizard: MyFirstWebDynpro for this example. Leave the checkmark for **Project Contents** as is, which selects the standard directory for SAP NetWeaver Developer Studios. Select the project language and then click **Finish**.

Metadata and structures

The required data and structures for the project are created. You will now see your project in the Web Dynpro Explorer with entries for *Web Dynpro* in *Applications*, *Models*, *Web Dynpro Component Interfaces*, and *Web Dynpro Components*, along with Dictionaries and *src*. Now create a Web Dynpro component that contains the functionality and that you can call later. Select the **Web Dynpro Components** node and right-click the mouse. From the context menu, select **Create Web Dynpro Component**. A new window appears, in which you now enter the details of your component. Select **MyFirstComponent** for **Component Name** and **Window; com.sap.demo.mywebdynpro** for **Component Package**, **Window Package,** and **View Package;** and **MyWebDynproView** for **View Name**. Click **Finish**.

All metadata and Java files are generated automatically. In your tool list, select **Save All Metadata**. You'll see the expanded structure of your project in the Web Dynpro Explorer: a component controller, a component interface controller, a configuration controller, and a standard window with the view. The controller listed under component interface is the only "public" access point to the component. All methods and attributes of other controllers are encapsulated and therefore invisible from the outside.

You will now create a model for a more complex example. Models represent the data basis for components. You can query the required data for the component from the model. For example, the model can refer to data called by RFC in an SAP R/3 system. To execute a BAPI call, the system landscape directory of the J2EE directory must be configured and the J2EE Engine must have access to the BAPI. However, because we're using a simple example for this demonstration, we'll use a view instead of a model.

Model

The view represents the interface to the user. Users are presented with various entry fields and selection buttons (GUI elements) to refine the data for a query.

View

The view has already been created for you. To edit it, double-click on your view, **MyWebDynproView**, in the list of views or in the Windows node. Both entries refer to the same object. The view editor of SAP NetWeaver Developer Studio will open and a layout will be displayed. In the outline window of the view in the lower portion of SAP NWDS, you'll see **RootUIElementContainer[Transparent Controller]** and a DefaultTextView. You can delete the **DefaultTextView**. To do so, select it directly in the view editor and press the **Delete** key on your keyboard, or select the entry in the outline window and delete it with the context menu.

Add a group element to your view. To do so, select the **RootUIElement-Container[Transparent Controller]** noted above and right-click the mouse. From the context menu, select **Insert Child**. Enter the new element under ID name, such as MyGroupBox. Next, set the type of the new element. Select **Group** from the drop-down box. Then, select your new element and click the right-click the mouse. Select **Insert Child** again and generate a **TextView** named MyText. Add an image element and name it MyImage.

Group element

You can set the properties of each individual element in the view with the **Properties** tab. Select your **TextView** and enter a text for the text property. Select **header1** for the design property. For the **MyGroupBox_ Header[Caption]UI** element, enter **My_View** in the text property. Then, insert an image. Select your image object and enter a file name as the value for the source property. An image must be located in your project directory under *src/mimes/Components/com.sap.demo.mywebdynpro.* Leave the layout of the group elements as **FlowLayout** to organize all the elements in a row. You have now successfully designed a view that was automatically inserted into the standard window of the Web Dynpro component.

Properties

Creating a Web Dynpro application

To be able to call your component from a Web browser, you must now create a Web Dynpro application. The only access point to a Web Dynpro component is a Web Dynpro application. To create it, select **Create Application** in the context menu of the application node of your project. Enter a description for the application, such as MyApplication. Select **Next**, **Use existing Component,** and then **Next** again. Now, you can select only the values available for the component and the view. Retain the values and the startup plug. Select **Finish**, and you will see a new entry under *Applications*—you now have a Web Dynpro application that you can call. You can now create Java code for event handling that reacts to the corresponding events in components. The Java code can be compiled and integrated into the SAP J2EE Engine.

Deployment

Now you must deploy your application, which you can do in one of two ways. With the first option, you can select the application with the right mouse button and then select **Deploy new archive and run**. This option deploys not only the application in the J2EE Engine, it also starts it immediately. We recommend that you employ this option to test the component. With the second option, select the project node in Web Dynpro Explorer and then select **Deploy** from the menu. To start the application, select the **application** node with the right mouse button and the select **Run** from the context menu. Your component will display in the Web browser.

You have now successfully created your first Web Dynpro component. Note that you did not have to program a single line of code. The approach is similar when you create a model and capture data from a BAPI call, although you would have to program a few lines for event handling.

When compared with portal components that you develop with the PDK, the advantage of Web Dynpros is that the views make it easy to design the component. Visual tools save Web Dynpro developers from complex work so that they can concentrate on the application, without worrying about its appearance. The application will not change as often as the design of the user interface (GUI). This approach produces a clear separation between the application and the design of the user interface: a desirable and future-oriented approach these days. Developers no longer need to worry about the design once the application can function and application designers no longer need to worry about programming.

A Glossary

Authentication Scheme: Users log on to SAP Enterprise Portal with a special authentication scheme. iViews are assigned to a type of authentication scheme. Users can access only the specific iViews for which they have authorization, based on the scheme stored during logon, or if they have more extensive authorizations. The related iViews must also be assigned to the scheme. Additional aspects of the authentication process, such as prioritization and so on, are associated with this term.

Breadcrumb: A path or tree view that reproduces the current navigational position within the portal. The component is placed above the detailed navigation area.

Business Package: Predefined portal applications that support related business tasks. Each business package contains a set of predefined, task-dependent applications available as iViews. User-related task assignments can supplement or enhance the applications.

Chain: A series of dependent portal objects, such as iViews, that are joined to each other by inheritance.

Child Object: A portal content object associated with or assigned to a single parent object. Child objects are units enclosed in parent objects.

Classification or **Categorization:** Content-based, partly automated assignment of documents to one or more categories based on hegemonic systematics.

Client Eventing: A mechanism within a specified iView that recognizes incoming (client-side) changes and notifies dependent objects in the portal. Such a notification might result in updating the contents of a target iView.

Collaboration: KM functionality for numerous forms of document-related communication between various portal users.

Container: A layout element that reserves a specific location area within a portal page. Containers can contain iViews or other containers.

Content: All functionality offered on the portal side that can benefit end users.

Content Area: The area in the portal desktop in which the embedded applications are executed or iViews displayed. For example, content areas display the results of navigation, portal pages with specific iView content, and administrative components.

Content Management (CM): KM functionalities to handle unstructured or prestructured data.

Copy: A copy is a duplicate version of an object. Both objects—the source object and the copied object—can be modified separately, without changes to one object affecting the other object.

Corporate LDAP Directory: Central, LDAP-enabled directory that contains basic data on portal users. Numerous systems within the system landscape use this data, which avoids redundancy in user data.

Data Source: The application used as the source of information within a database unifier project.

Delegated Administration: System-wide assignment of administrative tasks depending on role-based authorizations.

Delta Link: A specific type of portal object inheritance. It changes the parameter properties of object A when object B, from which object A inherits properties, is changed.

Detailed Navigation: A portal area that displays user-dependent folders, pages, and iViews normally placed in the navigation panel.

Detailed Navigation iView: iView for detailed navigation.

Discussion: A collection of documents assigned to a resource, which can be used to comment on or enhance content. A discussion usually involves several portal users.

Drag&Relate: A technology that enables cross-system transactions and queries to capture desired data and information stored in heterogeneous systems.

Drag&Relate Target: An iView capable of Drag&Relate that can be assigned to the remaining portal content objects.

Drag&Relate Target Area: Contains a list of links that point to specific iViews for which Drag&Relate functionality is available to end users, depending on their authorizations.

Drag&Relate Target Editor: This editor enables the definition of Drag&Relate targets for portal pages and iViews. You can call the editor from the portal content studio.

Eventing: An application that enables the exchange of data between iViews.

Example-Based Classification: An option to classify documents. Classification occurs based on a comparison of sample documents. Actual assignment occurs based on a calculation of similarity.

Example-Based Taxonomy: Systematics that can set categories for documents, in this case by specifying sample documents.

Feature Extraction: The retrieval of characteristics or properties for a document or a collection of documents.

First and Second Level of Navigation: Two horizontal navigation bars in SAP Enterprise Portal (directly under the header area) that can list menu entries, if necessary, up to the entire width of the screen.

Flat List View: Display mode in the "detailed navigation area" to display objects in a flat (i.e., non-hierarchical) list.

Forms-Based Publishing: A CM application to create and publish documents with a uniform structure. The application accesses the HTML structural elements, but is present in XML format.

Full-Tree View: Display mode in the detailed navigation area to display objects in a hierarchical list.

Full-Page Application: An iView that completes the entire content area of the portal. Examples include ITS transactions, Employee Self-Services, and so on. These types of applications are assigned directly to a role in the portal, without making a detour over a page.

Header Area: An area within the standard layout of the portal. It contains the masthead, the tool list, and top-level navigation.

Indexing and Retrieval: A service for searching for content by using several access methods.

iView: A small program that captures data from content sources and displays it in SAP Enterprise Portal.

iView Editor: A tool that you can use to create and modify iViews.

iViewStudio: A Web page that contains business packages and additional content elements. You can download the page if required. Business packages are assigned to numerous categories.

Java Application Server: A server that provides the infrastructure for Java applications. If the server supports J2EE, servlets, Java Server Pages (JSPs), Java naming and directory interfaces (JNDI), Java beans, and other J2EE services are supported.

Knowledge Management (KM): A component of SAP Enterprise Portal. It encompasses content management, data retrieval, and classification functionalities along with collaboration.

Layout: The basic structure of a portal page. A portal page can be associated with several layouts.

Logon Ticket: A data package required to authenticate a portal user or to allow SSO access to SAP applications. The logon ticket is created when a user logs on to an SAP system, as long as the system supports this functionality.

Masthead: Subarea of the standard header area in the portal. This area serves as an entry point and displays the company logo, user identification, and additional portal links (logoff, help, and personalization).

Navigation iView: A general expression that refers to various types of iViews contained in the navigation panel.

Navigation Panel: An area in the portal that can be opened and closed and used for navigation in the content area. The navigation panel can contain the detailed navigation area, the Drag&Relate target area, and so on.

Page: A page is displayed in the content area and contains the layout information required to format the content for viewing.

Page Editor: A visual editing tool for portal pages that allows administrators to define and modify the layout and content of pages.

Page Layout View: A view of the page editor that defines or displays the default assignment of iViews on a page.

Page List View: A view of the page editor that enables the selection of content that should be displayed on a page and the definition of the characteristics related to the content.

Parent Object: A portal content object that contains other objects (child objects). Parent objects are used to create modules and enable the generation of usable content for the portal.

Persistence Layer: A generic term that refers to a series of repositories that various portal components use for persistent storage of data. The repositories include the repository database and the portal content directory (PCD).

Portal application: Content created for a specific target group of users. A portal application usually consists of a set of dependent user roles with similar needs.

Portal Catalog: A collection of folders that contain roles, pages, portal objects, and additional content objects. You can also determine the basic characteristics of objects with the portal catalog.

Portal Content: A collection of predefined portal applications (business packages) and modules (depending on the role defaults and SAP BW Business Content) that can support customers in the creation of their own portal applications. SAP tests and certifies portal content. It generally includes information, applications, and services available in the portal.

Portal Content Directory (PCD): A repository for objects, particularly roles, and relationships between the objects that enables hierarchies and linkages, user personalization, distributed administration, and transports.

Portal Content Studio: A central environment for the development and administration of portal content.

Portal desktop: The entire portal area, including all content and layout areas. The preconfigured portal desktop consists of the header area, navigation panel, and the content area.

Portal desktop template: An enterprise portal normally provides several desktop templates, each assigned to a specific organizational role or subarea of the enterprise.

Portal Display Rules Editor: Enables rules-based definitions for the type of portal display.

Portal server: Provides the environment for the development and administration of portal content. It also provides a number of services so that iViews can run and assigns iViews in portal pages.

Portal Server Monitor: Displays the status of the Java–iView runtime environment.

Portal Web Server: The Web server is integrated in the portal server. It can process HTTP(S) requests transmitted by the portal client.

Project: A project is an application that can use Drag&Relate, is set up on the unification server, and contains the elements and data components required to present (display) dedicated sources. Sources can be databases or other applications

Property Editor: A generic content administration tool for simple objects. Other editors in the portal content studio (framework) use this editor to display and process generic object properties of the portal content directory.

Publishing Pipeline: A CM service to pass on the content, format, and layout of documents in the publishing process.

Query-Based Classification: An option to assign documents to a category according to a specific schema. Classification occurs based on search queries defined for individual categories.

Query-Based Taxonomy: A taxonomy that determines the content of categories based on search queries.

Related Links Area: Display of a flat list of links required to display content. You can use the portal content studio to define the links.

Related Links Editor: Enables the definition of related linked for pages and iViews.

Repository Filter: A CM component that is associated with the repository. It executes the transformation of content or metadata.

Repository Framework: A CM function for transparent handling of the contents of various repository types.

Repository Manager: Contains functions that enable access to the content of a repository from portal applications.

Repository Service: A service associated with a repository, such as subscriptions, indexing documents, and so on.

Retrieval and Classification: KM functionality and service to obtain information and classify documents.

Role: A collection of related tasks, services, and information made available to a group of users. The display of content and navigation structures also requires roles. A role can contain all possible types of data.

Role Editor: A tool for the role administrator. It supports the development and modification of roles stores in the portal content directory.

SAP User Management Engine: A Java-based component for user management. It supports centralized user management, SSO, and secure access to distributed applications.

SAP Enterprise Portal: A component of SAP NetWeaver that unifies and standardizes heterogeneous applications, information, and services that exist within an enterprise and combines them into one application.

Sibling Object: A child object that belongs to the same parent object as does a different comparable object.

Subscription and Notification: Services to inform users of possible modifications in content.

System: A group of properties required to set up a connection to an external application.

System Alias: The name associated with a system and that portal components can use to reference the system.

System landscape: The definition of several systems that serve as a source of information or data within the portal.

System Landscape Catalog: A hierarchical collection of systems within a system landscape.

Tab: Access point in the top-level navigation area. The name of the tab is derived from the appropriate role. A tab on a second navigation level can start a page with content or services.

Taxonomy: A hierarchy of categories used to classify documents, depending on their content.

Text Mining: Methods to extract information from regular or complex texts.

Theme: Coloring and images in the portal. Customers can choose their own theme for the portal by using the theme editor, including the templates it contains.

Theme Editor: Tool that enables users to modify standard theme templates and allow consideration of customer requirements.

Theme Template: A group of colors and images in the Theme Editor that users can employ as an entry point to adjust the portal's branding to a specific company.

Tool Area: A persistent area in the portal header that enables direct access to key applications, such as realtime collaboration or searching.

Top-Level Navigation: Two rows in the portal header that users can employ to access specific pages within the portal.

TREX Search Engine: A component of the search and classification engine that enables an intelligent search for information. It supports the following search options: exact, error-tolerant, phrase-based, Boolean, and attribute-related.

TREX Text Mining Engine: A component of the search and classification engine that supports the classification of and search for similar documents. It can also determine the properties of documents.

Unification: The basic idea behind integration of information sources in SAP Enterprise Portal. The unification functionality provided by the unification server and Drag&Relate technology supports access to information from the most varied sources, including historical databases and supplemental applications outside of SAP Enterprise Portal.

Unification Server: The technical infrastructure to set up database- or application-related unifiers that supports cross-project correlation and navigation.

Unifier: An application that enables integration of companywide systems in SAP Enterprise Portal with Drag&Relate. The unifier provides an extraction level that consists of the business logic of the target application and offers the target application a repository of metadata.

User mapping: Enables use of single sign-on (SSO) between systems even when the user's user parameters don't agree.

Workset: A collection of tasks, services, and information that are elements of a role and that belong to each other from a semantic viewpoint. Worksets cover a specific area of activity, such as controlling or budgeting.

Workset Editor: A tool for the role administrator that supports the development and maintenance of Worksets contained in the portal content directory.

XML Forms Builder: Tool to set up forms. The precondition here is the definition of a data scheme (XML-Template) and the creation of a form layout with the use of direct manipulation techniques. Based on this input, the tool generates XSL transformations used on the underlying XML templates and renders an HTML form.

B Object Model in SAP EP 5.0 and 6.0

The following table lists the availability of presentation objects in SAP EP 5.0 and 6.0.

Objects	SAP EP 5.0	SAP EP 6.0
Role	X	X
Workset	X	X
Page	X	X
Layout	–	X
iView	X	X
External Service	X	–
System	–	X
Folder	X	X
Transport Package	–	X
Page Template	–	X
iView Template	–	X
Layout Template	–	X
System Template	–	X

C Sources and Further Reading

- Fu, Biao: *SAP BW. A Step by Step Guide*. Addison Wesley Professional 2002.
- Goethe, Johann Wolfgang von: *Faust, Part I & II*. Princeton University Press 1994.
- Färber, Günther; Kirchner, Julia: *mySAP Technology.* Galileo Press 2002.
- Howes, Tim; Smith, Mark; Good, Gordon: *Understanding and Deploying LDAP Directory Services*. Addison Wesley Professional 2003.
- SAP: *Enabling SSL for the SAP J2EE Engine*. SAP Service Marketplace.
- SAP: *Installing Oracle 9.2 Database Server for SAP Enterprise Portal 6.0*. SAP Service Marketplace.
- SAP: *OS-Dependencies-Leitfaden*. SAP Service Marketplace.
- SAP: *Platform Availability Matrix*. SAP Service Marketplace.
- SAP: *SAP Enterprise Portal Security Guide.* SAP Service Marketplace.
- SAP: *SAP J2EE Engine Security Guides*. SAP Service Marketplace.
- SAP: *SNC-Manual.* SAP Service Marketplace.

D About the Authors

Arnd Goebel is a senior consultant at SAP Deutschland AG, where he concentrates on SAP Supplier Relationship Management (SRM), technology, and security. He started working at SAP while still in school and has been with the company for nine years. He worked on numerous projects as a solution consultant for SAP SRM, SAP Enterprise Portal (SAP EP), technology, and security, and has independently managed projects outside of Germany. He earned a degree in Management Information Systems (MIS) at the University of Mannheim, Germany and an MBA in international business in the U.S.

At SAP AG and SAP America, he worked in internal business consulting (IBC) and strategic enterprise management (SEM). He delivered an address on innovative technologies in SEM at the SAP TechEd 2000 meeting in Las Vegas, Nevada. He later worked as a consultant for SAP Enterprise Buyer Professional (e-procurement and SRM) and SAP technology in Germany and other countries. During the development of SAP Enterprise Portal in 2001, he successfully led one of the first portal projects for a ramp-up customer. In the area of SAP security, he has worked in project management and in presales; he has also delivered several lectures and held various workshops. He is currently working on several projects to implement digital signatures in global companies throughout the world.

Dirk Ritthaler is a senior consultant at SAP Deutschland AG and focuses on SAP Business Intelligence. He has four years of project experience that often involves cross-application topics, especially those focused on SAP Enterprise Portal (such as the development of Web-enabled applications, and so on). He has a broad range of MIS knowledge (SAP SEM—Management Cockpit) and experience in the automotive sector.

He earned his MIS degree at the University of Mannheim, Germany and is equally familiar with technological topics and business processes. During his studies, he collaborated with and worked on projects for many well-known companies. His extensive knowledge of Java and (OO)DB has made him well suited to work on development with SAP NetWeaver.

Index

Q

R

S

T

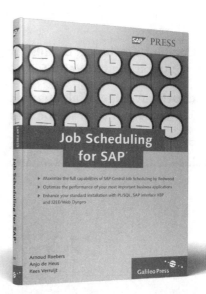

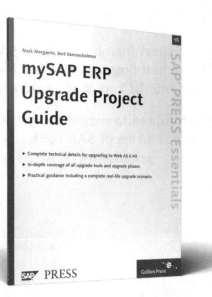